FIVE YEARS TO LIVE

FIVE YEARS TO LIVE

LUKE RICHMOND

First published in 2023 by Luke Richmond
and OLOC Adventures.

Port Arthur, Tasmania, 7182 Australia.
www.olocadventures.com

10,9,8,7,6,5,4,3,2,1

Copyright © Luke Richmond 2023

All rights reserved. No part of this book may be reproduced or transmitted in any form or by any means, electronic or mechanical, including photocopying, recording or by any other information storage retrieval system, without prior permission in writing from the publisher.

National Library of Australia Cataloguing-in-Publication entry:
Five Years To Live / Richmond, Luke.

ISBN: 978-0-6485947-9-6 (paperback)

Category: Memoir / Adventure Travel

Cover and internal design: Nada Backovic
Cover image: Yok Chaiwat and iStockphoto

The paper in this book is FSC certified. FSC promotes environmentally responsible, socially beneficial and economically viable management of the world's forests.

For Elise.

PRAISE FOR FIVE YEARS TO LIVE

'Intoxicating, exhilarating and pumped full of action, Richmond once again shows why living an adventurous life is super food for the human soul.'
GRANT 'AXE' RAWLINSON – Human Powered Explorer

'Luke is relentless. The amount of experience this bloke is jamming into his one life is amazing. His insightful understanding of the world comes from seeing it firsthand. Thanks for sharing another great chapter in your epic life.'
MARK DIREEN – SASR Veteran – Adventurer – Storyteller

'Luke's spirit of adventure is endless, and his incredible story continues across the world's most spectacular locations.'
DAVID KNOFF – Author of 537 Days of Winter

'This guy truly lives by his "One Life One Chance" motto. He lives and breathes extreme adventure and gives you a front row seat.'
MICHAEL ATKINSON – Alone Australia finalist – Adventurer – Filmmaker

'Redefine adventure's purpose with Luke's third book – a gripping read that inspires you to seize your own life's journey. These pages evoke laughter, tears, and contemplation as Luke shares his invaluable and vulnerable insights, on a crucial question we all deserve to explore in life.'
ERNEST HOCKING – Veteran – Explorer – Problem Solver

ABOUT THE AUTHOR

Luke Richmond is an Aussie adventurer who has conquered the odds during many internationally acclaimed expeditions. Growing up on various cattle stations across the Northern Territory, Luke joined the army at 17 years old, which gave him the discipline and world knowledge he needed, and lit a fire for adventure that he pursues to this day. Luke has climbed the highest mountain on six continents, completed a world record ocean row across the Atlantic, and was the first Australian male to trek 1800 kilometres across the Gobi Desert in Mongolia, dragging a cart that contained all his food and water. Luke's lifelong passion is to make adventure accessible to everyone, and to inspire others to feel the reward of conquering a physical and mental challenge. His life motto is OLOC which stands for 'one life one chance', a belief that has driven him into harder and longer challenges every single year.

CONTENTS

- ◆ Summit — XII
- ◆ Introduction - The Whisky Chat — 1
- ◆ Chapter 1 - Lobuche East — 8
- ◆ Chapter 2 - Ama Dablam — 30
- ◆ Chapter 3 - Cycle Across Australia — 45
- ◆ Chapter 4 - The Red Centre — 79
- ◆ Chapter 5 - The Treasure Hunt — 97
- ◆ Chapter 6 - The Larapinta Trail — 123
- ◆ Chapter 7 - Point Break — 151
- ◆ Chapter 8 - Three Peaks — 173
- ◆ Chapter 9 - The Deer Hunter — 206
- ◆ Chapter 10 - A River Runs Free — 232
- ◆ Chapter 11 - The Bay Of Bengal — 256
- ◆ Conclusion — 289
  - ◆ A Soldier's Journey — 292
  - ◆ Acknowledgements — 301

Summit

Bruised and battered he has been
Bones broken, flesh cut and torn
He could have died one hundred times
Since the day that he was born

He held a rifle in his hands
And he saw the damage done
He could have died one hundred times
When his life had just begun

Lost and lonely he has been
Tricked, beaten and betrayed
He could have died one hundred times
Then he found another way

I knew his path was always there
It was just so hard to see
He could have died one hundred times
But his searching set him free

From one hopeful step to a certain run
He felt the truth was near
He could have died one hundred times
Then it all became so clear

We have one life, one chance, one time to shine
Dreams can be caught, released, and followed
He could have died one hundred times
If he'd waited till tomorrow

A tear of joy, his woman's love
The mountains whispering in the dawn
And now he has lived one hundred lives
Since the day that he was born

Oh yes, now he has lived one hundred lives
Since the day that he was born.

Clive Richmond

INTRODUCTION

The Whisky Chat

Once again, the year seemed to vanish at warp speed and New Year's Eve had arrived. 'Where did the year go?' I asked my wife Elise as she handed me a glass of whisky.

She sat beside me on the couch. 'I know, another one down, old man.' She replied with a smile and took a sip from her glass. From the comfort of our couch, I scanned around our humble loungeroom. Mismatched 1970s linoleum covered the uninsulated floor beneath my feet. An old maroon leather armchair sat beside a large modern cream lounge, and an antique table with two chairs matched my writing desk at the window with views of the bay. The fireplace had a bent chimney, the internal roof sagged, nothing was level, and there would be a lifetime of work to keep her standing. None of that mattered to me; it was home, and it was ours.

What did matter was what covered the walls. Framed memories full of life experiences and adventures were beaming off every surface. Our personal showreel was nailed and screwed in place so we could reflect upon the incredible journeys we had been on. Mountains featured heavily in the kitchen and along the small staircase. Climbing the Seven Summits, the biggest mountain on each continent, was my first adventure goal as a young man fresh out of drug addiction. Being a veteran who had a tumultuous time following discharge from the Army in 2005, I experienced my cliché rock bottom moment in London where I woke up in jail. I knew I had to change. I reinvented myself, cleaned up my life, and set out to see whether I measured up against the great explorers of old, the stoics whom I had grown up reading about.

I attempted six of the seven summits that year and successfully summited five. Pictures show me smiling and holding sponsors' flags with snow, ice, and rocky views in the background. That same year, I was held captive in West Papua, almost shot in Russia, confronted death in Argentina, and rescued a climber from a crevasse in Alaska; it was a big year. Above all, I learned how to be a mountaineer and knew the adventure life was my calling.

A Guinness World Record was wedged into the corner of our lounge room. It was sent from the UK and arrived with a spelling mistake to keep me humble. To earn that record, I rowed a boat across the Atlantic Ocean from Europe to South America with three British comrades over 55 days, covering 6400 kilometres. I arrived on the shores of Brazil 15 kilograms lighter to Elise waiting for me in the shallows. We had to maintain two hours of rowing, then two hours of rest, 24 hours a day, to achieve our goal. I learned to be grateful for suffering on that journey, and it took me a year to recover. During this time, Elise wanted to join me on expeditions, so we took off together into the Gobi Desert.

A large wooden framed picture of us dragging our custom-made carts towards a bleak horizon has pride of place to the right of the couch. It took 57 days of living in a tent and walking every daylight hour to cover 1805 kilometres across the Gobi Desert in Mongolia. The temperatures in the desert ranged from minus 45 degrees in winter to plus 45 in summer, and during the middle period when we crossed her length, the sandstorms were biblical.

We discovered that communication was the key to surviving as a team.

Surrounding the Gobi picture is an assortment of images of us climbing in Switzerland, Thailand, Scotland, and the United States. There are pictures of us on the Murray River in our kayaks from when we paddled its entire length, 56 days covering 2200 kilometres, with Dad supporting us in his little fishing boat. There are dozens of pictures of me jumping off bridges, buildings, antennae, and cliffs worldwide while pursuing B.A.S.E Jumping. I learned how to control my fear in the sport that pushed me so close to death; I lived a thousand lifetimes in a moment.

Near the bedroom door is a poster for a documentary titled, 'The Sea Decides.' It showcases a friend of mine on his quest to row from Singapore to New Zealand. I made a cameo appearance halfway through when we joined forces to row the Tasman Sea. I nearly drowned on that one, and I learned the value of being able to self-rescue. Next to the poster is a collage of images of Nepal; we have been to the Himalayas every year for the last four seasons, and I can't wait to go back again. After all these years, it's soaring summits and remote valleys are a second home to us. And there were ten lifetimes worth of climbing to be experienced there, with smiling Sherpa, yaks, and the mountain gods guiding the way.

Nailed into skirting boards and placed on shelves are photos of our backyard and wilderness home of Tasmania. This wild, cold frontier is our base camp, and as a training ground for big expeditions, it was second to none.

Our walls are decorated with some big moments from the last fifteen years. But as I reflected, it wasn't the big moments that were most vivid in my mind but the small ones. Eating scones with my mum on the side of the road in the Northern Territory, fishing with Dad on the Murray River, or getting a hug from my wife every morning. It was the small moments shared with people I loved that I remembered first and valued the most. On my quest for big moments in life, I would strive to fill every space in between with small ones because that makes up the foundation of a happy life.

'That's a nice whisky. How much was this one?' Elise asked.

'Fifty-five bucks, we are bottom shelf babe, but it is nice, isn't it?'

I walked to the kitchen, grabbed the bottle, and topped up her glass. My mind drifted to the year ahead. We had ticked off our list of adventures, some successful, some failures, all fantastic experiences. Yet now we were in limbo. It was a blank canvas.

I looked over at Elise and sat back down beside her, she knew immediately.

'Is it that time again, time for the question, we haven't asked this in a few years.' She replied.

'Yeah, we have been busy ticking off the answers from the last time. What do you think?'

'Get a pen and paper,' she replied, pointing to my writing desk.

Sitting back down, I had the notepad and pen in hand. I took one more sip from my glass and placed it down.

'Ok, get in the right frame of mind. If we do this, we do it properly. We must believe this could be our reality. Are you ready?' I asked.

'Ok, yes, let's go.'

I scribbled the question down; one we had been asking ourselves every few years whenever we found ourselves without direction or full of distraction. I cleared my throat.

'What if we only had five years left to live?'

We both fell silent; it was a question to be respected, believed, and answered with raw honesty. Five years, it's a short time, but it was the right amount of time for this thought-provoking exercise. If it were one year, it would be too short and be answered with short-sightedness, filled with base desires and luxuries. If it was ten years, it would be too long and exposed us to distractions of careers, mortgages, and legacy. Five was the perfect time frame, long enough to achieve great things, short enough to keep the value and meaning of it all intact.

'I want to cycle across Australia.' Elise replied with authority.

'Wow, where did that come from?'

'We have never done a cycling trip; it looks amazing.'

'Ok, done.' I wrote it down.

It was my turn. 'I have always wanted to attempt Ama Dablam in Nepal. We should climb it.' This mountain had been calling me for 14 years, and if I only had five years to go, it was time to answer.

'Ouch, that will be tough. I'm keen to try. Write it down.'

Elise went silent for a moment, then spoke again.

'If we go to Nepal, let's bag a few more, maybe Mera Peak, Island Peak, and Lobuche East, to make the most of the trip.'

'Ok, done, mountain madness, I like it.' Our list was growing quickly.

'Dad had always talked about going bush into the Northern Territory with metal detectors looking for old coins and treasure; let's do that with him for fun.'

'Yeah, perfect.' Elise replied.

'Anything in Tassie?' I asked.

'Rafting the Franklin is supposed to be one of the must-do adventures down here. I'd be keen for that one,' Elise replied.

'Done. I want to get back in the air as well.' I said.

Since retiring from B.A.S.E Jumping three years earlier, I have missed the freedom of the skies. However, I couldn't get drawn back into that world, it was just too dangerous, and I barely escaped with my life.

'Keen to Paraglide?' I asked.

'I would love to learn. I heard there are courses here in Tassie.' On the list.

I sipped my whisky.

'Well, while we are learning new skills, I always wanted to learn to surf.'

'Absolutely, me too. Write that down for sure.' Elise replied instantly.

'Also, hunt a deer.'

'Umm, count me out of that one but go for your life,' I wrote it down.

'Ok, before we get carried away, what have we got so far?' Elise asked.

'Right, we have: Climbing Ama Dablam, Lobuche East, Mera Peak, and Island Peak in Nepal. Then cycling across Australia and treasure hunting in the Northern Territory with Dad. Here at home, we have rafting the Franklin River, and learning to fly again. We can learn to surf together, and then I will have to go solo hunting a deer by the sounds of it.' I said, grinning at Elise.

'Awesome, that's a solid list, anything else?' she asked smiling back.

'The only thing is the ski traverse across Antarctica and the South Pole, but that's a while away, and paragliding will be the first skill we need anyway, so we are working towards it.' I replied.

'What about Everest? That was on the list once.' she probed.

'Yeah, I have lost the desire for it, to be honest. The cost and crowding are not ideal, and my motivation for it has changed. In the early days, I wanted records and glory. These days I want adventure and fun. If I'm answering the question honestly, it's not on the list.'

'Ok, that's fine. We have plenty on there now. I think that's enough.' Elise took a sip.

'Yeah, it's a solid list. Are kids ever going to be on here?' I asked.

'No way!' Elise spluttered, almost choking on her whisky. 'Look, it's there, in a small sense, like I'm not sure if I will regret not having kids. But if I'm honest, I don't have a burning desire for it, and with kids, I think it needs to be a hell yeah from both of us, or it's a no. We are living an amazing life together, and it would be a huge sacrifice. It's not on the list this time.'

'Fair enough, I agree.'

My mind raced as I started to plan. We would need money, specialised build-up training, and a million pieces to fall into place to pull it all off.

'One expedition at a time, remember?' Elise's rule broke my chain of thought.

She knew how my mind operated; once given a mission, I was obsessed and couldn't relax until we had achieved or failed at our objective. It was my military mind taking over. I took a deep breath, sat back against the soft couch, and looked at her. She smiled back at me knowingly. We were living our dream adventure lives, no doubt about it.

'Well, babe.' I said, lifting my glass. 'Cheers to you and the next few years. We have our list. Let's do what we do best.'

Our glasses touched, sounding the end of one year and announcing the start of the next. 'Bring it on,' she egged. 'What's that thing you are always saying again?' she asked me sarcastically. I lifted my glass in homage to my life mantra, a few words conjured in the depths of a coal mine years before my first adventure. I sat up straight, cleared my throat, and spoke with pomposity.

'One life, one chance.'

CHAPTER 1

Lobuche East

I'm often asked, why do you want to climb mountains? What typically comes to mind is a quote from a famous mountaineer, George Leigh Mallory, 'Because it's there.' Yet I know the person asking the question is looking for a deeper understanding of why. Why take risks, endure hardships, and witness others dying in front of you? What is it all for? It does seem selfish.

In one way, it is a selfish pursuit. Even while climbing in a team, you are often climbing solo. It started as a personal ambition, following my ego towards the conquering of giants. I wanted records, titles, and to be an adventurer. I was continually re-inventing myself in my youth: from an Australian soldier to a lost backpacker with a drug problem, to a Muay Thai maniac, and then an underground coal miner with his sights set on the summits. I was on a quest to be more, to make more of my life, and to leave a legacy. Over the following ten years, my ambition and longing to climb evolved. Smouldering away in the background is still my ego, but today's driving force is to experience the suffering and witness the grandeur of the mountains. To be immersed in nature and enjoy a fleeting glimpse of glory during months of physical and mental struggle.

The most significant rewards in life never come easy. Neither did that lesson. We must earn resilience, confidence, leadership and courage; those noble traits often spoken about in conference rooms. I found them while enduring arduous expeditions where hardship and risk to life were a daily occurrence. With every journey, I refined them; they are now assets I use back in the 'normal' world. Even after all these years of adventures, I know without a doubt that there is more to learn. That is why I return each year to the highest peaks, the hottest deserts, and our world's vast oceans. That is why I climb mountains.

'What is the most incredible mountain in the world?' usually follows next. This question is subjective and can break down into a few categories: the highest mountain, the most dangerous, the most aesthetically pleasing, or even history could play a deciding factor. Mt Everest would be in the top three for many mountaineers, possibly due to their ambition to climb the tallest mountain on Earth. The Matterhorn, Eiger, Shivling, Siula Grande, K2, the list is near endless.

My answer without hesitation is Ama Dablam, a towering peak 6812 metres high nestled deep amongst the Himalayas in Nepal. I first laid eyes on her in 2006 during a trek into the Khumbu region towards Everest Base Camp. This was long before I had started my mountaineering career. I was young, charging up into the mountains, breaking the acclimatisation rules, and knew nothing about the power of mother nature. Outside a village called Namche Bazaar, my young eyes first saw her. She was tall, beautifully intimidating, and stood out from the surrounding valley. She called me. With zero climbing experience and terrified of the hanging serac on her western face, I vowed to return when I had the skills. I didn't know it back then, but I was being called into the extreme cold, gale-force winds, and one of the most challenging decisions of my life.

◆ ◆ ◆

I live in Tasmania, Australia, with my wife, Elise. It is one of the most beautiful places on Earth. Our land is far enough away from the civilised world to boast that we live an off-grid existence. When we were ready to depart on our expedition to climb Ama Dablam, we had to ask our neighbour Scotty for a ride to the airport. A first encounter with Scotty could be intimidating. He rides a Harley Davidson, is covered in tattoos, and has dreadlocks growing from the back half of his head into a reggae mullet. Once we got to know him, we realised his only danger was providing us with an extra hot cup of tea. When we asked him about a 3.45 a.m. lift into town, he replied, 'Of course, not a bother.' We crammed our duffel bags and ourselves into his small van and rattled off down the road dodging the wildlife in the pre-dawn light. Eighty kilometres later, we bid him farewell, pushed our trolleys into the quiet Hobart terminal, and checked in for our flights to Nepal.

After multiple connecting flights, 24 hours of plane cuisine, and a waning tolerance for air travel, we landed in Kathmandu. When it comes to names of places that instantly inspire thoughts of adventure, the capital city of Nepal must be at the top of the list, up there with Timbuktu, Alaska, or the Amazon. Navigating the arrivals area was always a challenge. The hall was packed with travellers, and there was no pattern or process for handling the hoards. My skin had taken on an oily pallor, as most have experienced after long-haul flights; I felt dirty and needed a shower. My stress levels move in the opposite direction to most people in these situations. As those around me start getting frustrated and snappy, I tend to ease back and wallow in the chaos. There was nothing I could do to improve the Kathmandu terminal's function, and after two hours of mosh pit madness, paperwork, and confusion, we were set free.

We exited the airport to our waiting friend Mingma Chirri Sherpa. Mingma was a mountain guide and climber in high demand and operated his own company - Extreme Ascent Trekking. He was born in the mountains and previously worked as an icefall doctor on Mt Everest, for large commercial expeditions. He was one of the guys who opened the route each season through the deadly Khumbu icefall, arguably the most dangerous job in existence. He humbly talks about fixing ropes to the summit of Everest while carrying a 30 kilogram backpack.

Driving through the dusty, dark streets, we absorbed a developing nation's sights, sounds and smells. It is always during the first drive from the airport on any adventure that my excitement begins to build, and my senses become heightened. My body was processing all the new sensory information and making adjustments, preparing itself for what was to come. As we made our way into Thamel, the city's tourist heart, I was in survival mode. I was watching angles, reading the traffic, noticing people staring, seeing wild dogs eating scraps of food from the street, breathing dust into my nose and lungs, smelling the open sewers, seeing a homeless and disabled person begging in the gutter, and watching a polluted river of Nepali, Indian, and European filth flow past. By the end of the expedition, when returning to the airport, we would be accustomed and in sync with our new rougher environment.

We disembarked at the Fuji Hotel. I have become a creature of habit over the years, and we have stayed at the same place during our last three trips to Nepal. It was a reasonably priced, clean, and friendly establishment with a solid breakfast buffet and a fully stacked second-hand bookshelf to pilfer. After a much-needed sleep, we gathered for coffee in the restaurant the following morning. It was the first time our entire climbing team would be together.

The first member at breakfast was Yok. He was a local to Phuket, Thailand, where he owned a climbing gym called Rebel and was the strongest rock climber in the team. He had joined us two years ago on a trek to Everest Base Camp and handled the altitude well. A skilled photographer and filmmaker, Yok would document our Ama Dablam climb. This expedition was his first ever mountaineering experience, and his strong climbing ability would be a vital tool.

Next to arrive were three Norwegian guys, Tobias, Vidar, and Kim. All were young, fit, and had grown up in the mountains of Norway. Tobias wouldn't be attempting Ama Dablam. He was only joining us for the trekking experience and to film the adventure. Vidar and Kim had successfully summited Island Peak

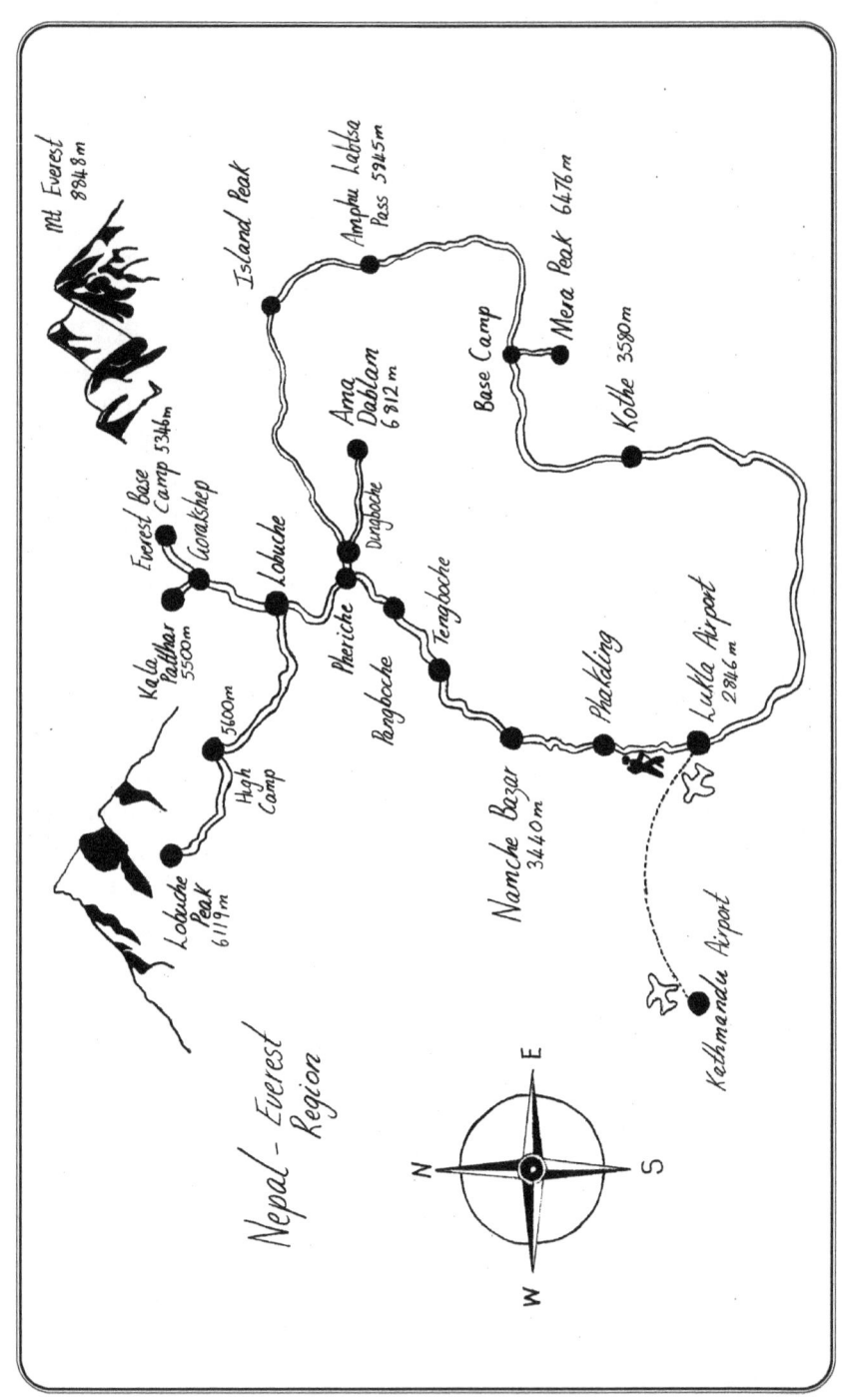

the year before and, like me, were smitten after laying eyes on Ama Dablam. Between all of us, we had a mixed bag of mountaineering experience and some strong technical climbers. Our team leader would be Mingma, who arrived last. We all ate breakfast together, got to know each other, and planned our departure from the hustle and bustle of the city.

The domestic part of the Kathmandu airport was under construction, which meant we couldn't get our direct flight to Lukla, the starting point for our trek into the mountains. Instead, we needed to drive four hours to another small airport in Manthali. I had travelled on Nepali and Indian roads many times before and grumbled internally. However, as with any expedition, our plans were always adaptable. After hearing the news,

I asked:

'What time are we leaving?'

To which Mingma replied, '1.30 a.m. tomorrow.'

We could use the rest of the day to buy any last-minute items, do a gear check, eat as much as possible, and then get a few hours of sleep. As we split up, Mingma said to us,

'See you in the morning' while wearing a cheeky smile.

I laughed and replied to him, 'See you tonight, bro.'

A four-wheel drive arrived at the hotel on time, the streets were empty, and we started loading our duffel bags. It was a very tight fit: seven climbers, the driver, a dozen big duffel bags, and seven backpacks. I was crammed in last, with my pack sitting on my lap; I knew I was in for a rough ride and so embraced the reality. The roads lived up to their reputation. Once the wheels left bitumen and onto the dirt, the real fun began. Dawn arrived, and the streets filled with pedestrians, bikes, cows, cars, trucks, and buses, all navigating the potholes and churning up dust. The condition of the main roads could only be labelled horrendous by Western standards. Unsuited vehicles were shaken and battered, with broken wrecks littering the roadside. When my head hit the window for a third consecutive time, I thought this must be the land of rich mechanics. They would have an endless supply of destroyed vehicles to fix.

I was looking forward to living a simple existence in the mountains with nothing to worry about except moving a little higher each day. However, this expedition was going to be different. Elise was climbing with me, and my continually risk-assessing mind was already working overtime. I wouldn't just be concerned about myself on this one; I would be watching every angle and keeping her safe too. Even though she had the physical and mental capacity to get the job done, this was her first mountaineering expedition.

After four hours of spine jolting, head thumping, and body-compressing dirt road travel, we arrived at Manthali Airport. The small landing strip was a scar on the Earth at the bottom of a valley and beside a shallow river. The terminal building was a derelict structure surrounded by a two-foot-high chicken wire fence. The solo security guard, dressed in full military attire, took his job seriously and shouted orders as we piled out of our truck.

This airport operated like the simple cousin of the Kathmandu terminal. No systems, bags everywhere, guides arguing with the check-in officials, and the mid-morning sun beating down on us all. The team retired to plastic chairs inside the tin-roofed coffee shack close by, letting Mingma fight the good fight. Three hours later, after seven hours of transit, we lifted off for our 17-minute flight to Lukla.

The pilot banked the plane towards the snow-capped peaks I could see in the distance. Below us, the terrain transformed from dirt roads and dust into farms and crops. The valley was covered with tiered crop fields, carved into its steep sides. Narrow winding dirt trails linked the small villages; no more roads existed. Dozens of peaks covered the horizon. I didn't know most of their names, but I wanted to climb them all. Yok and Tobias were busy behind their cameras, taking photos and filming. I envied their skills and what they could capture, but I also wanted to see the world through my own eyes, in real time, and not from behind a lens.

We landed in Lukla at what was rated the most dangerous airport in the world. Its short runway is daringly carved into the side of the mountain at a horrifically steep angle. Years earlier, when I first landed here, I saw fresh wreckage from a helicopter crash on the concrete pad. Today, it was vacant of debris, and after touching down, the pilot slammed on the brakes and turned sharply into the terminal building. Our Sherpa team was waiting for us on the tarmac. We grabbed our duffle bags, backpacks, and supplies then carried them to a nearby tea house.

Over a hot cup of chai, Mingma Chirri introduced us to three more climbing Sherpas. First was Kami Chirri, who had a mountaineering resume second to none. Second was Pasang Geljin, an incredible climber with multiple Everest summits whom I knew from a previous trip to Everest Base Camp. Our final member was Lakpa, the oldest in our team and Mingma Chirri's father. Lakpa had spent most of his life guiding tourists into the mountains, and even though he was now retired from climbing, he was coming with us as support staff. His energy and enthusiasm were infectious, and he always wore a toothy smile.

Our packs and duffle bags were strapped onto Yaks, owned, and cared for by a young boy named Krishna. For an expedition team, Yaks were the most reliable and efficient way to transport equipment into the mountains. The beasts were iconic, and their bells rang loudly along the trails and across the valleys. This symbiotic relationship between man and animal was commonplace when I ventured into remote regions—camels in Mongolia, horses in Australia, or yaks in Nepal. To thrive against mother nature in harsh environments, we needed to work hand in hand with the animals.

Lukla disappeared behind us as we started our ascent. The trail wasn't overly busy, and I fell into the steady rhythm of a mountaineer. The ideal pace to acclimatise is slow without ever getting exhausted. The time for hard work would come much later; first, it was about letting the body adjust to the altitude and get comfortable hiking. Elise and I had completed an extensive build-up training program before we departed Tasmania. Our home is surrounded by national parks dissected by some of the most famous trails in Australia. We started walking 5 kilometres carrying 10 kilograms, increasing the distance and weight weekly. Our final hike was 30 kilometres, with 30 kilograms on our backs. It was a tough day, but nothing compared to what a summit bid would entail.

Over two days, we hiked through the small villages of Phukding and Monjo and arrived at Namche Bazaar, the biggest community in the Khumbu region. Before moving higher, we would spend a rest day in this bustling mountain metropolis. Namche has evolved over the years into a tourism and trade hub. When I first trekked through this area in my youth, the choices were local cuisine, some simple accommodation, and very little else. Today, there was an assortment of comfortable tea houses, western restaurants, pubs, and cafes. Drinking a flat white while scrolling Facebook is now possible at the top of the world.

Depending on my sponsor commitments, I often unplugged entirely from technology while on expeditions, and during the first day of trekking, my brain began calibrating to inputs from the natural environment. I then drifted away into my imagination, something rarely done by adults in our bigger, stronger, faster world. It would only last a few seconds at first, but by the end of the day, I would drift off for minutes. On the second day, my brain had rediscovered its youthful and unrestrained imaginary landscapes, and I could lose hours exploring other realities. This ability to imagine and daydream is a fundamental asset. It can inspire new ideas, conjure future possibilities, or discover a strategy for success that has been clouded by technology. If every idle second continued to be consumed with Instagram, Facebook, and Twitter, we would risk eventually losing this evolutionary tool.

In Namche, a small Sherpa museum showcased the history of these mighty mountain men and women; it's a must-visit on your first trip. Outside the museum is a small grassed area with a statue of Tenzing Norgay on its northern boundary. Tenzing is a hero to the Sherpa people and a Nepalese icon. He rose to fame when he stood on the summit of Mt Everest with Sir Edmund Hillary on the 29th of May 1953. They were the first men to stand on top of the tallest mountain on Earth and make it back down safely. I admired Tenzing's statue and then looked past it into the distance at what I had come to see.

Ama Dablam stood prominent against the blue skyline. It was a clear day, and I felt like I could reach out and touch her. The green of the farmlands and forest transformed into scree and rock at the mountain's base. Black cliffs loomed in the shadows before the brilliant white of the snow line. I began to visually and find it decorating the interior somewhere. Travellers from every corner of the world had left their mark.

I'd forgotten that many years before, I had visited this pub with a group from the United Kingdom on an overland tour named OZ BUS. Our route took us from London through Europe, then through Iran, Pakistan, India, Southeast Asia, and on to Sydney. We had passed through the Northern Territory on the final leg. In the corner of the bar, dusty and faded, I found the blue Oz Bus T-shirt still pinned to a rafter and signed by all of us.

Elise and I gorged on bacon and egg sandwiches for lunch before moving to the campground to find a secluded spot for our single tents. Being secluded turned out to be a struggle. The grounds covered two football fields, but it was filling up fast. From paying attention to the movements of the caravans and travellers on the road the previous days, I knew there would be many more checking in around sunset. We set up far enough from the bar to enable sleep and as far away from the caravans as possible. Our afternoon evolved into showering a few times, reading, doing bike maintenance, and then returning to the pub's restaurant for more calories.

A live band fired up at sundown, and the place was heaving. After ordering the Barramundi and steak combo with the added 'all you can eat' much-needed salad bar, we squeezed onto a long table with a family who introduced themselves as the Morgans.

Stephen and Kristy, with their two young kids, Max and Ellie, were from Newcastle and had taken a year off to hit the road in a van and explore Australia. It was the perfect opportunity for them with all the COVID drama and school closures. The kids were home schooled to keep up their education, and from my childhood, I knew the road would give them a PhD in street skills, face-to-face social interaction, and life experiences.

Leaving the party that seemed to be just firing up, we retired early to our tents. With earplugs and eye shades, I drifted into sleep, although only briefly. One thing I had realised, and something new travellers must be aware of, is that caravan parks and campgrounds are loud and often lit up like Christmas trees. For some reason, which must revolve around safety and insurance, the grounds have spotlights everywhere, keeping all areas void of darkness. Sleeping in a caravan or cabin might be okay, but it is challenging for tents. While coming to terms with the brightness of my surroundings, the bar had closed, and a group of drunk French travellers decided to form a circle ten metres away and carry on the party. Talking loudly with no regard for their surroundings, I was sure one of the dads from the abundance of families around us would get up and say something. They didn't.

I gave them 20 minutes until my temper and adrenalin had built up enough steam to increase my heart rate, powering me off the ground. I unzipped the tent, and with a calm fury building, I said, 'Guys, can you shut up and piss off up the road? There are families here all trying to sleep.'

With the tremors in my hands signalling a surge of adrenalin and expecting some back chat, I was pleasantly surprised when they all gathered up their chairs and crept away. It took another hour for my brain and sympathetic nervous system to calm down before I could finally drift off again. Before doing so, I vowed never to stay in campgrounds again; it was the bush or cabins from now on.

South of Daly Waters, the road straightened towards the horizon. The view reminded me of art class in high school, learning to draw perspective landscapes and vanishing points. Two lines come up from the bottom corners of a page, getting closer together to meet in the centre, giving the illusion of depth. Or if you're not an art enthusiast, it's like in the Bruce Lee film, Enter the Dragon, where he battles his enemy in the room of mirrors. When one mirror reflects the other, it creates the same effect. If you are not an action film fan, it was a long, endless, bloody road.

We woke to a headwind on the morning of day ten, and Elise was not having much fun in the saddle. The wind knocked seven kilometres an hour off our speed, eroding my resilience hour after hour. I struggled to focus on the ground we covered and slipped into dwelling on the distance we were not gaining. This was not a healthy head space.

> *Elise's journal: After the first few kilometres, it was clear that it was going to be a somewhat painful day as I had already*

begun to crack my neck and stretch my back, a ritual that until now had only come on during the late hours of the day. We broke early after only an hour and a half, my saddle sores sending dagger pains into my raw butt. You would swear by the feel of it that I would have open gaping wounds, but it's no more than a small pimple. However, with a lack of sleep comes a lack of other things. Lack of pain tolerance, lack of motivation, lack of evaluation, and lack of patience.

My gypsy parents had contacted me and told us they were about to leave their home in Charters Towers, North Queensland and travel to work at Ammaroo Cattle Station in the Northern Territory. It was a 2500 kilometre drive for them, and they were excited to get on the road again. This also meant they were due to intersect our planned route and had offered to be support crew for a few days. We planned to meet at a junction where the Stuart Highway met the Barkly Highway heading east into Queensland. It was a point where a traveller had limited options. North to Darwin, south to Alice Springs or east to Queensland. This unique cluster of buildings was aptly named Three Ways. We were still a few days' cycle away but agreed that whoever arrived first should set up camp at the roadhouse and wait. I told Dad I was carrying a handheld UHF radio for emergencies and to chat with the truck drivers. He took a similar setup in his vehicle and said he would make contact when they were within range.

Elise's journal: Luke has a radio he's using to contact the truckies about us being on the road. He flicked it on. 'Yeah mate, nah yeah but, nah mate...' Are they speaking English?
    The conversations between the truckies are so country that I can't even figure out the general gist of the content.

We cycled into a small community called Elliot which, from the exterior, looked rough. Burnt cars filled side streets, the police station was corralled behind eight foot high double barbwire fences, and cheap housing was in varying degrees of degradation. Every storefront was abandoned or closed, and the only open business was the fuel station with a grocery store attached. We pulled up for lunch and quickly realised there were limited options on the shelves. The only healthy food we could find was four apples, which we snapped up for $10, and a cooked chicken, which sold for $20.

On the way out, we stopped in front of a laminated health poster hanging on the wall. To our surprise, it was produced by the Northern Territory Government and detailed health advice for those suffering from diabetes. In Australia, Aboriginal communities have vastly higher disease rates than the rest of Australians and have a shorter life expectancy. This could be explained away by the fact that the majority chose to live remotely, far away from emergency medical care. However, the poster on the wall helped explain the underlying conditions. The poster was for diabetes prevention and listed under 'What to eat if you have Diabetes,' the Government advised bread, pasta, cereal, and crackers. No joke.

I couldn't believe what I was reading and thought it was fake. The Government was so wrong with this advice; it was literally the opposite of what someone should do. These foods were the ones that created and accelerated diabetes in people and would only make their condition much worse. As we read the information, we were rooted to the spot, feeling obligated to tell everyone around us not to believe this, or even better, rip it from the walls and burn it for the greater good. We did neither and walked to a bench nearby to eat chicken sandwiches and a semi-rotten apple. We watched the procession of locals leaving the store with Coke, Fanta, chips and fried food. As we cycled away, I felt like I was abandoning them to their fate, just like the Government had abandoned them many years before.

It was early afternoon, we were spent, and scanning the side of the highway for a camping spot. I wanted to move at least a few hundred metres off the road, preferably into the rough country, where the chances of a vehicle visiting us during the night were slim. The black flies were out in force, and I studied the annoying bastards as we rolled along. Even at top speed, the flies could stay right next to me, hovering in front of my face and landing on my lips, in my eyes, or up my nose. Their flight capability was phenomenal. The further south we travelled towards the centre of Australia, the more flies we would encounter. They flourished in the desert country and dominated daylight hours. They only disappeared half an hour before sunset while we were cooking dinner.

We found a spot, scraped out a small area of scrub clear of thorns, and set up our tents. The window of respite from the flies was glorious until about 30 minutes after sunset when the whine of the mosquitos signalled a new air force was taking over for the night shift. I'd take the bugs, thorns, snakes and spiders over drunk French tourists any day. I crawled into my tent and slept like a baby.

Our goal for lunch on day 11 was a dot on the map called Renner Springs Roadhouse, and I was salivating at the thought of bacon and egg burgers as we rolled in. We found a shady spot next to some outdoor tables and noticed a sign that read, 'Showers - $10.' It had been a few days since our last wash at Daly Waters, and with the temperature rising to 30 degrees Celsius, the bush doctor ordered a cold shower. We knew a rough scrub camp awaited us once we departed the roadhouse, so we were in no rush. I dined on a few meals, and gulped litres of cold drinks before relaxing in the shade after my shower.

I had been reading the Harry Potter series while on the road and was enjoying the escapism of wizardry and children's fantasy. I had put off reading J.K. Rowling's series for years, calling them kid's books, but now I gorged on them like a literature-starved academic. I had finished book number four two days earlier and had abandoned the extra weight at a fuel station. While chatting with Mum earlier in the week, I asked her to bring out book five, so I could continue the journey with Harry and Ron, but she couldn't find any Harry Potter books in her hometown. So, there I was, relaxing after my shower, thinking about what adventures the Hogwarts kids could get up to next, and then along comes Georgia.

Georgia was a single mother on the road from Queensland with her two sons in a campervan. They were home schooling and exploring the Outback, which was becoming a common theme for families. We started chatting and eventually got onto books about cyclists she had read, and she asked me if I had read them.

'No, I haven't read those. I'm working through the Harry Potter series.' I responded.

'Those books are so great, aren't they?' she replied, with her two boys lighting up and adding, 'We have read them all.'

'Wow, that's so good, I just finished book four, but now I can't find book five; I'll have to wait.'

'We have two copies of book five in the van.' The boys chimed in together.

'Go and get one to give away boys,' Georgia told them.

They raced off and reappeared moments later, beaming smiles holding a well-read copy of book five. I took down their address in Queensland and promised to send over copies of my two books to say thanks. They continued their adventure, and I couldn't believe my luck. The one book I needed was given to me at a roadside stop in the middle of the Outback. Maybe magic was real after all.

We started packing the bikes, and I watched a man returning from the showers who settled himself at a table opposite us. He was wearing board shorts and what I first thought was a singlet but turned out to be a singlet sunburn, the worst I'd ever seen. He was scorched bright red in contrast to his milk-white skin. He was missing a front tooth and covered in tattoos. Never one to be put off by appearances, I fired up a conversation. Jim was a truck driver travelling from Alice Springs to Darwin and Darwin to Adelaide. His truck overheated, and he pulled over for a shower and rest. He lived in Alice Springs, was married to an Aboriginal woman, and had five boys to provide for.

'I fucken hate truck driving, but it's easy money.'

'Yeah, it's a tough job, mate. I couldn't do what you do. I'll stick to cycling. What do you do for fun in Alice?'

'Not much, we spend lots of time by the river, I like my burnout comps and AFL footy, but most of the time, I'm on the road these days.'

We got on to the unavoidable subject of COVID-19, and Jim told me his theory of why it's spreading so quickly in the cities.

'I drove down to Melbourne for a job once, and I tell ya what mate, it's spot the bloody Aussie down there. Anyway, I was watching that city mob, and they all kiss and cuddle each other when they say g'day. They don't just shake hands like us. No wonder it's going rampant. I stopped for a pizza down there, and on the door was a sign saying Halal. I turned around straight away. They wouldn't want my bald head and white skin in a place like that.'

Jim came across as a good bloke trying his best to support his family. He imparted a few local pearls of wisdom onto me about the flies, which were once again flying sorties into my nostrils.

'When you camp, get a little smoky fire going; that will get rid of the bastards. Then, when you sleep, put up a tarp wall with two small fires at either end. The tarp will direct the heat from the fires onto your camp and keep away the mozzies. My wife taught me that one.'

Jim had to keep moving down the highway, and so did we. The food and showers were a nice respite, but too many luxuries will weaken the knees. It was back onto the highway and into the bush for us.

Up with the sun on day 12, we were 118 kilometres from Three Ways, where we would rest for a few days and meet up with my parents. With a plan to make it by sundown, we eased our battered backsides onto the seats and started the first rotation. The surrounding country had begun to thin out. Thick scrub gave way to patches of shin high golden grass with stunted hardy trees dotted throughout. The seemingly lifeless grass would be the perfect fuel for a bushfire. However, it would transform into a vivid green after the wet season and fill the land with life. Some termite mounds were visible, yet far fewer and smaller in stature. The Earth underfoot was evolving into a rocky red martian landscape the further south we cycled, with miniature versions of Uluru beginning to appear. I couldn't wait to see the ancient monolith up close.

We endured a constant headwind as the landscape started to undulate and throw hills at us. The inclines felt like the Himalayas after almost two weeks of flat highway. They were a gift and a curse. First, you had to pay the price to reach the crest, but then you could enjoy a downhill rush with no effort and a free kilometre. I felt strong and stubborn and viewed the uphill slogs as a personal challenge. Elise was a little more composed.

> *Elise's journal: By the time we hit our first big hill, I was dropping gear; by gear, by gear, I was zapped. 'I'm getting off.'*
> *'What.' Luke replied.*
> *'IM GETTING OFF; go ahead.'*
> *'Okay, meet ya at the top!'*
> *I jumped off the bike and walked my arse up the hill. After a moment and a talking to, I climbed back on. It's crazy how at kilometre 40 you think, 'I can't do this,' and then eight hours later, we are rolling into Three Ways after 118 kilometres.*

The Three Ways Roadhouse was different from the oasis in the desert we were hoping for, but it had a small caravan park around the back, hot showers, and cold drinking water. We checked into a small cabin but immediately regretted it. The air conditioner sounded like it would rattle off its wall mounts and kill us in our sleep. It also discharged warmer air than the atmosphere outside. The free market rule of supply and demand was in full swing at this remote crossroads, with our little hotbox costing $140 per night for the privilege.

We had covered 970 kilometres in 12 days and were in dire need of some rest days and re-feeds. We devoured two roast dinners each, hobbled back to the cabin and lay down to the cacophony of trucks pulling in, men shouting, doors banging, and a rattling heating system. I was so exhausted that it was all a sweet lullaby.

The following morning was spent lounging inside the airconditioned roadhouse, and we chatted to the German manager Sofia about a small town located 25 kilometres south named Tennant Creek. Sofia had been working in the area for five years, had seen it all, and was frustrated. I asked her, 'What's Tennant Creek like?'

'The locals run the show around here,' she replied. She was gesturing towards a car full of Aboriginal people pulling up.

'Guess how many police we have in our tiny town of 3500 people?' she asked.

I had no idea, but I did know our community in Tasmania, with 3000 locals and 7000 tourists in summer, had one police officer.

'We have 53 full-time police; that's how bad it is. They burnt down the grocery store last week, so now we don't have one. The locals are only allowed to buy alcohol between 4 p.m. and 7 p.m. each day, and there is always a huge line up. Be careful if you head into town after dark.'

We left Sofia to her work and returned to the park out the back just as Mum and Dad arrived driving their big Toyota Land Cruiser and towing a caravan. It was an iconic scene watching them pull up, and it took me straight back to my childhood. My parents lived in a perpetual state of travel and adventure, and I had grown up on the road with them. They only paused their gypsy life for six years to put my sister and me through high school in one location. They were back on the road after my graduation when I shipped off to the Army. We spent the afternoon eating Mum's homemade cheesecake and catching up, and they agreed to be our road crew for the next 500 kilometres to Alice Springs.

During our rest on day 14, we drove into Tennant Creek to hopefully resupply with groceries for the next leg of the journey. We pulled over at an old telegraph station where an information board detailed the area's history. I was captivated by a story of a fellow cyclist who was a pioneer with none of our modern engineering or comforts.

Jerome Murif was an Irish-Australian engineer and bushman who was the first to cycle across the entire Australian continent from south to north. His 1897 route took him from Glenelg, a suburb of Adelaide, to Darwin. He was given food and assistance at Tennant Creek telegraph station, where the blacksmith produced new pedals for his bicycle. He was starved from his hazardous journey and recorded in his journal,

> '*At Tennant Creek, during the many days I remained at the telegraph station, I could eat almost continuously. My happiest thoughts were centered around the dinner table, and there was a savage delight in the partaking of every meal.*'

In 1911 another adventurer named Frances Birtles cycled from Sydney up the east coast, across to Darwin, and then down through the centre of Australia. Upon reaching the telegraph station, he wrote,

> '*At Tennant Creek I was most hospitably received. I had a good clean bed, which was a longed for luxury and a splendid meal of beef and vegetables, after which I had a look at the garden. The vegetables were growing as well as I had ever seen them anywhere, and I came to the conclusion that even the desert will grow anything when water is obtained.*'

These two early explorers were humbling to read about. Sometimes, I was naive while planning adventures and forgot that great men and women had often been there before me. Not being the first didn't mean the experiences were not worth pursuing. The valuable lessons gained from physical and mental challenges in the natural environment transcend technology and time. The adventure would be new for me, so I never worried about following in the footsteps of others. I could learn from their hard-felt mistakes and go even further.

After growing up in remote regions of Australia, I knew what to expect before arriving in Tennant Creek township, but Elise had never seen anything like it in her own country before.

> *Elise's journal: We took a day trip into Tennant Creek. We hadn't heard great things, so expectations were low. And the reality was a fairly derelict, slow and sad town. If there wasn't a*

high gate around it, there was wire fencing, and if there wasn't wire, there were security screens on all windows and doors.

'Is there anywhere to get groceries?' We asked the butcher as we grabbed some meat for the next few days on the road.

'Well, there's some fruit and veg at the United petrol station. It's slim pickings though.

We headed to the United and grabbed what we could, then found out a temporary grocery store had been erected in a shed next door, which had everything we needed to get us 500 kilometres to Alice Springs. It's funny how, after just two days resting, I feel like we haven't ridden in weeks. I'm refreshed and ready for the road again.

Up with the sun again the following morning, we had planned to set out first and meet Mum and Dad for smoko, which is Australian slang for morning tea, out on the road somewhere. An old guy aged about 70 came up as we hopped on our bikes. He was dressed for his daily run, and before he slowly bounded off, he said, 'You gotta stay active. Sitting down is the new smoking, have fun.' I couldn't agree more. We had unloaded two panniers and our water barrels into the caravan, and my legs felt strong. With a tailwind and lighter bikes, we flew down the highway.

Mum served up scones with jam, cream, and hot coffee for our first break. This was the way to adventure. One hundred and thirty one kilometres south of Three Ways and powered by baked goods, we cycled a dirt road into one of the most iconic sites in the Northern Territory, Karlu Karlu. Also known as Devil's Marbles, Karlu Karlu is an Aboriginal name translated to *round boulders* and is a sacred site to the Kaytetye, Warumungu, and Warlpiri people. One minute we stared blankly at the barren flat Earth, and the next, the landscape was covered with spherical red granite rocks. Some sat solo; others stacked atop each other forming monuments. It was as if two Gods were playing an intergalactic game of marbles, and when one was victorious, the other tipped his bag out to scatter them haphazardly across the human Earth below. There could be some different story of erosion and time to explain their appearance, but not in my imagination. We scrambled to the top of the largest stack of stones and watched the sun slowly descend into God's playground. It was a special place to visit for anyone travelling through the Outback.

Two days north of Alice Springs, we stopped for fruit cake and tea at a memorial built for one of the legends of Australia's pioneer history, Ned Ryan. Edward (Ned) Ryan was born in Tipperary, Ireland, in 1835 and immigrated to Australia as a young man. He worked as a labourer for the South Australian Government in 1865 and was recruited for a wet season survey in 1866 to Arnhem Land in the Northern Territory. The survey team became trapped without food on the East Alligator River and was menaced by hostile Aborigines.

To escape, Ned and a fellow bushman built a makeshift raft using the skins of their 27 packhorses and were followed by hungry crocodiles and sharks on a six day voyage. The raft blew 13 kilometres out to sea before being beached and finding safety for the team at Escape Cliffs. On a separate expedition, Ned and his brother Jeremiah ventured into the Outback again as surveyors, leading a group of 140 people for the Northern Territory government, where they discovered the outpost which is Darwin today. They were also lucky enough to witness the planting of the first pole of the Overland Telegraph Line (OTL), which eventually connected Darwin to Adelaide.

In 1885 Ned was appointed foreman of a well sinking party to drill wells for permanent water along the OTL. He pioneered methods utilising camels and horses to rotate machinery and penetrate deep into the unyielding red Earth. Ned died in the Outback in 1893 of appendicitis, amongst a geography so unlike his birthplace of Ireland, but a country he seemed to relish and called home. The well he drilled north of Alice Springs was renamed Ned's Well as a shrine to this legend of the bush. Reading about Ned while sipping my cup of tea, I wondered if I could ever experience adventures like his in today's world. Was there anywhere left in the world so remote and hostile that it could deliver up the adventure Ned endured? I stared out at the horizon, squinting from the glare, and watched the heat shimmer off the ground. There must be somewhere.

❖❖❖

At this stage of a cycle expedition, you must be wondering if we were ever getting flat tyres. We were using tubes inside our tyres, which sounds common. However, these days tubeless, and special sealant liquids inside the tyre, are gaining popularity. The sealant acted as an instant fix if a thorn punctured the tyre, but we were told there were often leakage issues. Tubes sounded easier to repair in remote areas, so we stuck with it. The first flat was almost exciting, and I went through the process of removing the tyre, pulling out the tube, patching the hole, and reassembling it, all with good temperament.

By the fourth or fifth time, I resorted to throwing in the spare tube and repairing the punctured ones in the evening. A couple of times when we bush camped, we both received flats while walking our bikes 300 metres off the road. Thorns and prickly scrub would go through our weakened outer tyres like Delhi belly through a backpacker. After a big day in the saddle, nothing was more frustrating than noticing we had three flat tyres needing repair before bed. This forced us to carry our fully loaded bikes off the ground whenever we departed the bitumen. By the time we were nearing Alice, I was well and truly over fixing tyres, but just like building snow walls around tents every day in the mountains for protection from the wind, it was a pain in the arse but all part of the adventure.

On the morning of day 19, we stopped for smoko on the Tropic of Capricorn, an invisible circle of latitude crossing the centre of Australia. Mum had outdone herself and whipped up bacon and egg sandwiches, coffee, and fruitcake. With an easterly breeze hindering us slightly but knowing we would make it to a comfy caravan park in Alice by the afternoon, Elise and I became excited kids and took to songwriting as we powered along after our break. Hoping for the road to turn west and gain a better angle to the wind, we sang out loud to the tune of the Village People.

*'Go west, down to Alice Springs. Go west,
we'll eat all the things.'*

*'Go west, where we'll fry some eggs. Go west,
and we'll rest our legs.'*

With roughly an hour remaining to arrive in town, I was looking forward to a few rest days and visiting the tourist attractions the red centre was famous for. The final five kilometres into Alice were all downhill. With a tailwind assisting, we went rocketing down the valley into civilisation. Alice was a big place with a permanent population of around 30,000, accounting for roughly 10 per cent of the Northern Territories population. The town sits alongside the often dry Todd River and was established in 1872. I flicked on my radio to connect with Dad and find out where he had chosen to camp. After several attempts to raise him, his voice crackled onto the airwaves.

'You there knackers?'

'Yeah Dad, where did you pull up mate?'

'We are at the G'day Mate Tourist Park, on the other side of town, through The Gap.'

'Roger that mate, see you soon.'

I had no idea where that was, but with modern phone technology alive again, we found it in seconds and cycled towards them. The places were aptly named, and at a point where the road dissected a mountainous ridge running through town was The Gap. Its sheer walls hugged the highway, and once through, we located the park and rolled into a lush green oasis full of caravans to find our faithful roadcrew sitting under a big tree. We had travelled 1500 kilometres from Darwin in 19 days, and even with the support crew for the last 500 kilometres, we were well and truly ready for a break. We were halfway across the country, and the bikes needed some maintenance, but most importantly, we wanted to take some time to visit one of Australia's most iconic attractions, Uluru.

CHAPTER 4

The Red Centre

I realised quickly that the people who called the Northern Territory home had a distorted understanding of distance and language. We were asked by the reception manager at the Caravan Park, 'Are you gonna pop down to Uluru for a look while you're here?' The answer was yes, but then we realised popping down to 'the rock' comprised a 1000 kilometre return trip from Alice Springs. Cycling that far would add two weeks to our expedition, and I was never a fan of backtracking the same path. We thought a lazy guided tour would be an ideal way to relax. Unfortunately, the COVID-19 pandemic, or more accurately, the Government's policies surrounding social distancing rules, had forced all tour companies to close. The only other option was to hire a car.

A day after arriving in town, Elise and I hit the road at 135 kilometres per hour, which felt like warp speed compared to our pedal power. When we cycled along slowly, our brains absorbed tiny bits of information from the environment. I noticed cracks in the road, the varied colours of the rocks, and vapour coming off the bitumen in the afternoons. I could watch lizards, birds, grasshoppers, and other critters going about their lives on the side of our route. I could also take in the symphony of the country surrounding me and think deeply about its origins and future. Inside the car, cruising along slightly faster than allowed, with the air conditioning reigning in our discomfort, the environment was a blur off to my right, and I was disconnected from it. It was like trying to watch a movie in fast-forward; I understood the basic idea but not the finer details. The driving experience became an internal one. How was I feeling? Do I have enough fuel? Am I hungry yet? The natural world no longer breached my consciousness. It made me realise that, as a species, if we ever want to tackle our climate issues and look after this land like the indigenous had for 40000 years, we must slow our lives down and learn to walk the earth once again. Only then will we see the detail and understand its priceless value and what we were risking. If my mind had slipped into environmentalist mode on the drive out, it was compounded tenfold when we finally lay eyes on Uluru.

> *Elise's journal: I've wanted to see this place since my friend visited here when I was nine, and she brought me back a little rock from Uluru or Ayers Rock, as they still called it then. After a few hours of driving, passing Mount Conner (which we thought was Uluru until we saw the sign), we pulled into the tourist resort/community they had purposefully built for visitors. Everything matching, everything in its place. A stark contrast, Luke says to the Aboriginal communities that live just a few kilometres from here. We drove towards the national park and Uluru.*

The Aboriginal people have a unique way of remembering and sharing their knowledge of the land, called song lines. These song lines were walking routes that crossed the country, linking essential sites and locations. Before colonisation, these paths were maintained by regular use, burning off, and clearing. One example of a song line was a 3500 kilometre route connecting where we stood in the central desert to the east coast of Australia, where

Byron Bay is located. This trail allowed desert tribes to visit the ocean, and coastal tribes to travel inland, visiting their culturally significant sites.

I couldn't imagine the sensations the early coastal tribes must have felt walking inland through the desert country to arrive at the monolith of Uluru. Sitting in our comfortable car as it came into view, we were silenced by how enormous it was. The steep sandstone grew out of the flat country, projecting an ancient and godly atmosphere. It looked fake due to its contrast with the surrounding land, and the deep red hue forced me to remove my sunglasses and capture the richness un-tinted. I understood instantly why a tribe would walk months to visit this site. It had an energy that echoed a message of creation, something far more important than the individual. It was a sentinel and a marker in time, showing us how insignificant we were to the universe's grand scheme. It was humbling and changed my internal dialogue from 'Me, myself, and I' to 'Why are we here?' These were the same thoughts that captured the stoics of Rome and undoubtedly initiated campfire conversations amongst the Australian tribes, ideas that are as timeless as the rock itself. Visiting Uluru for the first time will leave you questioning the meaning of life.

The western face of the rock was the iconic image you see on every postcard, but Uluru has many faces, and the best way to see them all was to walk around its base. No one can climb to the top of the rock anymore; that liberty ended in 2017 due to erosion issues and the site's spiritual significance. The steep 400 metre ascent also claimed 37 tourist lives while in operation since the middle of last century. There is now a well maintained 11 kilometre dirt path around the bottom. The trail hugs the base of the rock, which allowed us to touch the flaky stone and see its many features up close. In some places, the formation wrapped over itself in waves; in others, it has been carved out by water. The dark algae staining the grooves told the story of the wet season where, at certain times, Uluru was transformed by waterfalls cascading down its flanks. Even now, at the end of the dry season, there were small ponds and caverns containing fresh water.

I am not familiar with the details of the song line that connects Uluru to the ocean, but it almost certainly must contain verses about the permanent fresh water and the cool overhanging shelters dotted around the rock. It was an oasis, a place that would have attracted game animals and humans alike. It would have been an important meeting place where tribes could share knowledge, settle disputes, and recover from long journeys. It was now a tourist attraction, yet because of COVID-19, we were alone to experience its power. Just like the diseases brought by the settlers that decimated the native population, the fear of another virus had cleared the land of tourists. While standing there alone in total silence, I was grateful for the latter.

We spent the night at the tourist village, paying $60 for a patch of grass to erect our tents. The following morning, we decided to shout ourselves a luxury breakfast at the resort restaurant; however, after being told the price, we ended up back where I was more comfortable, boiling oats on a camp stove in the dirt. The Aboriginal communities lived alongside these luxury resorts where every food imaginable could be eaten at the buffet. Yet, simple fruit was hard to find inside the local grocery stores servicing the communities. It was a conflict I was having trouble reconciling.

We drove into the park again to visit the Olgas or Kata Tjuta, as it's known to the local Anangu people who have inhabited the area for 22,000 years. The first non-Aboriginal person to see the incredible rock formation was explorer Ernest Giles in 1872. He named the highest peak Mount Olga after Queen Olga of Wurttemberg, a kingdom of Germany at the time. The nickname of the Olgas stuck when the area was opened to tourists in the 1950s.

> *Elise's journal: The Olgas aren't spoken about much, but the bulbous sister to Uluru is just as stunning. A viewing platform as you get closer allows you to see it in the morning glow, and its highest points tower 200 metres higher than Uluru. We did a short walk into the gorge and were awed by the huge*

walls of smaller rocks compressed together by mud and sand to form this giant in the desert.

On the way back to Alice, we took a quick detour of 322 kilometres over to Kings Canyon, another geological formation we couldn't miss. The land had been home to the Luritja people for 20000 years and is now the Watarrka National Park covering 71000 hectares. We slathered on sunscreen, filled our water bottles, and hiked up to the top of the canyon for a six kilometre walk around its rim. The geology was different from the other sites we had visited so far. This area was once sand dunes 400 million years ago, which were compressed and eroded over time to form a layered canyon with multitudes of beehive shaped domes across its roof. The colours, textures, and ancient structures were unique.

Elise's journal: We could only assume that there had been many people overestimating their ability and underestimating the heat in this place, with an emergency medical station every kilometre on the short walk around the rim. This place was so different from Uluru, or the Olgas. It's incredible to see such variation of rock in close proximity. Luke caught me a goanna like he'd promised and got bitten in the process.

We were hoping to make it back to Alice by nightfall but only made it to the Erldunda Roadhouse on the highway intersection at sunset. We were back on the road at dawn the following day, enjoying the last hours of comfort and speed. We spent the afternoon restocking supplies, fixing punctures, and doing bike maintenance. With Dad's help, Elise fitted a piece of yoga mat and a thick sock over her seat for added comfort for the second leg of the journey. Mum and Dad were off to work at Ammaroo Cattle Station, a vast piece of cattle country spanning 3.5 million acres. I would love to go and explore the land with Dad, but as Elise often told me, one adventure at a time. We had 1500 kilometres remaining to reach Adelaide, and after four days of luxury, I was keen to get back on the bike and back in the bush.

The next key location to rest and explore was Coober Pedy, a famous Opal mining community 700 kilometres away. Apparently, half the town lived underground, where it was cooler in the summer months. I wanted to see if this was true or a tourist myth. To be in Coober Pedy within a week, we needed to maintain 100 kilometres daily. We bid farewell to my parents, thanking them for being road crew, and cycled out of Alice heading south. We had a strong tailwind, a downhill trajectory, and minimal traffic. My legs felt refreshed and powerful underneath me, but my adaption to the seat had weakened due to days off, and I needed to suck up a bit of discomfort before finding my flow again.

It was a fast morning, and we pulled into Stuart's Well rest stop for lunch, where I devoured coffee, biscuits, bacon and eggs inside the eclectic bar room out the back. They had a two metre python in a glass enclosure, a world class Smurf collection, and a family of camels in a pen outside. I was chatting with a friendly Vietnamese girl who had worked at the roadhouse for two years. She became concerned when she heard we were going to bush camp for the night.

'You must be careful,' she began to tell us.

'A year ago, some tourists decided to camp in the bush but were lost when they drove off the road. There were three of them; they got bogged down, one stayed with the vehicle, and the other two walked in different directions to find help. It was two weeks before they located two of them, but one was never found.'

It was a story I had heard many times before, and I had trouble understanding how these situations could occur. Why didn't they stay with the vehicle? Why didn't they follow their tracks out? When faced with a survival situation, stress and anxiety often surged and could cause people to rush and make the wrong decisions. It wasn't fair to blame the tourists entirely; they underestimated the harsh reality of the Outback. Just like Ranger Rod's friend in Katherine, it could happen to anyone. One thing to always remember about desert country is that such a vast land void of water, and with very few people around to help, a small mistake can have deadly consequences.

Elise's journal: Feeling fresh, we covered another 30 kilometres before finding a suitable rest stop with water, a table, and shade, our 5 star rated rest stop accommodation. 4 star is no shade, 3 star is no water, 2 star is no table, and then you have one star, which is a truck stop with just bins and none of the above. There was a creepy van parked at the stop, yet no one surfaced the entire time, but we still scurried off into the bush to be safe. I thought it would be cooling off by sundown, but after putting up the tents, I was in a lather and walked back to the tap to have a splash. As I came back, there was my husband, standing there wearing nothing but a head torch, trying to cool off. The wonders of the desert and wide-open spaces.

It was day 25, and I was staring down the highway at nothing in particular when I noticed movement up ahead. Someone was walking on the bitumen, on the wrong side of the road, in the middle of nowhere. At first, I thought it could be a stranded tourist, but as we got closer, I realised it was a fellow adventurer pushing a large cart and powering along. We pulled up and introduced ourselves. James was completing a modern day song line. He was walking across the country, starting on the Sunshine Coast north of Brisbane in Queensland, and had planned to walk to Perth in Western Australia. COVID-19 border restrictions had forced him to detour north from Port Augusta in South Australia, so he was heading to Uluru, where he would finish his trip. He had covered 2000 kilometres with his 50 kilogram cart leading the way, and it was like a Rolls Royce version of a shopping trolley. He was a great guy who, like us, was making the most of this new COVID-19 life. We wished him luck for the remainder of his journey.

◆◆◆

I have shared many beautiful aspects of the outback and some of its darker secrets. I always strived to tell a truthful story about how I saw and experienced it. As beautiful as most of the environment was, we also witnessed civilisation at its worst. Campgrounds and caravan parks were meeting grounds for humans, and as mentioned earlier, they were bright and loud party scenes that were conflicted with our needs: rest and recovery. I have touched on the Aboriginal story in Australia, and I hope my observations provide a foundation of understanding.

The one thing we weren't expecting was the sheer volume of rubbish and human filth that built up on the sides of remote roads and highways. The trash seemed to fall into a no man's land of jurisdiction. Countless burnt out cars, tyres, rims, bumpers, and other vehicle wreckage were scattered across the country. Broken glass, plastic bottles, cans, wrappers of every variety and an unquantifiable number of plastic bags. We encountered nappies by the hundreds, bottles of urine in all shades of yellow, and soiled adult underwear at truck stops, all discarded as if it was a rubbish dump. Where does this type of selfishness come from? It was such strange behaviour, and I couldn't come up with any explanation. As with all my adventures, I will share the good, the bad, and what humans do.

Our first raindrops and a cooler climate greeted us on day 26 as we crossed the invisible border into South Australia. As we approached, I was expecting a border checkpoint with armed police guarding the state against quarantine breakers. Instead, there was only a plastic table with a solo police officer who radiated frustration and didn't even look over as we cycled past. On either side of the highway, the country had recently received a soaking, and I noticed tiny green shoots of grass beginning to emerge from the earth. It was an early wet season, and like the Gobi Desert, the rain gave rise to new life amongst the desolate landscape.

Elise's journal: We stopped for the usual meal of bacon and eggs at Kulgera Roadhouse, the last roadhouse in the Northern Territory, before crossing into South Australia. A chirpy woman came for a chat. 'Husbands are great, aren't they,' she said, as mine went to get me food and hers went to get her a coffee. 'Yeah, I found that they come in handy a fair bit.'

'We've been married forty years, and the sex is still great!' I laughed out loud at her honesty, and we chatted for a while longer. Luke is currently taking the gold medal placing for punctures, his tally reaching six by the time we pulled into the bush. I have successfully avoided all thorns, screws, glass, and other paraphernalia. I assume Luke would be the one to change my tyre anyway... even if I did get one.

While we carried our bikes into the bush for our first camp in South Australia, I thought cyclists who read about this would shake their heads at our amateur skills. There is likely a simple fix to avoiding punctures. However, with no remedy at hand, I was happy to do the grunt work. A simple fix wouldn't have made any difference on this particular night, because where I rolled my bike happened to be straight into a thorn minefield. Once again, I had a flat tyre to fix before bed. I noticed Elise's front tyre was also flat, and she changed it out herself. She decided not to patch the tube, leaving her with no spare. I mentioned to her,

'You should fix that now; otherwise, if you get a flat tomorrow, you won't have a spare and will have to patch it on the side of the road.'

She gave me a look that told me to mind my own business, and I didn't push the issue. We woke to dingoes howling, and I joined them for a chorus at dawn. One cheeky dog must have resonated with my vocals because he came in for a closer look. I saw him 20 metres away, and we made eye contact before he bolted for the safety of the scrub. Dingos are very wary of humans, being their biggest predators who hunt them relentlessly. As a kid, I remember a dingo pelt fetched $20 as part of a government-funded eradication program. We packed up our heavy bikes and humped them back to the highway for sunrise.

> *Elise's journal: We carried our bikes through the spikey minefield back to the road, not wanting to change yet another tyre, but within the first five minutes, my front wheel went flat. I know, I know, I should've fixed my spare. Luke stared at me with the 'always listen to your husband' look. He fixed the tyre for me, not because I can't, but because he knows he's quicker, and he hates waiting for me to do things if I fumble when he knows how to do it.*

There were several Aboriginal communities connected via rough dirt roads to the highway, and we received many waves from smiling people in overloaded cars as they passed us. We could easily pick the vehicles belonging to the communities because they were always borderline not roadworthy, with different sized wheels, broken windows, odd paint jobs, and blowing smoke. We had a private game to guess from a distance who owned the car. If it was a nice four wheel drive pulling a caravan, it was definitely a white fellas' car, and we wouldn't get a wave. A small van, loaded with water barrels and swags; it was backpackers wearing dreadlocks for sure and they waved half the time. If smoke poured out, moving slowly, with a different coloured bonnet, it was a black fellas' car, and they always waved.

> *Elise's journal: Each car was more beaten up than the next, spluttering with broken windows and bits falling off. However, there was always a cheery black arm waving at us out of them.*

With the assistance of the wind, we had been covering over 100 kilometres each day since Alice Springs. On day 29, we had only 154 kilometres remaining before Coober Pedy, so we decided to go for it. With 4 star hotel luxury in our minds, we set off at dawn and powered all day. The landscape had slowly changed throughout the week, slowly shedding itself of scrub and trees. It was the bleakest view we had seen on this trip, with flat pebbled Earth and the occasional tuft of straw grass as far as the eyes could see. I also started noticing small mounds of dirt scattered randomly across the country on either side of the road.

The piles varied in size from two metres up to small hills, and as we ticked over the kilometres, vast numbers of them began to appear. The piles were an assortment of different coloured dirt, like an Indian marketplace selling spices in red, orange, white, and gold. All the shades of a desert rainbow were lit up in the afternoon sun. We were entering the famous Opal fields we had heard so much about. It clicked that what we were seeing was the spoil from core drilling when searching for Opal. I noticed a sign telling everyone to stay out of the areas due to the danger of open shafts. I would learn the following day that I was seeing a tiny fraction of the 2 million abandoned mining shafts drilled into the Earth.

It would be easy to judge Coober Pedy by what you first saw on the surface, a small country town with little going on. Yet like a book cover, we had judged too soon because most of the towns homes and infrastructure were buried below the ground. We checked in at the Desert Cave Hotel, and as the manager walked us to the entrance, we realised the accommodation had been dug into the side of a hill. We entered through a door in the cliff, and the temperature dropped ten degrees. We were allowed to keep our bikes in the room, and as we walked through the passageways, the clicking from our wheels echoed off the rock walls and ceiling. The room was spacious and, as you could imagine, felt like a cave. It was sensory deprivation with no natural light and total silence due to the thick rock walls separating guests. We decided to splash out in true Richmond style, buying a cooked chicken and picnic spread from the grocery store. We had covered 2185 kilometres in 29 days, and we toasted our success with wine and beer in our underground grotto.

A full rest day in Coober Pedy involved maintenance on the bikes, eating copious amounts of food and booking a town tour in the afternoon. Noble Tours, operated by Aaron, a knowledgeable Opal miner, was an eye opener to this unique mining community. Coober Pedy was established in 1915, and the name evolved from an Aboriginal term 'kupa-piti,' which roughly translated to 'whitefellas holes'. The town is situated on the edge of the Stuart Ranges, on beds of sandstone and siltstone 30 metres deep and covered with a stony treeless desert. Very little plant life exists in the area due to the lack of rainfall and topsoil. The Arabana people traditionally own the land, but the Kokatha and Yankunytjatjara people are closely attached to some ceremonial sites in the area.

Most of the town lives in dugouts. Like our hotel, they carved caves into the hillsides and renovated. We visited a lovely multi-bedroom dugout, a museum, a Serbian church, and a mine filled with a labyrinth of tunnels. The temperatures in summer could exceed 45 degrees Celsius on the surface, and living in a dugout created a more forgiving habitat hovering around 20-25 degrees Celsius. Seventy per cent of the world's Opal comes from the mines surrounding Coober Pedy, and only 10 per cent of the expansive Opal fields have been mined. A claim could be purchased for $200, and anyone is welcome to come and try their luck. Aaron explained,

'First, you drill a hole and hope to find some sign of an opal seam. If you find some, you dig; if not, you move and drill again.'

He went on to say that the holes were not allowed to be filled for safety reasons, and people have died by falling into shafts covered with a layer of dirt. Better to leave them exposed and visible.

The tour finished at the Breakaway Mountains, a layer cake of colourful hills outside of town protected from mining due to their cultural significance. We stopped for a photo of the famous Dingo Fence on the way. I knew about this unique fence and had a future expedition idea waiting on the shelf, that involved cycling along its length. Initially, this might sound like a boring trip, but it is one of the longest structures in the world, stretching 5614 kilometres from South Australia to Queensland. It was constructed two metres high with wire mesh between 1880 and

1885. The goal of the huge project was to keep dingoes away from the relatively fertile southeast part of the country and protect the sheep farming industry. One unlucky farmer lost 11000 sheep in a year due to dingo attacks before the completion of the fence. To cycle it would be an expedition of logistical challenges, but one I will attempt in the future.

Our rest day also coincided with our fourth wedding anniversary. To celebrate, we recreated our picnic from the night before, and I settled in for a drink with my best friend and adventure partner for life. Elise and I were married in Las Vegas at the end of a three month American road trip full of climbing, B.A.S.E Jumping, and hiking all over the country. We decided to do the ceremony a little differently by having it at 5000 feet elevation inside the basket of a hot air balloon. I was wearing my B.A.S.E Jumping parachute, and we hired a parachute for Elise. The celebrant married us, and then we held hands on the edge of the basket before sealing the deal by jumping off. The Nevada desert landscape looked incredible during the freefall, and our parachutes opened safely before we landed on a patch of grass in front of a casino. It was a unique start to a marriage, and I am the luckiest man alive to call Elise my wife.

On day 31, we packed up and walked our bikes through the tunnels of our recovery cave, ready for the next leg of our journey. We were immediately met with howling winds and thunderstorms as we opened the big doors allowing the environment to flood inside. We both knew it would be a rough day as we donned our wet weather gear. The hammering rain and cold wind made the first two riding blocks of the day some of the toughest of the whole trip. We were fighting a headwind all day and were both struggling with the conditions. To break up the monotony, I hopped off to catch a blue tongue lizard lying by the side of the road; then, I found a unique grasshopper. He was small, the size of a ten cent piece, and had evolved to look identical to one of the red pebbles covering the ground at my feet. Evolution was incredible, and this little guy had adapted to avoid predators where no trees or grass could protect him. Elise wasn't too interested in my new little friend; the conditions had crushed her enthusiasm.

We managed to cover 92 kilometres with plenty of rain, wind, and heartache before finding a roadside stop with a sheltered table we could erect our tents alongside. A thunderstorm rolled in with torrential rain, flooding the entire area. I frantically dug trenches around the tents to keep our sleeping bags dry. Before crawling inside, I quickly checked our gear was ready for tomorrow, and noticed my helmet was missing. After searching and coming up empty handed, I realised I had left it on the ground while I examined the grasshopper on the side of the highway 12 kilometres north. I lay in my tent, trying to understand how I could be so stupid, not to notice it wasn't strapped to my head. The conclusion I came to was stress. This was the most stressful day we had endured; with storms, wind, rain, and trucks speeding passed. I was stressed and anxious, causing my sympathetic nervous system to kick in, and my fight or flight response to take over. When this happens, sensory dampening comes into play. My system dedicates energy to keeping me alive and neglects the missing sensation of a tight strap under my chin. This is why staying calm and composed in critical situations leads to better decision making.

Elise's journal: After much deliberation, I snuck out of my tent at midnight to relieve myself and was confronted with the most incredible light display nature had to offer. The storm had moved into the distance, and the entire horizon was getting lit up every second with lighting.

By the time we officially woke up, the clouds had cleared, and all that remained were deep puddles and cool air. We pushed off and were greeted with a tailwind that didn't leave us until the end of the day.

After waking up to a northerly wind, I decided not to go and retrieve my helmet. It was only 12 kilometres away, which doesn't sound far, but with a strong headwind, and then 12 kilometres back, it could cost us almost two hours. We hit the road and started making progress south.

I noticed the type of rubbish on the side of the road was changing. Every town, state, and country had unique alcoholic roadside trash. Previously, during our Gobi Desert crossing in Mongolia, we always knew when we were close to a town by the build-up of glass vodka bottles. In the Northern Territory, it was green VB cans announcing civilisation. In Queensland, it was GOLD XXXX beer cans, and now that we were in South Australia, we saw Coopers Pale Ale cans littering the roadside. It was tribalism at its purest, like spear tips or cave paintings of rival mobs. It told a story and created a social boundary.

◆◆◆

Woomera is a small town situated in the middle of South Australia's flattest moonscape. There is literally not a tree to be seen in any direction. The town is home to the Australian Governments Department of Defence aerospace and systems testing range covering 122,000 prohibited square kilometres. What occurs out in the desert and what's tested is all secret, of course. If we stick to the Aboriginal theme of our journey, my family had a song line that came right through this area many years ago. My grandparents, Harry and Jean Richmond, decided to leave their lives behind in England, pay ten pounds to board a boat with two kids, and voyage to the great southern land. They arrived in Adelaide and boarded a bus the following day, which brought them 450 kilometres north into the desert, arriving at Woomera. My grandfather was a clever man and had been employed to work with the aerospace department fixing rocket fuel systems.

The change of environments between England and Woomera was like going from a wet lush forest to Mars. The town was named after an Aboriginal spear throwing implement, that extends the range a spear can be thrown, called the Woomera. It's a fitting name for a place dedicated to testing modern apocalyptic weapons. I wondered if my grandparent's sense of adventure caused their immigration here. They could have stayed in a nice comfortable life in England, but they chose to uproot and plant themselves on the other side of the world in one of the harshest environments imaginable. As I looked to my past, I could see that at times when my life could have become easy and routine, I had consistently turned my back on it to seek adventure instead too. The Richmond blood from my grandfather and gypsy parents still flows pure in my veins. Who knows where it could guide us next.

We spent the morning exploring the town, and I stood on the plot of empty land where my family's first tiny house had been. It was an empowering feeling to know more about my history and where it all started for us in Australia. I could get a tiny sense of what it must feel like for Aboriginal people returning to their country knowing the ancient stories connecting them to it.

The weather was cooling off, and we enjoyed a peaceful bush camp on night 34. The following morning, we powered along towards Port Augusta, a town on South Australia's coast. It is a crossroads for the southern highways leading east to Adelaide and west to Perth. It was also a big town where I could get a replacement helmet before the last stretch into Adelaide. The traffic was building up considerably as we progressed closer to the coast. We got a few honks from drivers out of annoyance, saying hello differently than they were in the Northern Territory. After seven hours in the saddle, we cycled into a lush caravan park in Port Augusta. Camping on the freshly cut green grass was a nice change, and we splashed out on salmon and vegetables for dinner.

Dawn had us up and recharged, with some jobs to do before we departed. I serviced the bikes, and then we went to the ocean. We had started this cycle with views of the Timor Sea north of Darwin, and pulled up 36 days and 2800 kilometres later, cycling into views of the Indian Ocean south of Port Augusta. The salt smell and the humidity were a thick brew, in contrast with the crisp desert air from the weeks before. We enjoyed a coffee to celebrate our big milestone before joining the road heading east.

Elise's journal: We had a few errands to run. First, now that we were in the place of cities and with that rules, we had to get a new helmet for Luke. A nice hearty breakfast had us heading off around 9 a.m. to the bike store two kilometres away. As we crossed the bridge, a cop car went passed in the other direction ... and sure enough, by the time we had reached the other side of the water, they had spun around to pull us up.

'Where's your helmet, mate?'

'We are literally going to get one right now.'

'I'll have to write you a caution, I should fine you, and you'll have to walk your bike the rest of the way.'

So, we walked next to our bikes on the footpath to the cycle shop. Naturally, Luke got a puncture. On approach, it wasn't looking promising, and sure enough, it wasn't open on Wednesdays, Thursdays, or Sundays... today was Wednesday. So, we sat out the front, watching two men without teeth enter the house across the road, score some drugs, and leave, as we fixed Luke's tyre. The irony. After all that, we walked our bikes back to where the cops pulled us up, to Big W, and grabbed a shitty helmet that slipped off backwards... at least it looks like Luke is following the law. So, we were finally on the road.

The road out of town was packed with cars, buses, and trucks, all fighting to get to their destinations. There was only a tiny strip for us to cycle on, and immediately we were copping abuse from irate drivers. With a large traffic volume in both directions, drivers couldn't get around us, and it wasn't long before we received our first indication of human annoyance, the mighty middle finger.

Elise's journal: This new highway was not like the Stuart, and almost immediately, we felt the wrath of city drivers. People couldn't take a wide berth around us with so much on-coming traffic, and it only took us 10 kilometres and a few middle fingers to pull over.

'City riding sucks.'

'Yeah, I'm not loving it. Bloody dangerous.'

Within the time it took us to eat a banana, we decided to cycle back to the wharf on the waterfront and finish our expedition in Port Augusta. We weighed up our two options: Victoria was closed due to COVID-19, and Adelaide was another 300 kilometres away. If the early indicators were anything to go by it would be a rough and dangerous three days to Adelaide, leaving a bitter taste in our mouths. So before the ants had even located the banana skins on the side of the highway, we were back at the water, taking our final photos together.

We had evolved physically to cycling over the days and weeks, met some amazing people who called the outback their home and learned about Australia's history. We had heat, wind, rain, and often all seasons in one day. We lived in the bush, explored the desert, and embraced every second of it. I love the physical and mental battle of expeditions and the logistical challenges, and whenever I hear someone say, 'That's crazy and can't be done,' I know I am on the right track. But what I cherished the most was seeing the real landscape replace the one I had conjured in my mind. When we started the trip, we had an imagined reality of what the Outback would be like, often with a foundation of glossy tourist images. After we ventured through it, and took the time to feel it, we knew what it was really like. The original landscape in my mind had altered and was no longer fictional; it was now based on experience. The good, the bad, and the ugly make up this landscape, it is uniquely Australian, and even with its problems, it is my home and a place I love.

A tourist couple took our photo for us, returned the phone, and asked about our trip. After hearing our stories from the previous month, they said,

'Wow, well done, so what's next?'

I turned to Elise, who was giving me a look I had seen many times before, and I asked her,

'Should we buy an Opal mine?'

CHAPTER 5

The Treasure Hunt

I found a two dollar coin on the side of the road. Its gold shimmer caught my eye, and I dove on it like a Bowerbird. It was my lucky day. I threw it inside the centre console of my truck. Then, on the drive home, I wondered how the coin ended up in my possession. What journey did it take to arrive in the dirt at my feet?

It would have started at the Royal Australian Mint in Canberra. The mint opened in our capital city in 1965, right on time for decimal currency to begin circulating on the 14th of February 1966. Fresh off the press, my coin landed at a bank and was handed out as part of a small business float by Tammy, the young teller. Inside the till of the local fruit & veg shop, the coin mixed with many of its kind before touching the palm of Billy, a young lad buying milk for his mum on the way home from school. After a long haul drive from Melbourne, Billy's dad borrowed change from the kitchen counter for a quick schooner at the local pub.

My coin was passed around the noisy smoke filled bar from palm to palm, pocket to pocket, as the nectar flowed. It departed with an Irish backpacker named Aidan, destined for the southern colony of Van Diemen's Land; he was seeking adventure. The coin set sail across the Bass Strait, arrived in Devonport, hitchhiked south to Hobart, and then further towards the famous Port Arthur. Aidan sat on the side of the road thumbing for a lift; unbeknown to him, the coin shuffled out and tasted pristine Tasmanian air before hitting the gravel. Along came a man with a propensity for imagination who, on his lucky day, found the treasure and drove home.

Of course, this scenario might not have been the coin's actual trajectory. I was succumbing to these imagined journeys more often recently since taking up a unique hobby, one undertaken solo, with intense focus and an anticipatory dopamine injection like no other. It helped to have a love of history for this craft and an active imagination a necessity. I had become a modern day treasure hunter, a headphone wearing Indiana Jones. I had become a metal detectorist.

As cool as this persona might sound, I remember watching the beachcombers and old men with detectors creeping around the local parks as a kid. I associated them with homeless people looking for change; how naive I was. I was nervous when I first took to public areas with a detector in hand. However, after the first find, all the anxiety and perceived societal shame disappeared, and the hunt was on. Let me take you back to where it all began and where the addiction first wrapped its arms around me in an archaeological bear hug.

◆ ◆ ◆

My dad, Clive, has been a part time amateur prospector most of his life. He often panned for gold or went metal detecting with my grandfather while I was still in diapers. A fond story Mum enjoyed telling after a few cold beers was about when I decided, as a helpful toddler, to wash Dad's gold for him. He had accumulated a small plastic tube full of gold dust from countless hours panning in outback creeks. The glittering specks obviously needed an extra shine because I took it into the bath, opened the tube, and tipped the contents in. Following a good soaking of myself and the gold, which I had quickly forgotten about and would currently be worth AUD 2389.19 an ounce, the plug was pulled, and I carried on with my day.

With this story in the back of my mind, and the COVID situation still limiting our overseas expeditions, I thought it was time for another adventure with the old man. We spoke on the phone and brainstormed a location where we could take a family treasure hunt. We wanted to search for gold first, and then look for pre-decimal coins, which Dad assured me were more exciting to hunt for. Our call coincided with his next working contract out at Ammaroo Cattle Station, and he suggested we head to the Northern Territory and spend some time prospecting on the station before he started work. I agreed, and just like that, we were off on another Outback adventure.

Crammed into a Jetstar seat, the plane took to the air above Hobart and turned north for warmer climates. A male passenger behind me, fitting all the stereotypes of a Tasmanian bogan, was listening to death metal music on his phone, minus the headphones. The stewardess asked him politely to turn it down twice, but he didn't seem to have the cognitive ability to comply. Passengers on either side of him avoided the situation and fixed their eyes on the fascinating carpet at their feet. I failed to comprehend why people behaved the way they sometimes do, and as the seconds ticked by, and the music blared, my heart rate climbed. I knew I had to say something to this bloke.

I turned around,

'Mate, can you turn the music down?'

With glazed eyes, the guy looked up and replied,

'You better say please, or we will have a problem when we get off the plane.'

Stunned, I turned back around as adrenaline surged throughout my system, with my fight or flight response being well and truly initiated. Now, let me put this in a clear picture for you. I'm 93 kilograms, above average fitness, have a shaved head, was trained to kill or capture humans in a former life, and was cranky at this particular moment. My opponent was probably 60 kilograms, looked like he hadn't enjoyed a meal in days, or a haircut in years, yet projected a scary enough demeanour under the dim overhead light to intimidate most of the public. His behaviour created fear in people, allowing him to continue with his actions without consequence. I imagined a scenario where I turned around, stealthily relieved him of his consciousness and enjoyed a peaceful flight. Instead, I took a few deep breaths, and the stewardess arrived just in the nick of time to berate the passenger again about his music. He turned it down, and I looked at the fascinating carpet at my feet.

The plane descended into far north Queensland and landed in Townsville, where we spent a few days with my sister and her family. I reflected upon the very relaxing lifestyle Elise and I enjoyed. With no kids, we choose to travel a lot, work when we need to, and often enjoy months away on expeditions every year. My sister Kim and brother in law Wesley were real adults with three small kids, full time employment, a mortgage, and a small farm to maintain. Luckily, my sister has an endless supply of energy and patience to see it all through. Mum and Dad arrived towing their caravan, and between nursing my baby niece, feeding the cows, and playing with my two nephews, we caught up and planned our drive into the middle of the country.

Crossing the border from Queensland into the Northern Territory was currently allowed. However, this period of COVID craziness had proven we were one political tantrum away from being shut out with no notice. We were all feeling healthy and had bowed to mandatory vaccination, so there was no reason we wouldn't get through. However, my baby niece was sporting a runny nose. I watched the mucus descend from her cute little nostrils and contemplated the robustness of the human immune system, right before she sneezed directly into my face with the force of a petrol powered leaf blower. I wiped my cheeks hoping my system was as robust as hers and that I wouldn't show any symptoms.

The swords we would swing for our modern day treasure crusade on foreign land would be Garrett AT Golds, a fancy name for a metal detector at the budget end of the spectrum. I realised the detecting world is no different to any other hobby. There were entry level devices and also $10,000 setups for professional gold hunters. We opted for something in the middle, and after assembling them in Kim's driveway, Dad led us into the yard to show us the basics.

It was more complex than you might imagine. It had multiple discrimination modes to eliminate unwanted metals like iron from discovery. High, low, and mild tones differentiated the size of the hidden objects, adjustable threshold levels, frequencies, and volume controls. Rapid audio information illuminating the underground landscape streamed through my headphones constantly as I waved the detector back and forth at my feet. I was receiving audio input and needed to translate this into an unseen physical world to try and answer a question on every metal detectorists mind; to dig or not to dig?

At first, I dug for everything, quickly producing a pile of nails, tin, bottle caps and wire fragments. Then, I only dug for something if it fell within the required settings. Gold, for example, would read between 40-50 on the display, modern coins between 50-75, and pre-decimal coins, such as copper pennies and silver shillings, between 75-85. This made sense to me until I quickly realised ring pulls, foil, beer cans, and an abundance of other trash also fell within these ideal parameters. The effort required to dig out a target is marginal, yet after my 20th ring pull and disappointment, I was over it.

One then started to become very selective about what to dig. An object might sound and read well on the monitor, but so did the last ten pieces of garbage. I would continue forward, only to start second guessing my judgement, imagining a gold ring or silver coin buried just below the surface. A line from a hilarious TV series, 'Detectorists', would echo in my mind. 'If in doubt, dig it out.' I would backtrack and dig the spot with new vigour to unearth a ring pull once again.

In 1962 Ermal Cleon Fraze, from Dayton, Ohio, had a unique idea for attaching a metal ring to a can utilising a rivet, for pulling open its contents. His timesaving pull tab was able to detach completely and be discarded. It would revolutionise fast food and be utilised in canned beverages worldwide. I'm sure Ermal couldn't foresee during his moment of enlightenment and invention that following a few billion of his brainchildren being secreted in the soil, the 'ring pull' would become the bane of existence for futuristic metal detectorists.

We bought supplies in Townsville, including tools for digging hard ground and a Pinpointer from the local prospecting shop. The Pinpointer is a handheld metal detector the size of a small torch. After locating a target with the ATGold, and removing the top layer of earth, the pointer could be used to zero in on the object. It is rocket science accurate, and I found 60 cents worth of change inside my sister's garden bed before it was time to hit the road.

◆◆◆

Heading west from the North Queensland coastline, we passed through Charters Towers, a gold mining town founded in 1870 that boomed in the last quarter of the 19th century. The small town produced 200 tonnes of gold between 1871 and 1917. It hosts a population of 8000, including some of my family, who have adapted to 40 degree summer temperatures. We stopped for lunch at Aunty Vicki and Uncle David's house. After producing a mountain of chicken sandwiches, Vicki said, 'We have just paid to get the pool heated, it's too cold.' As she spoke these words, sweat poured down my butt crack, and I looked outside to where the 27 degree spring sun glared off the inviting pool. I wiped the sweat from my face, then took another bite of my sandwich before replying, 'Ok, perfect.'

We drove a few hours west from Charters Towers and found our first night's camp near a Telstra communication tower a few hundred metres off the highway. Once our caravan was settled onto a flat section of hard dirt, I was off into the scrub with my detector. It was a high trash area, and I was exposing all sorts of scrap metal. Screws, tin, air rifle slugs, and assorted rubbish were raised to the light. Even though I wasn't receiving the reward I was chasing, my excitement was high, and it motivated my search until sundown.

Motivation is a fascinating topic. What motivated me to keep scratching in the dirt for hours, finding nothing of value? The answer was dopamine. Dopamine is a neurotransmitter molecule that influences brain pathways involved in motivation, movement, and cognition. It drives our pleasure pathway and plays a vital role in all reward driven behaviour. When we receive a reward, dopamine is produced, and we experience pleasure. However, there is an even more fulfilling side to this addictive neurotransmitter, which is the anticipation of the reward. Studies featured in Robert Sapolsky's bestselling book, 'Why Zebras Don't Get Ulcers', conclude that an even higher dopamine spike occurs moments before a reward is expected. As I am scratching in the dirt, getting ever closer to my perceived reward, dopamine is flooding my system, giving me enough motivation and pleasure to keep going until I find it.

In the peaceful world of metal detecting, this feature of human biology has minimal downside. However, if you partner dopamine and anticipation, with a uniquely engineered algorithm for slot machines, you have a recipe for disaster. The designers were well versed in neurotransmitters and their effect on human behaviour. They designed a computer system that required us to keep pushing a button in anticipation of winning our reward. Pleasure is gained, motivation is covered, and some of us will choose to keep pushing that button all day and night. The downside is that each push costs hard earned money, and with ever longer delays of our reward, our finances disappear long before dopamine ever does.

Road trips with my parents are always a fun time. Mum and Dad are seasoned travellers, nothing seems to stress them, and they have driven more kilometres on Outback roads than most Australians combined. However, one part of the day must occur for Dad to maintain his sanity. The long held British tradition of morning tea, aka smoko, was ingrained in my upbringing and was the critical nourishing feature of my dad's day; it must never be missed. It didn't matter if we had only been on the road for an hour, our boat sank on our Murray River expedition, or if we were about to pilot a shuttle to the moon and it was T-minus five seconds to lift off. At 10 a.m., we had to stop, boil the kettle, and have a cup of tea with a biscuit. As long as this throwback to colonialism occurred, Dad would fight all day and drive all night without complaint.

It was 10 a.m., so we pulled over for smoko west of Cloncurry at a roadside stop with a stone memorial built at its centre. The small stone wall was covered in square copper plates with poetry engraved. It was a tribute to the Kalkadoon people native to the area, and on closer inspection, I noticed piles of small rocks stacked at its base with the word 'sorry' written on them. The people leaving the rocks were referring to Australia's brutal past and its treatment of the locals. Above the rocks was an engraving that read,

You who pass by are now entering the ancient tribal lands of the Mitakoodi, disposed of by the European, honour their name, be brother and sister to their descendants.

During the frontier wars between 1788 and 1934, the atrocities committed by the British settlers against the natives were well documented. The short poems engraved into the metal were an acknowledgement of our history.

Up this track that's now a road,
Spear in hand brown Adam strode
His was everything bare the back that knew no load
Naked but a king.

Earth, sun, and the sky
Knowing not where for nor why
They each saw me roam
Happy to live and to die in the bushland, my home.

Bounds the kangaroo they stalked
Cattle graze where the wild men walked
And their camps have been

> Silent bush, where they laughed and talked
> And there, slates are wiped clean.
>
> Spear can never conquer gun
> Man no more the horse outrun
> By the gun blast tossed
> Still in death lies everyone, and the battles lost.

At the top of the stone wall was a square metal plate featuring the face of an older Aboriginal man. He wore a red bandana around his temple and white paint made from local clay on his face. It would have been a lovely image apart from one scarring feature, bullet holes. Someone had decided to use the picture as target practice and fired six large calibre rounds through it. I couldn't determine whether it was racism that compelled someone to shoot at the memorial or if it was simply another thing to shoot at. Most road signs, power poles and big trees were scarred similarly. Elise spoke with a valid point, 'If you placed a picture of Scott Morrison (our current Prime Minister) or any sports star up there, someone would shoot at them too.'

I tried not to read too much into it, but shooting at the Prime Minister for disagreeing in politics, speed limit signs because I enjoyed driving fast, or even sports stars because they beat a favoured opponent told one story. But would we shoot holes into a picture of a fallen soldier? Or a picture of a loved one in a cemetery? I don't think so. Firing those bullets carried more weight and much bigger statements. The shots fired through the memorial carried the echo of the frontier wars, a generational disregard for fellow humans, a prejudice we have not managed to eradicate in all these years. It was the symptom of a historical and modern blind eye that has been allowed to remain so. Mum pulled me out of my reflections, calling me over for morning tea, and I shunned one symptom of colonisation as I walked over to partake in another.

After smoko, we drove through the large mining town of Mt Isa, where shafts and tunnels under the city descend to a depth of 1900 metres. Then further west to Camooweal, where I had my knee stitched back together after putting it through a windowpane as a boy. Thirteen kilometres from Camooweal, we hit the Northern Territory border and a checkpoint. Where once was barren ground next to the highway, now stood a cluster of buildings and police guarding the state against an invisible enemy. After a few quick questions regarding COVID-19, we were all allowed through. Shortly after departing, we passed the turnoff for Avon Downs cattle station, where we once lived.

As a ten year old, this country was a boundless landscape full of adventure. I would spend hours exploring dry riverbeds, hunting anything that moved with my air rifle and was content to live a country kids' life where my sole ambition was to become a ringer, the Australian version of a Cowboy. With adult eyes and 15 years of exploring under my belt, I still saw adventure in the surrounding bush, but I also felt the isolation. Around the time when my sister and I were due to start high school, my parents packed up all our possessions, drove 1300 kilometres to North Queensland, and showed us the other side of the coin. We left their beloved Outback behind and were introduced to big towns, big schools, and hundreds of kids. We played team sports, learned street skills, and developed friends for life. We were shown the best of both worlds and allowed to make up our minds. I could never thank them enough for their foresight and sacrifice.

Later that afternoon, we pulled off the highway into the bushland to camp, and I was immediately scouring the ground for treasures. Still not solidly grasping what the detector was telling me, I dug for everything. I found wire, ring pulls, a Levi Strauss button, brass .22 calibre spent cartridges, alfoil, and beer cans, but no coins. I could read tracks from lizards, beetles, goannas, and small birds in the sand at my feet. Their prints gave me an insight into the nocturnal dance that occurred while I comfortably slept in my tent.

At dawn, I poked my head out to see a white coloured dingo patrolling the campground. He wasn't afraid and focused his attention on searching the surrounding trees. I got up to investigate what he was feeding on, and upon discovery, I was glad I hadn't consumed breakfast. The native dog had been digging up and eating the campgrounds buried turds. I found multiple holes relieved of their waste, with left over toilet paper strewn across the ground. That's why it is always best practice not to bury the toilet paper and to instead take it away with you. One man's waste in another animal's breakfast. Dad came out of the caravan just as the dog took off at speed across the flat; he noticed the canine at full gallop, and without missing a beat, he said, 'Look at that turd burglar run.'

We were approaching Three Ways, the same cluster of buildings indicating the junction of the Stuart highway we had stayed at on the cycle trip. I watched Dad in the driver's seat scan the roads ahead, he was once renowned for his driving endurance in his younger years. 17 hours and 1500 kilometre hauls were standard practice at one point in his life. These days Dad moved across the country like desert sand, guaranteed to arrive but when exactly would depend on which way the wind was blowing. I noticed similar trends in my behaviour after completing an expedition. Ten years ago, I would endure any discomfort or hardship in-between adventures, notching it up as resilience training for the next mission. These days I enjoy a soft mattress, a climate controlled home, and warm drinks on demand. I now told myself that the next round of suffering was coming, so enjoy a few luxuries.

After setting up camp at the caravan park, we travelled out to a fossicking area called Mad Micks. The area is one square kilometre of country open for anyone to come and prospect; no permissions or permits were needed. It was originally a gold mine in the 1970s owned by a man with eastern European origins who the locals remember well. Nigel Skelton, a Tennant Creek local, tells the story.

'Mad Mick used to work at the Warrego Mine (about 50 kilometres west of Tennant Creek) until one day he found a decent lump of gold. He took out a miner's lease and started working a small shaft on his own. He was nicknamed Mad Mick because his English was hard to understand, and when he became agitated, he'd talk fast and loud in his native language.'

The mad European worked alone for over ten years, going weeks without being seen in town. One day a man mysteriously went missing near Mick's lease while attending a barbecue, and the body turned up nearby a few years later. Shortly after the body was discovered, Mick went missing and was never seen again. Dad used to come out to the fossicking area with his dad, looking for gold using metal detectors. After hearing stories about these trips, I don't know how dedicated they were to actually finding gold. They would search for an hour or two and then drink beers at the nearby rock pools. Either way, there was a Richmond family tradition to adhere to.

Mick's derelict old camp and mining shaft marked the location of his claim. We pulled over into a random area of bush and started the hunt. I wasn't overly optimistic; most likely thousands of prospectors had been out here over the years. However, the year before, an 8 year old boy found a two ounce gold nugget with his dad; it was worth a shot. We had driven past Warrego Mine on the way in, and while we scanned the earth waiting for an audible cry of victory, Dad recounted days gone by living in the area. My grandparents, parents, and uncle Neil all worked at the mine at one point. Dad told us a story about Grandfather Harry.

'He built a trailer in the workshop once using all the mine's steel and parts, but then he had to figure out how to smuggle it out. Security was tight. He towed it up to the security gate and told the guard he was delivering it to the mine manager Brian's house in town. The guard was sceptical and asked for the paperwork, or it couldn't leave. Harry said in his rough English accent, "Well, you call bloody Brian and ask him what he wants to do with it." The guard hesitated. Apparently, Brian was a real hard arse and didn't suffer fools lightly. He didn't call and chose instead to let him through.'

The trailer was exceptionally well made, and it currently sits on our block of land in Tasmania, where I still use it weekly.

Just as we were about to pack it in for the day, a loud beep in the 50-60 range startled me through my headphones. It was the perfect range for gold. I started to dig, scraping away inches of earth and then locating it with my pin pointer. My heart was thumping as dopamine flooded my system. I dug a little deeper, and out popped a small lump, rounded on the edges and the size of a 20 cent piece. I threw off my headphones and grabbed the nugget. It was heavy, and when I rubbed off the layer of dirt on this ancient mineral, it revealed itself as a piece of lead. Elise and Dad turned to see me kicking dirt into a freshly dug hole. The disappointment only made me want it more.

◆◆◆

Driving into Alice Springs a few days later we planned to resupply with provisions for a few weeks out bush, pick up some deliveries for Ammaroo station, drop off the caravan, and then get back on the road. Before we departed, we caught up with my uncle Neil, one of the most unique characters you will ever find in the Outback. Pulling into his driveway, we were greeted by two enormous dogs, Penny and Zeus, followed closely by Neil. He was dressed in a blue singlet and shorts, while a freshly rolled cigarette clung to his mouth. He was fifty years old, only a short man, but he had trained daily like he was preparing for the Olympics. His muscles were ripped, veins bifurcating like the roots of a tree, and when we shook hands it felt like holding granite.

He was a hardworking, training, drinking, smoking, bush-loving, fighting machine. Yet underneath his rough veneer was a good heart with country morals and values. The beers started flowing, and stories began to be retold before long. From Neanderthal man to Greek philosophers, sitting around a fire and sharing stories was as natural to humans as breathing air. Trying not to laugh when my uncle and dad laughed was impossible. They were infectious, and the stories varied from fights, fishing, and sexual conquests, to love lost and fathers never forgotten.

'While I was caretaking a place once, this bloody donkey…' Neil begins his story, referring to an actual animal and not an annoying person. '…it kept giving me the shits, and I just cracked it. I gave it one good punch to the head, and the bugger staggered, then fell over.'

Neil went to school in Tennant Creek, considered one of the roughest towns in the Northern Territory, and he grew up fighting. Violence was a part of life, a way to protect yourself in a community where the weak were often singled out. He left home at 16 years old, for a life on the road, working, drinking, and fighting his way around the northern regions of Australia.

'Then, in the gym the other day, this bloke kept dropping his weights, and the banging was doing my head in. I flipped it, went over to the guy, grabbed him, and started to choke the bastard. They got it all on CCTV, and I got a warning from the manager.' His laugh boomed as he retold the tale. I couldn't help but chuckle along; the Richmond mob were renowned for many things, a short fuse being one of them.

For fun, Neil raced dirt bikes along rough desert trails at speeds of more than 175 kilometres per hour. He had completed the formidable Fink Desert Race and told me he was his calmest after riding. I understood what he was referring to. I struggled to stay calm inside a Westfields or Kmart; the whole scene and the desperate shopping drove me bonkers. Shopping is a task I often handballed to Elise while I stayed with the truck in the car park. However, put me 6000 metres up a mountain, with high risk, frostbitten teammates, and an extraction to execute, and I will be calm and in control.

Neil never sat down; he stood from dawn until bedtime. I asked him why he doesn't sit to relax, and he said he had his chair pulled out from under him once when he was young and was injured. Since that day, he had chosen to stand. The funniest tale and one that I'm sure left another scar from his youth, involved him learning to swim. Dad retold the story.

'Neil had to learn, but me and Paul (Dad's older brother) couldn't be bothered slowly teaching him. We took him to the river, encouraged him into the water, and got him to hold onto us as we took him out into the middle. Then we pushed him off and swam back to shore. He thrashed around for a bit, then finally saved himself; lesson over, he could swim.'

The longer the night went on, and the more stories I heard, I finally understood why my uncle Neil was labelled the menace of the Outback.

◆◆◆

It is a 315 kilometre drive from Alice Springs to Ammaroo Station, most of it along a rough dirt road. The truck was unburdened of the caravan and Dad drove carefully, avoiding potholes, ruts, and corrugations. 'We are all fat and shiny now hey,' Dad said to Mum in the front seat. 'What's that mean?' I asked from the back.

'Out on the stations when everyone comes back off holidays, they have usually put on weight, are well rested and look healthy. The black ringers (Aboriginal cowboys) used to say we all looked fat and shiny. However, everyone would be skinny, tanned, and broken again before too long.'

It sounded very similar to the physical evolution of expedition life. I would usually start an adventure in top condition, injury free, sometimes with added layers of fat, depending on the adventure. Then return home riddled with tendonitis, muscle wastage and probably a few brain cells short due to altitude. Over the years, my body has adapted to the yearly transformation. These days, when I return to good food, sleep, and training, I recover in unprecedented time scales, and I am ready to go again within two months.

Before turning off the Plenty Highway and onto the Sandover Highway, Dad said to me,

'Keep going down this road, and you come to Harts Range. We lived out there once, well before you were born. Nanna and Grandfather worked at the Over The Horizon Radar site. There was a purpose built little township for all the employees. Whenever they turned that radar on, it wiped out all VHS tapes and made everything jittery.' Dad went quiet for a moment, then spoke again softly, more to himself than anyone else.

'I reckon that machine is why they deteriorated so quickly as they got older.' It took me a second to catch on; then, I realised what he was saying. My nanna and grandfather had both ended up with dementia and withered away before our eyes when I was a teenager. It was tough to see, but harder on Mum and Dad, who cared for them till the end. Dad thought the radar had something to do with it.

The final 100 kilometres of dirt road towards Ammaroo was rough, and Dad threaded through the obstacles kicking up clouds of bulldust in our wake. Large lizards called bearded dragons scattered from the red baked earth as we ploughed forward across corrugations. We passed by the local Aboriginal community of Alparra which had its own shop, school, Police Station, football oval and power station. As mystical and modern as the name might suggest, it looked more like a third world war zone than a paradise.

Trees appeared in the distance, an abundance of green in a sea of red. We had arrived at an oasis. Thick grass and luscious gardens surrounded a large homestead and cluster of buildings. Steel cattle yards and enormous sheds were constructed close by. As we slowly drove in, I counted twenty or more Landcruiser utes, three road trains, workshops, storage sheds, lay down areas, a helipad with a hanger housing two helicopters, worker's quarters, and machinery scattered everywhere. I said to Dad, 'Bloody hell, no wonder you have been coming here for ten years; you would never be short of things to fix.' Dad laughed and replied, 'I won't be fat and shiny for long.'

The station owners, Anna and Stewart Weir, invited us to dinner that night. One thing guaranteed on a cattle station is that there will always be an abundance of beef to go around. Anna and Stewart were fourth generation owners of Ammaroo. Their property was comprised of five smaller cattle stations totalling 3.5 million acres. The oldest of the five is Old McDonald, built in the early 1900s. I asked Stewart's dad David, who was seated next to me,

'How many cattle have you got out here?'

He replied, 'That's like asking me how much money I have in my wallet,' before he started to chuckle.

I didn't receive an answer. One common theme throughout all the stories shared that first night at dinner was that these country folk are tough as nails. Anna told me a story about her own Dad who at 72 got bogged and decided to walk back home. Apparently, he hated wearing shoes and, on this occasion, walked 20 kilometres bare foot until the soles of his feet peeled off and he was, in Annas words, a little foot sore.

I picked their brains about the old settlements, before we devised a plan for the following two weeks. Our goal was pre-decimal coins. Three pence, sixpence, shillings, and florins, coins made from .925 silver, or old copper pennies. They were taken out of circulation when Australia changed to decimal currency. A jackpot find would be a 1930 penny valued at over $40,000. Or the infamous Holey Dollar, a name given to Spanish silver coins brought to New South Wales in 1812 to remedy a coin shortage in the new colony. The Governor at the time, Lachlan Macquarie, imported 40,000 Spanish reals. To prevent them from leaving the country, he ordered convicted forger William Henshall to cut each centre out and counter-stamp them. This doubled the number of coins. The centrepiece, known as the 'dump', was valued at 15 pence, and the outer coin was valued at 5 shillings. Finding this innovative coin from 1773, restamped in 1813, would quickly pay off our house. Its estimated value today is more than $300,000.

The following morning, we loaded into one of the Toyota trucks and entered the bush. We had a limited time to search a vast area, and our first stop was Dingly Bore, where a ringer supposedly picked up an old florin. A bore on a cattle station is a water point, a shaft drilled into the underground water supply, traditionally with a windmill above ground to draw the water up. Small diesel engines replaced windmills over the years, and solar pumps and surface tanks replaced combustion engines. One of Dad's roles on the station was the 'bore run.' This entailed days of driving around the station, checking all the bores, starting the engines, and making sure the cattle had enough water in their troughs.

Australia's harsh interior evolved into an agricultural heartland and cattle producer due to the Great Artesian Basin, a massive underground freshwater sea. It is the largest and deepest artesian basin in the world. Spanning 1,700,000 square kilometres with measured water temperatures ranging from 30 to 100 degrees Celsius. The basin is 3000 metres deep in places and is estimated to contain 64,900 cubic kilometres of groundwater. Some believe it will never run dry and is replenished yearly during the monsoon. Scientists are not so confident. In one study, a concerned official stated, 'The Great Artesian Basin is a closed system; it will run out, but whether it lasts 20 years or another 100 years depends entirely on how we manage it.'

Dad told us a story about these days of water discovery. 'When the bore drillers worked through this area, they told us about some strange things over the years. Once, when drilling deep, they pulled the bit out, and water gushed from the hole containing fish with big bug eyes that died straight away from the sunlight. Another time when the drill behaved strangely, it seemed to be penetrating soft material. As the crew withdrew it, there was meat and blood 15 feet along the steel drill shafts. They reckon they went through something monstrous. Who knows, maybe they spent too much time in the sun, but it does make you wonder.'

Driving along the rough dirt roads, dust billowing behind us, I felt at home. Like the little kid I once was growing up in these remote places. I'm glad I had country values instilled in me while I was young. As well as learning about the real cycle of life and death of what we eat, and the actual cost of what goes into a slab of steak bought from the butcher.

We arrived at Dingley, and I was out the door with the detector in hand, scanning the ground with raw enthusiasm. Steel cattle yards were next to the road, and old campgrounds were scattered along a nearby riverbank. It was anyone's guess where to search, and I watched Dad head straight over to the biggest tree and search around the base. One thing was certain, in this harsh environment, someone would always sit under a big shady tree for a rest, whether in the 1800s or 2022. Within minutes he found a modern one dollar coin and some brass bullet casings.

After an hour, I looked up from the red earth and noticed the three of us had entirely different styles of treasure hunting. Elise chose an area of ground, overlayed a mental grid and then proceeded to sweep every inch of it until certain nothing was hidden before moving on. Dad would spend two minutes under one tree, walk somewhere else, another five minutes, then change again. His style was erratic and had no pattern at all. I often noticed him sitting under a tree enjoying a tea, and watching us hunt. Maybe he was channelling the spirits of the early explorers and planning his next move. My detecting style was a combination of both. Searching thoroughly once I was in a 'good' area, but happy to wander off to find another at the drop of a hat. Time would tell whose technique would yield the rewards.

We spent five hours hunting, and for our efforts, we unearthed kilograms of scrap metal in various configurations, creating our own modern art gallery. Welding rods, brass bullet shells of many calibres, ring pulls, cans, iron tools, and a handful of modern coins but no old silver ones or copper pennies. Covered in dust, with the scent of cow manure nested firmly in my nasal cavity, we drove back to the homestead. The strikeout had dampened my enthusiasm slightly. This wasn't going to be as easy as I thought.

Over the following week, we explored Anna and Stewart's enormous property, and each afternoon we would debrief them on what we discovered. Stewart loved the history and gave us insight into each area we were venturing. We drove two hours one morning to reach Deniper on the southern boundary of Ammaroo. It was once a full time homestead and station but was now only utilised during mustering season as an outpost. Some grassed areas around a cluster of buildings yielded over nine dollars in modern coins, but nothing old. During our cross country drives, we'd check the bores, fix broken engines, and assisted with any small jobs Stewart needed done. On the way back, Dad mentioned offhandedly, 'There is a meteor crater over there; I'll take you in for a look.'

Not grasping what he was referring to, we pulled up at the rim of Boxhole Crater. It was 170 metres in diameter, roughly 30-40 metres deep and estimated to have struck the earth 5000 years ago based on the cosmogenic terrestrial age of the meteorite. A local shearer Joe Webb took geologist Cecil Madigan to examine the crater in 1937. At the bottom, they found metallic fragments and iron shale balls. On further excavation, they unearthed an iron mass of 82 kilograms which now sits at the Natural History Museum in London. It was an impressive site, and it wasn't lost on me that this cattle station was big enough to have its own meteor crater.

Before we pulled out the following morning, Stewart yelled, 'Hey Clive, there is a dead cow in the yards at Dingly. Can you drag it out for me, mate?'

'No worries at all,' Dad replied.

We drove over and could smell the carcass before we could see it. Then we noticed the flock of circling crows, their spiral flight indicated both death and food. We walked upon a heifer that had died giving birth. The calf would have briefly tasted the fresh air and taken one look up at the sun before becoming stuck. Instead of one life being born, two had perished.

This complicated death typically happens when a calf is too big. To avoid this loss of life some cattle stations use workers to try and assist the births. However, trying to save every calf would be a perpetual challenge due to their genetic defects, that never die off. On stations like Ammaroo, they tend to let nature take its course, knowing that the cows with a genetic mutation birthing larger calves will eventually die out. They were allowing only those that had smaller calves to survive, eventually eradicating the problem. This is natural selection at its purest, but due to our modern technology and values, it is one of nature's rules that no longer applies to our own primate species.

We estimated that the heifer had died 4 or 5 days ago. What lay before us now was a bloated mass close to the water troughs, and to avoid contamination, it had to be removed. The best way to do this was to hook her onto the Toyota with chains, and hope that she hadn't decomposed too much and would stay intact. The stench was incredible, an invisible ripeness that hung in the air. Flies swarmed, feasted, and laid their eggs in the moisture of blood, guts, and gore. The belly had been torn open, and all I could see were maggots, a gyrating ball of small white worms. The black calf hung, frozen in desperation, and was being consumed in the cycle of nature; it was a grim scene. Elise hadn't seen anything like it before, but Dad had seen plenty. He once pulled 42 dead horses out of a dam where they had all perished from a lack of water when a bore broke down.

I looped the chains around the legs of the cow and onto the tow ball of the truck. Dad took the slack, and I prayed it would hold together. Slowly the legs took the strain, stretched, and quivered with false life; it held, and the mass began to slide. We towed it through the yards and into a paddock. In its wake remained a carpet of maggots fallen from their prize, they would be consumed by the birds, and the cycle would continue. The smell reached new and unforgiving heights as the contents of the stomach emptied onto the ground. It soaked into my nostrils, clothes, and pores. Nature is not always beautiful; it is often harsh and gives us a glimpse into our futures, exposing our softness.

Arriving back at the station in the afternoon, all hands were at the cattle yards. Clouds of dust were thick in the air, and a cacophony of anguish from the mobs of cattle set the scene; I had to check it out. I climbed onto the perimeter fence and held the top rail as I took in the barbaric symphony. Stewart and Anna's 23 year old son Will was bleeding from his hand, the consequence of shoving a six inch needle through it, and Anna was quick to slap on a plaster before encouraging him back into the fray. Stewart's arms were covered in blood up to the elbow, and a small pocketknife was still open in his hand. Anna worked frantically with anaesthetic sprays and ear tag contraptions, back and forth to the weaner held in a steel cattle cradle. One by one, the cattle were mustered by two other station hands, into a cradle; the walls would constrict, locking it in place, before it rotated the animal onto a 45 degree angle.

One of the workers would seize the back leg and tie it off, exposing the underside of the young beast. Stewart was quick to slice open the scrotum and remove the testes, a process I had witnessed before while growing up on stations. As he worked his minor surgery, Will removed the horns with a large medieval dehorning knife, a curved blade designed to remove the entire horn, bud, and skin. This eliminated any chance of horns re-growing. Cattle with horns would injure other cattle, or injure ringers, it is standard practice to remove the danger.

Anaesthetic was sprayed onto the open wound; vaccines were given, and then he was handed the tags and a pellet insertion needle. A $10 hormonal growth pellet was inserted behind the ear, slowly releasing low dosage hormone into the animal over the next 200 days. This promoted significant weight gain, often up to a 30% increase over untreated animals. It was a tried and tested safe procedure and has been utilised in the beef industry since 1979.

The last step was picking up one of the red-hot iron brands resting on a gas furnace within reach. The lettering was scorched into the hind leg, a burnt hair stench mixing with the dust, blood, manure, and sweat. Within 90 seconds of entering the cradle, the animal was released back into the yard. The speed of the operation was incredible. Stewart took a moment while the next mob was rounded up to brief me on everything I witnessed. 'When we really get going, we can do one beast per minute all day.'

When a delicious steak, wrapped in plastic, is taken from a shelf inside a grocery store, the consumer often doesn't have a clue about the amount of physical labour and work that goes into each slice. Every gram of beef carries with it the metaphorical sweat of the land. Suppose you factor in every aspect of the process, from the calf being born into the dust, fattened on the land, transported, killed, sliced in the abattoir, and eventually sizzling in your pan at home. Fifteen dollars for a T-bone is a bargain.

◆◆◆

As we started our second week of detecting, we had accumulated plenty of metal, piles of modern coins, and I had been enjoying the process, but we hadn't located any old coin areas. Stewart mentioned an old bore close to the homestead that could be worth a look. We loaded up and drove out to find it.

It was known as Depot and had been a government operated bore in the early days. A string of old Government bores stretched from the Northern Territory into Queensland. It was a promising location because it would have seen lots of traffic over the years from cattle drovers, military convoys, and anyone needing water. We found the windmill easily, then started searching the nearby bush until we found an old car shell and tonnes of rusted parts scattered about. The wreck had an iconic antique structure; we were in the right area. A stone's throw away, we found a small concrete slab, lots of old bottles, and what seemed to have been an old drinking bar. This is where we started the hunt.

Joining us for the day was Kat, Ammaroo's former governess, who had recently joined the ranks of the South Australia Police and was enjoying some vacation time. She was interested in our hunt and decided to tag along. I found an old one cent piece from the United States within the hour. Then, minutes later, Kat bent over and picked up a .925 silver one shilling coin from New Guinea. Dated 1938, it had a hole through the centre and was in excellent condition. It was the first old coin we had seen on the trip, and Kat had found it without a bloody metal detector. I had mixed emotions, elation because we had found something and surging jealousy that I hadn't found it. However, the coin confirmed we were on some good ground; it was time to get serious.

Over the following few days, I became a slave to my neurotransmitters; my anticipatory dopamine was red lining. I was addicted to the hunt. I found my first Australian kangaroo copper penny, dated 1943, then another from 1952. They were in great condition with the dry outback climate and minimal annual rain being ideal for preserving their fragile material. As the hours ticked by, I became more attuned to using the detector. I could tell instantly if I was hovering over copper, iron, or aluminium, which limited the number of times I was digging dry holes. I had been searching over a small area where I assumed an old washing line had once hung after finding a few old metal clothes pegs, when I heard another high pitched tone. It read 82 on the screen, and I assumed it was another penny. I dug down and flicked out the spoil noticing a flash of silver. My heart pounded, and I reached down and picked up a 1910 .925 silver Australian one shilling coin.

I was ecstatic at finding my first shilling. It was well worn on both faces, and thinner from many years of circulation. As I returned to hunting, I imagined how this silver coin arrived in the desert. Who carried it? From the mint in London, across the seas, to the new colony of Australia. It could have spent years palmed around in Sydney or Melbourne before being banked and then paid in wages to a drifter heading north to the frontier. Into the Outback it travelled. By train? Or by horse? Eventually, it was traded over the counter for a beer inside a tin shack bar in the middle of the Northern Territory. It was handed out as change to another patron, who forgot to remove it from their pants before washing and hanging them to dry on the line. The coin fell and buried itself into the dry soil, was quickly covered in dust and lost. To be unearthed many years later by a Tasmanian with a detector. I spent hours imagining different scenarios, and the only parts I knew to be true were where it started its journey and where it was now.

The next day Depot delivered again when I found my first .925 silver three pence coin. It was in perfect condition, a shiny little brother to the large copper pennies. Another 1952 penny appeared after lunch, then one more mid-afternoon. By this point, I had found all the coins and knowing that Dad and Elise would be growing tired of it; my excitement was beginning to dampen. When I found another kangaroo penny from 1945 and yelled out to my comrades, I received a 'Bloody hell' from Dad, and a 'You're kidding' from Elise. I took two more steps and hit a high tone of 82 on the screen, and I thought, another penny for sure. I hesitated to dig because if I found another one, I might be murdered and buried in its place. I also wanted Elise to share in the excitement. 'Elise, come here and dig this spot, it might be something.'

She walked over, scepticism shining brightly, and dug where I indicated.

'What have you got me digging...' She paused mid-sentence, then yelled, 'It's a Penny! I found one!'

We burst out laughing together. I had barely escaped with my life, and Elise had found her first pre-decimal coin. An hour later, Elise yelled when she discovered a 1927 three pence coin; she didn't need any more help from me. It was found in an area I had been over at least twice. She was more patient and had moved some trash out of the way that was causing a false reading before finding the coin. We wrapped up our final day by sharing a cup of tea and sitting in the dirt like the drovers, explorers, and soldiers would have done 100 years before us. Our first of many treasure hunts had been a success, but the time spent in the wild with my dad and wife was the highlight.

Back at the station, we enjoyed a farewell dinner with our amazing hosts and their staff. Stewart sat next to me, he looked worn and tired from a big day, and I noticed his hands. They were big iron mitts, larger than usual, thick from a life of hard labour. Deep grooves covered his fingers like the cracks of a dry riverbed. They were tinged in red from the dirt, tinted forever, connected to this land. Like the coins, he held history in those hands. Moving the station forward one day at a time, they could tell a story of hardship and endurance. Their appearance reminded me of crocodile skin, and their ability was on par with the reptile. A crocodile could gently hold eggs in its mouth, liberating slow hatching babies, or it could tear animals apart and shatter bones. Stewart's hands had held his children at birth, gently bringing them into the world, protecting them. They have also inflicted pain, carried loads, wielded weapons, and taken life in the cycle of natural selection in the bush.

I pulled myself back into the conversation at the table, realising how weird it was for a man to stare at another man's hands. 'How's the cattle business this year, mate?' I asked Stewart.

'One of our best yet, record prices; it's going to be a great year.'

'Fantastic, where does your beef end up?'

'All of ours is live export. I'd love to keep it here in Australia, but to kill an animal here costs upwards of $100 per beast plus extras. I can ship them to Vietnam, where it's $10, and earn a hell of a lot more. That's the market these days. I know where they end up; they do a great job over there. Everything negative you see on the news about animal cruelty is just politics.'

As we chatted, Dad pulled out his guitar, and we settled in for a few songs, drinks, and laughter. We didn't find our 1930s penny or the infamous Holey Dollar. These two coins will be my Mt Everest of detecting, a lifetime ambition, and a driving force to keep me hunting. I had found a hobby for life. Detecting calmed me down as hours fell away in focus and flow. It also kept me outdoors in nature, where I have always felt at home. I couldn't wait to get back to Tasmania and start hunting. It is one of Australia's oldest settlements, and if there was one place the holey dollar was lying in wait, it was there.

Driving back to Alice Springs along the rough corrugated dirt road, I thought about the piles of modern money we had pulled from the ground; almost $30 in change had been lost from circulation until we had discovered it again. How much money could be buried in parks and beaches around the country? What percentage of our currency is lost annually to the earth and oceans? It could be a lot more than we think. As I contemplated the mathematics and what it would take to find out, Elise, sitting quietly beside me reading a tourist guidebook, spoke up.

'Babe, there is a bush walk west of Alice Springs called the Larapinta Trail, 230 kilometres through the West McDonnell Ranges. They say 12 days to do it, but we could do it quicker. Should we go?'

For about five seconds I contemplated winter back in Tasmania and compared it to more time in the Outback and stretching my hiking legs. I replied,

'I ain't busy. Let's do it.'

CHAPTER 6

The Larapinta Trail

'Are you ok?'

'Yeah, I'm fine. I just twisted my knee.' Elise replied as she rubbed her right leg. I heard her stumble under the weight of her pack.

'Just go steady. How's it feel to put weight on it?'

'Bloody painful, she'll be right; let's keep going.'

It was day one on the Larapinta trail. We had started in the middle of the MacDonnell Ranges, 230 kilometres from civilisation. It was not an ideal start. Ahead of us lay 12 days of gorges and rugged mountain ranges. I started to have doubts. My brain processed all the 'what if' scenarios of how to evacuate her if she couldn't walk anymore. We were in remote country, yet there was an access road a few kilometres away with sporadic traffic; we had plenty of supplies, motivation was high, and it was within my scope of risk. She is a tough cookie; she'll be right.

◆◆◆

Three days earlier, Dad dropped us off at the G'day Mate Tourist Park in Alice Springs, and we started planning. It was all relatively straightforward. The tourist information centre had maps of the trail broken into 12 sections. It was recommended to take 12 days to complete, and each section finished at a designated camp with fresh drinking water. This eliminated the need to carry large amounts of water each day. The trail had a few locations where food resupplies could be deposited and picked up later during the hike. These were small shipping containers dropped in the bush and one storage room at a tourist cafe in Ormiston Gorge. These cache drops allowed us to cut weight and only carry 3 to 4 days' worth of food at a time. Finishing in under 12 days was looking like a safe bet.

We were reading through blogs online, harvesting intelligence, and most people started the trail at the Old Telegraph Station in Alice Springs and finished 12 days later at Mt Sonder in the west. Hiking in that direction meant we would need to organise a pick up from the end at a designated time. I tried to avoid putting time restraints on completion; we could be late or early for several reasons. We decided on the reverse. To get dropped off at Redbank Gorge near Mt Sonder and walk back to town. We needed a lift. Some local tour operators quoted me $300 per person for the service, which I thought was a bit steep. I knew there was only one solution. We required the menace of the outback.

I messaged my uncle Neil asking if he could help.

'A carton of beer and one bottle of vodka, and you have a deal.' He replied via text. Our plan was coming together. We loaded our three food resupplies into sealed plastic tubs for days three, six, and nine. They were filled with noodles, salami, tins of salmon, and an assortment of calorie dense snacks. Expedition food was purchased with endurance fuel in mind, not vitamins and minerals. Our little treats on resupply days would be coconut water and tins of fruit.

The Larapinta Trail was conceptualised in 1989 and opened for its first walking tours in 1990. It was initially half as long as it is today, extended and developed to its current size in 2002. The trail traverses land traditionally owned by the Arrernte

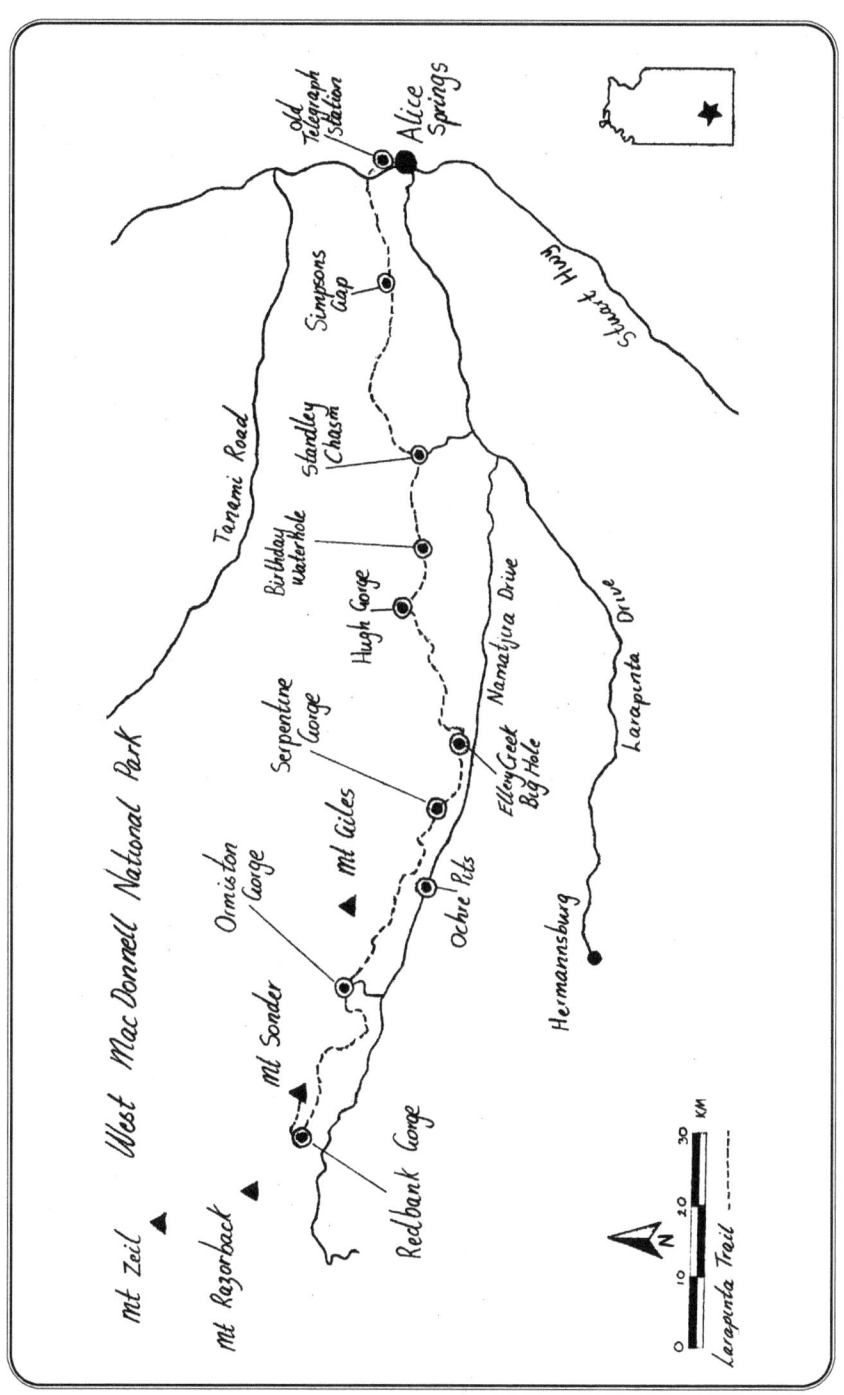

people (pronounced Ah-runda). They are the original Indigenous inhabitants of a land rich in water holes, gorges, and spectacular mountain ranges. The Arrernte are one of the longest continuing cultures on the planet, dating back more than 40,000 years. I couldn't wait to immerse myself in this ancient landscape and experience another aspect of the beautiful desert country.

Up early and on the road, Neil drove at a sensible pace considering his passion for speed, dialling back his throttle foot for the sake of his passengers. The trail was logistically easy to access due to a bitumen road built parallel to the mountain range. Namatjira Drive is named after Australia's most celebrated Aboriginal artist Albert Namatjira. It enabled quick reaction for rescue when required, aided the National Parks service in maintaining and filling water tanks, and gave easy access for tourists to experience the famous gorges spread along the trail.

Neil had worked for the parks service as a ranger for a few years when he was younger, and he loved the bush and the remoteness. The countryside whipped by as he retold stories from those years. His passion for the animals, the history, and the land came across with a gentle enthusiasm and softness I wasn't expecting. This type of talk came from teenaged hippies with dreadlocks eating a bowl of acai, not from the full throttled hard charging menace Neil Richmond.

'It sounds like you really loved it out here. Why did you leave the rangers?'

'Politics', he replied.

'What do you mean, like management policies or something?'

'Here is a perfect example.' He started to explain. 'One day, some female tourists were down at one of the waterholes sunbathing topless. Apparently, this was against the rules, and I was sent down to tell them to cover up.'

I looked over at Neil as he recounted this story; he had an expression of disgust on his face, pure confusion.

'I didn't get it; I got down there, and as I walked in, the girls came out of the water and rushed to cover themselves. I started yelling, no, no, no, it's all ok. Don't worry about that. They asked me if it was ok to sunbathe topless. I said absolutely and sat down with them for a chat. I just couldn't do it mate. That rule made no sense to me. So yeah, politics.'

We dropped off our food tubs at Stanley Chasm, Serpentine Gorge and Ormiston Gorge and continued to the end of the official trail at Red Bank Gorge. Neil bid us good luck with a firm handshake.

'Beer at mine when you get back.'

'Sounds great mate, thanks for the ride, behave yourself.'

With a big smile and wave out of his truck window, he was off down the road towards Alice. We were alone in the bush; the initial silence was filled with birds chattering and flies buzzing around my eyes. It was mid-morning, and the heat was beginning to have an effect as sweat soaked through my t-shirt; it would be scorching by the afternoon. We dragged our packs to an information board at the trailhead to orientate ourselves. We couldn't see Mt Sonder; the surrounding thick vegetation blocked our view, but we knew it was close by. The 1380 metre tall peak, the fourth highest mountain in the Northern Territory, kept watch over the gorge.

The maps I bought in Alice showed the entire trail broken into 12 recommended walking sections. They detailed campgrounds, water refill tanks, and the topography of the land. I dug out the last map as we were doing it in reverse. From where we stood, the trail forked, and the first trail followed a creek one kilometre into the gorge to a picturesque water hole. As tempting as a shaded lounge by cool water would be, I turned my attention to Mt Sonder. The second trail went up 14 kilometres to the summit and back, 600 metres of elevation gain with the afternoon sun beating down. It sounded like a fun start to me. We set up our tents on soft sand in a dry riverbed, not an ideal spot to camp during the rainy season but fine this time of year. We ditched some food and equipment from our packs to lighten the load, then set off.

The trail wound through the wooded lowlands of the mountain slope; birds took flight from trees as we trudged by. The grey headed honeyeaters were abundant, surviving well off the many insects we could hear barracking us along. I expected a harsh desert landscape, but the country was in bloom. Bright pink mountain hakeas with their bottlebrush shaped flowers were scattered amongst the mallee scrub, a stark contrast to the dry red soil and spinifex.

I hadn't felt the comforting embrace of a backpack for a while, and my legs vibrated in protest, pumping lactic acid as the trail started to ascend. We were setting a cracking pace, keen to reach the top and be back for an afternoon swim in the gorge. The initial steep ascent topped out at a saddle; from there, a steady incline followed the ridge to the top. The crystal clear sky allowed an unimpeded view of the horizon. The foreground was full of rich red rocky outcrops, with mallee forests and desert spinifex filling every spare patch in between. A quick break on the top to cool down, rehydrate, and eat snacks before throwing packs on and starting the descent.

The trail steepened as we passed the saddle for the second time when I heard Elise stumble behind me.

'Shit, my knee!'

'You ok? What happened?'

'It was a sharp pain, and it just gave out.'

'Just rest for a minute. How does it feel to put weight on it?'

'It's not great, but it will hold; let's keep going down.'

'A cold swim will help with the swelling. Let's head straight into the gorge.'

Taking the first fork in the trail, the afternoon heat evaporated once we reached the bottom, and high cliffs grew on either side of us. The soft sand underfoot crunched and gave way, it was over five hours since we set off for the summit, and I was frothing at the mouth for a swim. Elise was in obvious pain from her knee and keen to ditch her pack. The gorge had abundant bird life, wallabies, lizards, and insects. Creatures great and small, all trying to avoid the heat of the late afternoon and stay cool. It was the end of a long dry season in the Northern Territory, and I was beginning to doubt there would be much of a waterhole to swim in when it appeared. At the base of a naturally forming cul-de-sac of rock walls towering 30 metres above us was a pool of water the size of a tennis court. It wasn't flowing, but it was clear. I ditched my boots, stripped off to my bike shorts, and waded in.

The temperature took my breath away; it was freezing, an abrupt difference to the scorching sun above the canyon rim. The sand bank sloped into a deep pool, and I couldn't touch the bottom. Its depth allowed the temperature of the water to stand its ground against the sun, maintaining an icy embrace. Elise followed me in and soaked her knee; the natural ice pack would help alleviate the swelling and pain. Cicadas sang their chorus, birds sipped at the water's edge, and I sat on a smooth boulder with goosebumps covering my legs, totally content.

We hiked back to our tents on the riverbed and inhaled a culinary delight of noodles and sliced salami, then crawled into our sleeping bags. The first night back camping for anyone is usually an uncomfortable experience. I had grown soft with beds, blankets, and climate controlled environments over the previous six months. I rolled over 400 times during the night as my body adapted to the inflatable sleeping mat, with a jacket rolled up and stuffed in a sack for a pillow. Desert mice scurried and scratched a few feet from my head, and tiny frogs which remained buried during the day, would emerge and get their exercise on the leaf litter around us. The symphony of nature denied me the realm of a deep sleep.

After a few days of hiking and camping, I knew my sensory system would once again habituate to this new environment. I would sleep eight hours straight in a week, but the first night was always a battle. I lay awake and thought about every weekend warrior who went camping, spent a night or two feeling like I did at that moment, then returned home Sunday afternoon just to put the tent away in the shed, never to be used again. If only they had stuck with it.

There is a primitive beauty to re-habituating to nature. Our senses increase, and our hearing and sight begin to function in high definition. After only a week in the bush, I could hear a human moving across leaf litter during the night at 100 metres and smell chewing gum at 25 metres. That's how in tune our systems would become. It is an evolutionary survival skill that comes back online after an immersive period in the wild. Unfortunately, it has been pruned back, if not numbed, in most people due to modern technology. I pondered all these ideas as I tossed and turned that first night. With my back aching, I rolled one more time and drifted off to sleep.

I woke with puffy eyes, and with a hint of sarcasm, I greeted the dawn and Elise. 'Best sleep ever, coffee?'

'Oh, yes, please,' she replied.

With enough black magic on board to ignite motivation, we packed our camp away, loaded our backpacks and stepped onto the trail on day two, heading east. Over the years, we had fine-tuned our packing procedures and were super efficient. I would make coffee first, and while I did this Elise packed her tent and equipment. When coffee was ready, I would start my own pack up routine, and Elise would make oats for our breakfast. We would then both sit to enjoy coffee and food together. Once done, it was a quick stroll into the bush with a shovel before throwing our packs on and setting off.

One of the reasons we decided to attempt the trail from west to east was the rise and fall of the sun. We thought it would be much better to have the warming sun in our faces early as we trudged towards the sunrise instead of a sweltering afternoon sun heading the other way. From my experience in the mountains, the sun could inspire motivation during a tough time or be the element that breaks you.

Elise's knee seemed stable again, and I didn't want to ask her how it felt. Giving an injury too much attention could be a bad thing. In our nervous systems, we often create feedback loops of information. A knee injury begins as sensory information from the environment, like what happened the day before when Elise took a tumble coming down from Mt Sonder. This ignites pain receptors in the knee, which send messages back up the spinal cord to the brain. The brain processes this information and responds by either dampening the pain or keeping the receptors in the knee firing to inhibit behaviour and further injury. So after Elise woke with no pain, if I then asked, 'How's your knee?' It may have caused her to give attention to it, unconsciously rubbing it every time we stopped.

The brain processes this behaviour as important and starts to send signals to the knee again, firing up pain receptors and keeping them active. I have worked with athletes who have no mechanical problems with their knees anymore, but because of their constant attention and over awareness, they continue to have pain from previous injuries. This is a feedback loop. The worst thing you can do for a sore back is wake up every morning and rub it to see if it's still painful. Try to focus on something else for a few days, change the environmental stimulus, and you will most likely feel a pain reduction as the loop dissipates.

Our next goal was to reach Finke River by the evening. As the name suggested, it was located on a river, and we hoped for a swim to finish the day. The trail was well maintained, and even though I carried maps, a compass, and a PLB (Personal Locator Beacon) for emergencies, it would be near impossible to get lost. Little blue arrows on signs with distances were positioned every two kilometres.

Our pace averaged four to five kilometres per hour as we paralleled the ridgeline of Mt Sonder to our north. Halfway through the morning, as the sun started to make its presence felt, we crossed through Rocky Bar Gap and into flatter country north of the ridge. Big goanna tracks were visible in the sand at our feet. To my inexperienced eyes, the country looked in good health. Green spinifex outnumbered the grey, and native flowers were scattered in abundance. A flower garden of white, purple, yellow, green, and desert colours bloomed a welcome as we trekked by. We decided to top up our water at a small tank at Rocky Bar Gap, and by 10.30 a.m., we were glad we had. The heat beat down while we rested in the shade, and then changed into long sleeve shirts, big hats, and coated on sunscreen. Heat stroke was no joke, and we were playing it safe.

The trail ascended the ridge 300 metres in elevation up to Hilltop Lookout. I loved Australia's names for places; they were always direct and to the point. Rocky Bar Gap was a rocky gap in the ridge with a sandbar underfoot, and our lunch stop at Hilltop Lookout was literally that, a scenic spot at the highest point of the ridge. Grab a map of Australia and scan the names one day. Black

Water, Boat Harbour, Double Island, Emu Park, Green Island, Hat Head, Kangaroo Island, Longreach, Mole Creek, and Wiseman Ferry, it will make you chuckle. In the military, I was stationed in a town that couldn't decide on a name and went with Townsville.

The descent from the ridgeline during the afternoon heat was a sweaty affair. We were fully loaded with gear, and heat pulsed off the rocks underfoot like a fan-forced oven. We both started the trek with old shoes that had seen better days, and the rubber soles were already beginning to peel back from the effort. Ending up barefoot in the desert would be a severe character building exercise and I doubt I was as tough as Annas' dad from Ammaroo.

With three kilometres remaining to Finke River, we stumbled upon a small creek full of water with lilies around its edge and birdlife galore. It was too tempting not to indulge. We stripped down to our underwear and waded in. The surface water to a depth of about ten centimetres was warm, but below that it began to cool and by waist deep it was cold. I ventured in deeper until fully submerged. It was freezing below, and the shock to my system going from hot to cold caught the breath in my lungs.

We walked into Finke River campground, having covered 25.9 kilometres for the day. Our imagined oasis was nowhere in sight; the leaning shelter with one side open to nature was built atop a bare patch of rocky ground with no trees for shade. The shelters were basic but modern, with two elevated sleeping platforms and two more elevated bunks. Another couple and a separate younger man had arrived before us and were in various forms of disarray while recovering from the afternoon heat. There is always a slight awkwardness in the air when entering inhabited campgrounds. Those already in place wonder who is coming to wedge in amongst them and take up space and those approaching hope for a spot all to themselves only to be greeted with little room and judging eyes. The couple broke off their conversation and greeted us. The solo male, dressed like Lawrence of Arabia crossed with an adventurous hobo, also said hi.

They were very friendly and welcomed us before returning to their conversation. It was toasty inside; a hot wind blew across the exposed ground, and the tank water was warm. Signs hung to the tank warning us it was unsafe to drink and do so at our own risk. Another outlined the procedure of boiling the water to make it safe. I had grown up on bore and rainwater, where every cupful was either brown or contained varying amounts of animal urine. I decided we would be fine and gulped it down.

I watched the other three as they chatted about trekking equipment and laughed at private jokes. The couple was very white, with fully loaded packs containing all the latest and greatest from an outdoor camping store. They didn't look in the best shape but seemed to enjoy the adventure together. The young male was different. I had seen his kind many times before all over the world. He was on a spiritual journey. Skinny to the point of sinew, vegan I guessed; he carried the bare minimum, wore his hair long, had an impressive unkempt beard, and wrapped a shemagh around his neck. His skin was covered in tattoos from an assortment of countries and religions. With protective symbols from Thailand, Japanese characters, and bamboo markings from Bali, he was searching for something.

'Have you seen Trail Jesus?' The girl paused her conversation to ask me. I hesitated, thinking she might be referring to her starving friend on a quest opposite me.

'No, we haven't. Who is that?'

'Oh, he is this guy from Victoria who is on the trail now. He started hiking just as COVID-19 hit and his state went into lockdown. He decided to just keep hiking and has done it four times already, end to end. He survives off donated food and water tanks.'

'That is impressive. If we see him, we will make a donation.' I replied. The three returned to their talk, and I turned to Elise.

'Let's camp back down in the riverbed.' She looked at me, knowing my patience for talking about equipment and noise at bedtime was finite. We filled our water bottles, bid farewell to the others and hiked into the dry riverbed. A few hundred metres away, we found exactly what we were after. On a slight lean, an enormous paperbark tree provided shade over the soft sand, a perfect camp. We settled in.

The following morning, I wandered shirtless into the bush to perform my morning rituals. The soft sand made for easy digging, and once reaching the required depth, I removed my pants entirely. When possible, I prefer to disrobe to avoid any risk of soiling my limited trekking clothes. It was also liberating and natural, this was how it was supposed to be done. I stood up, refilled my hole, and then, standing there in all my naked glory, I noticed the couple from the day before walking my way. We made brief eye contact, and as embarrassment and annoyance overtook me, they did the polite thing and pretended to look at a fascinating piece of spinifex off in the other direction. I pulled up my pants and slunk my way back to camp, where Elise was laughing.

I felt great trekking after a better night's sleep in the soft, quiet riverbed, and our bodies were slowly habituating to bush life. Up and over ridges and steep inclines, my heart beat steadily from the work. It was another ten kilometres from our Finke River camp to Ormiston Gorge, where we had our first resupply tub of food. We hadn't even eaten what we had been carrying and realised we had overestimated our food for the trip. Always better to have too much than not enough; there would be a few items left over for Trail Jesus. Ormiston Gorge is one of the highlights in the MacDonnell ranges. A sandy beach welcomed us to a secluded canyon sheltering a deep pool of water. Large shady trees hung over the sand, providing the ideal spot to sit, relax, and wait out the hottest part of the day. In many Australian cities, I had noticed attempts by councils and developers to replicate the incredible scene before us. Nothing came close to what nature had created.

I stripped off to shorts, not my birthday suit, as there were tourists about, and walked into the water. It was exactly what my aching legs desired. The pool was deep, cold, and refreshing. We spent the afternoon gorging ourselves on salami, noodles, pringles, and tinned fruit; eating everything we were reluctant to carry. Hot coffee and a book completed the affair, and I didn't want to be anywhere else in the world. It was perfect.

The sun had dropped below the gorge rim by 3 p.m., and we decided it was time to gain a few extra kilometres. From Ormiston to Serpentine Chalet Dam was an estimated 12 hours and over 29 kilometres, with a sizable mountain in the middle. We hit the trail fully loaded with food and water and immediately wanted to return to the gorge. The afternoon sun was scorching and sweat soaked through my shirt in minutes. We covered five extra kilometres and scraped ourselves a flat camp out of the rocky scrubland just before sundown. An evening brew and another day spent in the Outback. This country could be beautiful and brutal at the flip of a coin, and I loved it.

Up early on our fourth day, we were on the trail by 5.30 a.m. We wanted to make the most of the cool morning and cover as many kilometres as possible in the shade of the mountains. The path wound its way along the southwestern base of the ranges for the first two hours before taking a sharp turn skyward. The steep switchback ascent of 300 metres landed us on top at 1100 metres elevation.

A breeze that had kept us company from dawn dropped away, signalling the arrival of the heat and squadrons of tiny black flies. Their relentless attack lasted about 45 minutes before they found some level of calm and became more of a symbiotic partner. Initially, they loved my eyes, nose, ears, and mouth, but these areas were within my arcs of fire, and I could kill them on mass when they dawdled in these regions. Eventually, they accumulated on the top of my head, back, and other sweat soaked patches out of reach. I could live with this, and we settled into a mutual peace agreement; they could enjoy the salt of my labour if my face remained a demilitarised zone.

Water is our most precious commodity in desert country. We had departed Ormiston the day before carrying 4.5 litres each, enough to see us through to the next camp. Due to the heat, we consumed more than we had rationed for and ran low. I looked at the map and Waterfall Gorge jumped out. I doubted it would be much of a waterfall this late in the dry season, but if we were lucky we could refill our bottles. We started our descent from the high point.

The switchbacks were steep, with loose gravel underfoot making it precarious. When walking downhill carrying a load, the force from the weight on your back shifts from your glutes and hamstrings into the quadriceps in the front of your legs. It also puts an overload on the tendons and ligaments supporting the kneecap. These essential pieces of anatomy keep the knee in alignment, but with every step at such an acute downward angle, the knee inevitably fatigues. The front of the knee is a common spot for pain in older people when walking downstairs or in athletes with overuse injuries. If the knees are healthy, strong, and trained for the extra load, they will cope with the strain. Elise and I had been hammering our bodies lately on multiple adventures, and our knees were barely hanging on. Her knee gave out halfway down towards the valley floor.

Knowledge of anatomy and why an injury occurs doesn't help with the pain. We stopped and strapped her knee for extra support, then, conscious of not creating feedback loops, we carried on slowly. The trail wound its way into a deep gully and further along inside a dry gorge. We started to hear chatter from flocks of birds, an early sign there could be water close by, and then we found it. Trapped at the base of what we assumed would be a magnificent, tiered water feature during the wet season was a stagnant pool about four metres in diameter.

It looked deep and was full of life, with algae blooming along its surface and tadpoles swimming in abundance around the edges. Water skippers, spiders, lizards, and hundreds of birds all relied on this tiny pond to see them through until the rains came. I checked for any dead animals lying close by or in the water; there were none. The water was clear, and birds were drinking from it, another good sign it wasn't poisoned. Unlike the water tanks at the camps, if we wanted to drink this water, we would need to boil it for safety. It most likely contained a collage of bacteria that was harmless to animals but would wreak havoc with our biology.

'Time for a brew,' I said, as Elise sat in the shade.

'Boil the hell out of it,' she replied.

I set myself to the task. A symphony of bird life surrounded us while I made our coffees. Three different varieties of budgies, red-headed finches, and small grey pigeons; all fearlessly landing inches from me and taking a drink. Their evasive survival instincts were overridden by their desire for water. I remembered Neil telling us in the car that it had been a buster season for seeds, and the bird populations had exploded.

I put a big bowl full of water on the stove and let it boil for two minutes, then sat back with a hot cup of black magic and took in the natural world around us. I watched a flock of 50 or more budgies swoop and fly together in unison above the pond, stunning in their synchronised trajectories. A flock of birds is an analogy we utilised in our NeuroPhysics Therapy strength and conditioning training. The seamless flight of the flock represents the flow of energy and information throughout a healthy nervous system. When attacked by a predatory bird, a flock of birds will temporarily split apart and then reform before carrying on with their flight. The predator was a significant stress to their system, but they were not overly perturbed by it and flew off in the same seamless pattern.

When training I mimicked this behaviour while moving about in my gym environment. I could take on a big set of weights or 'stress' into my system, keep my composure, and then move along to the next movement seamlessly. No grunting, growling or becoming overly aroused. The nervous system doesn't know the difference between the gym and the outside world, it only knows how I feel about what I am doing. This approach to training taught me how to handle all of life's stresses in a calm and composed manner, like a flock of birds.

Before departing the pond, we soaked our shirts to give us some respite from the heat, then hit the trail. We entered a gently sloping southern valley, and the going was easy for 13 kilometres before the route turned south into the Inarlanga Pass. The pass cut through a deep red rock gorge filled with old smoky green fronds of the MacDonnell Ranges cycads. Thick seams of quarts, squeezed tightly into its curves over 300 million years ago, wound through the glowing red walls. The place held power, and when we arrived at the Serpentine Chalet Dam, it was vacant; however, the cooling swim I had dangled as a carrot all day didn't eventuate. The dam was almost dry, with a few stagnant and unenticing pools scattered throughout. We settled into the evening routine, set up tents, hydrated, and finally lay down to rest our legs after covering 24 kilometres.

Hitting the trail before dawn the following day to avoid the heat, we were walking into our next camp at Serpentine Gorge by lunchtime. We had punched out a quick five hours and 13 kilometres. Although a shorter day, it did entail a 300 metre ascent back up on top of the ridge to Counts Point Bluff and the best views of the lower valleys we had seen. Then, of course, down again to the camp. I was starting to see a pattern developing on this trail.

The flies were in abundance and aggressive, and they swarmed like a D-day landing whenever I stopped to take a leak. If I stood still, they would land and crawl all over my nether region, while an exciting sensation in a weird way, not very hygienic. Their relentless attack forced me to swing back and forth, and as urine hit the dry earth at my feet, it created the familiar sound of a sprinkler. This transported me to our backyard sprinkler at home when I was a kid. It was my job to systematically move the hose to ensure a watered lawn and the mission was to try to get in, move it, and get out again without being soaked. All the while avoiding land mines laid by our dog Bruce. Every time without fail, I would be sprinting for safety when a rapid-fire blast of water drilled my back like a retreating soldier being shot in a Hollywood war epic. The joys of a kid's life before technology.

Serpentine Gorge was an official sacred site to the Aboriginal people, and they requested that no visitors swim in the water. The few trekkers that were there when we arrived were all respecting this wish. We rested in the shade on a sandy beach overlooking a large pool of water wedged between stone pillars. The contrast between the hot, barren conditions in the valleys and the shaded gorges was unreal. These waterholes really were a lifeline to people living off the land. Unlike the Arrernte tribe, who harvested bush tucker from this country, we needed to gather our next food tub from a shipping container near the car park. It was resupply day again already, and time to gorge ourselves at the gorge.

A solo trekker, Marie, was departing the campsite as we walked in to set up our tents, we had struck it lucky again and would have the place to ourselves. Marie was from Darwin, seemed well equipped, and was keen to push on to Chalet Dam throughout the afternoon. Often in passing, fellow trekkers would ask, 'How far is it to go? Is it hard going?', desperate to figure out what was ahead for them. I avoided ever asking these questions, they were very subjective. Someone could answer, 'Super hard going; it took hours,' only for Elise and me to knock it out quickly and easily. Or the reverse, someone saying, 'Just a little further and you're done,' only to realise their 'little further' is four hours of strenuous hiking. I also never wanted to put someone in a risky situation out of their depth. With our experience, something relatively easy could be a lifetime achievement for someone else, which they may not be ready for. Marie didn't ask any questions. Being from Darwin, she was used to the heat, and I asked her, 'Have you got plenty of water?'

'Yep, full up with six litres', she replied.

'Perfect, have a great trek.'

After a solid night's sleep and fully loaded with food, we enjoyed another short day of 13 kilometres following a new trail skirting the northern side of the mountain range. We arrived at Ellery Creek Big Hole's north side. The heat was already ramping up above 30 degrees, and the northern valley was sparsely vegetated, dry as tinder, and had a Mad Max vibe about it. We descended into a sandy riverbed and followed its curve south into the gorge.

The temperature dropped ten degrees as the enormous rock walls rose on either side of us. A cool breeze blew through the canyon, skipping off a large deep waterhole as it passed us. We paused at the edge of the water and dropped our packs. I had seen pictures of this waterhole in brochures, it was one of the most popular tourist attractions on the entire Larapinta Trail, yet no photo had done it justice.

'How good is this.'

'So beautiful,' Elise replied.

'We are spending the whole day here; it's too good.'

We were the only people on the north side. We could see the waterhole expand through a narrow canyon like the top of an hourglass on the south side, surrounded by a large beach, slowly filling up with travellers. We had the north all to ourselves, and there was no way anyone could walk to our side. The cliffs were sheer on both sides to the water's edge; to come across would mean swimming 150 metres or initiating some world-class climbing. I sat next to a rippled rock formation, the pattern reminding me of an original Dunlop Volley sole, and removed my boots. It was time to swim, eat, brew up, and relax.

Three hours later, after we had enjoyed a few rounds of these luxuries, a skinny trekker appeared with a spring in his step.

'G'day mate, how are you going?' I asked.

'Really good, thanks. I'm Matt.'

'Great to meet you, Matt, I'm Luke, and this is my wife, Elise.'

'I took a wrong turn; I'm supposed to be on the south side where my resupply container is.'

'You're on the best side. No tourists here, and you can swim over and get your tub; it will be great fun.' I suggested.

'You're right, good idea, I'll do that now.'

We watched as he stripped to shorts, entered the frigid water and started crossing. A mixture of wading, rock hopping and scrambling evolved into freestyle swimming as he crossed the open section. The Southerners were taken by surprise watching this semi-naked man emerge from the water. He wandered off to locate his supplies before returning with a large plastic tub on his shoulder. He entered the water again and pushed the floating food container in front of him as he slowly swam back. It was a top effort.

He crawled onto our beach and lay in the sun to warm up.

'That was harder than it looked.'

'I bet it was.' I replied.

Matt was 37 and on a solo trip after a recent failed relationship. He had moved to Alice Springs from Cairns to be with a girl, but it didn't work out. He decided to go bush while he figured out what to do next. He worked for defence in procurement and owned a map and chart shop back in Cairns. He was planning to finish the entire trail in a week, which meant covering big kilometres each day, and was nourishing himself on a budget. He opened a cold tin of baked beans and sausage, his so-called treat, and shovelled it down. He was skinny but moved like he had once been an athlete; he sported a long unkempt beard and gave off a gypsy vibe. He was a lovely bloke, and we hit it off, chatting late into the afternoon.

Matt swam his container and rubbish back to the north side and then decided to hit the trail and cover more kilometres before sundown. We chose the opposite: spend every second by the water till dark, then camp nearby in the riverbed. We bid him farewell, and as he walked off into the dusty horizon, I wondered, was that Trail Jesus?

Our seventh day started at 4.40 a.m., up early, fed, and stimulated; we stepped off 45 minutes later. We planned for a massive day, 30.3 kilometres to Hugh Gorge in the northeast across undulating country. While most of the Larapinta Trail leads hikers along ridge tops and through gorges, this section traversed vast rolling hills that separated Heavitree Range in the south from Chewings Range in the north. Luckily, we had cloud cover, a slightly cooler day, and possible rain.

On long days where monotony and workload are compounded it's great to have an overactive imagination. I could drift away for hours following Alice through Wonderland, and down rabbit holes of adventure. I planned expeditions, remembered past adventures, created lists of tasks to execute upon arrival home, and often wondered about the finite aspect of our most valuable commodity, time.

We are born with an average life expectancy of 79 years. We sleep about a third of this time, leaving 52 years of conscious living. We go to school and university; on average, this will chew up two whole years. Then we embrace the workforce and trade every second of 10 full years for currency to survive. Forty years remaining. We spend a year in traffic, a year brushing our teeth and getting ready for work, two years planning meals and shopping, six years of yard work, chores and cooking our food, and five more years eating and drinking it. Twenty five years remaining. Two years we will dedicate to caring for our kids and loved ones as part of human evolution and degradation. Twenty three years of precious time remain, and what do we pour this valuable commodity into most? Eighteen years on average, spent watching TV, playing video games, or scrolling through social media.

This leaves five precious years to discover who you are, fall in love, travel, write a book, hold hands, start a family, build a house, or even sit and think about life's most profound questions. Just five years to do all that. Five years to live.

◆◆◆

Clouds had been building throughout the day, the humidity reaching new heights of sweaty irritation. Something had to give. Respite came around midnight at the Hugh Gorge campground, the heavens opened, and rain saturated the land, our tents, and the heat. The cool change was welcomed after the 30 kilometre push from Ellery Creek Big Hole. We were exhausted, but the flapping of my tent's rain cover in the breeze kept me awake. I got up, crawled outside, and pegged it down, hoping for quiet. Within minutes the flapping had begun at a different spot. I crawled out again, the frustration building, and wedged the side flap with my full water bottle before getting back inside. Five minutes later, I was dying for a drink, and my bottle was outside. I crawled out a third time as the rain stopped; I tore off the cover and packed it away, with nothing left to flap I went back to bed and slept till dawn.

While packing up the following day, I swindled a few extra pieces of our equipment into my backpack. I had secretly stolen supplies from Elise's pack to lighten her load and save her knee. If I had asked her to give me extra, she would have said no.

Section five was my favourite part of the entire trail. There were no waterholes, but the mountain's razor-back ridges, scrambling portions, and picturesque gorges were impressive. It was a 15 kilometre section, but due to the topography, it would take us nine hours to navigate. The weather was perfect, and almost cold during the day due to the cloud cover, sporadic drizzles of rain, and strong wind. It felt like the Tasmanian outdoors. Although the grey outlook was not ideal for photos, the climate and conditions were excellent for human performance. We could push hard all day, needing fewer breaks and not succumbing to the heat by the afternoon. After arriving at 4/5 Junction campground and feeling euphoric, we threw an idea around.

'Should we try to finish the trail in the next two days?' I asked.

'How far would that be?'

I pulled out the maps and did some rough calculations.

'Well, if we get to Standley Chasm for our last resupply tomorrow, then crack on as far as we can for the afternoon. It would leave us about 50 kilometres in a day to finish.'

'What's the biggest distance we have ever walked?' Elise asked.

'42 kilometres on the Gobi Desert expedition.' I replied.

'But we were dragging carts.' I added.

'Let's do it.' Elise sounded confident.

'Awesome, I'm in. It will be good training for summit days in Nepal.'

'Let's get a few more kilometres in today,' Elise replied, 'I'm feeling good.'

'Done. Stewarts Pass is another four kilometres; let's get there.'

We filled up with water, devoured some snacks, and returned to the trail, knowing we would be loaded up again the following day. Stewarts Pass sat at the base of Brinkley Bluff Summit, with a high point of 1209 metres, and was our ideal camping spot. A soft sand riverbed shaded by paperbark trees, a cool breeze keeping the flies at bay, and we had it all to ourselves. We set up tents an hour before sunset, feeling accomplished, and gazed up towards our next objective.

'Spicy uphill start to the day tomorrow,' I said.

'After coffee, we will crush it,' Elise replied.

With dawn barely on the horizon, and powered by strong coffee, we charged up the steep ascent of 500 vertical metres in two hours, arriving at Brinkley Bluff Summit. Red granite escarpments were glowing in the early morning sun, cliff faces dropped away, and we could see the trail winding its path eastwards along sharp ridges we had grown accustomed to. The rock features were unique, layered flakes so thin in places they were brittle to touch, like stacks of Pringles. I relished the steep sections where we needed to use our hands to hang on. The touch of the rock added a new sensation to the experience; with some exposure and a little risk to life thrown in, you've found my happy place.

We traversed the ridge for the morning and descended into the centrepiece of the area, Standley Chasm. Due to its popularity, modern amenities had been built near the entrance, including a café, toilets, and ample parking for travellers. The area is traditionally known as Angkerle Atwatye, meaning 'the gap of water,' and located in a reserve privately owned by the Iwupataka Land Trust. Tourists pay to access the site; however, you gain free access if you are a through hiker on the Larapinta Trail. The deep granite gorge was originally named Gall Springs by Europeans, then renamed to Standley Chasm in honour of Ida Standley, the first schoolteacher in Alice Springs who taught for 15 years between 1914 and 1929.

The gorge was impressive, but just like a trip through Europe when seeing countless cathedrals or pieces of incredible architecture, I was more focused on the tourist café after a week of breathtaking scenery. We arrived at 11.45 a.m., bang on lunchtime, and I ordered up big. Two toasted chicken and salad sandwiches, extra fried eggs with chips, and large coffees. We also picked up our resupply container and reloaded our packs while waiting for lunch to arrive. The abundance of fatty food washed down with three milk coffees required a visit to the toilet block before we stepped back onto the trail.

Refreshed but feeling every extra kilogram of our resupply, at 2 p.m., we hiked up and over the gorge as the Northern Territory heat returned with vengeance. We scrambled amongst the rocky riverbed as it meandered its way through the Chewings Range with bluffs rising on both sides of us. A Dreamtime story from the Arrernte people tells how their spirit ancestors found the passage through this country. One of them was the serpent, and the entire area is now a sacred site associated with its deeds.

We tried to limit our rest breaks, but my feet were beginning to burn with fatigue and pain from two full days of sharp ridges thrusting into the flimsy soles of my boots. However, as every kilometre we covered during the afternoon subtracted from the total of our final day; we pushed on. We passed through Millers Flat, Tangentyere Junction and arrived at Fish Hole, named after the native species of Spangled Grunter inhabiting its small deep pool. This location was once a frequented rest spot in the 1900s for camel trains linking Hermannsburg in the south to Hamilton Downs homestead in the north. Camels didn't appreciate stones or steep slopes when carrying heavy loads, and the creek bed was ideal. No swimming was allowed because our sunscreen would be enough to wipe out the vulnerable fish, and with no camping permitted either, we carried on. Following the ever present blue arrows, we arrived at Jay Creek campground on dark. It had been a massive day, our feet were throbbing, but at least we enjoyed another peaceful night to ourselves.

I stripped off, had a splash bath from the water tank, and then consumed noodle and salami wraps, chocolate, and electrolytes to recover.

'Are we doing this tomorrow?' I asked Elise.

'How far till the end?'

'About 51 kilometres. It will be a big day, and we need to start early.'

'My knee is not the best, but I'm keen to try,' she replied, forcing down a mouthful of noodles.

'Game on.'

I lay awake most of the night, as I did every night before a summit attempt on a mountain or a physical battle in the outdoors. The anticipation of the suffer-fest to come caused anxiety, and the rat in my brain was sprinting on its wheel. I knew I had to sleep to perform at my best, which worsened my anxiety. I tried to read and covered my eyes from the full moon. I counted sheep backwards from 200, but nothing worked. I started tuning into the sounds around me. Tiny frogs were hopping about, and spiders with diamond eyes under my head torch were scattered across the sand like stars. I heard mice battling for dominance in the scrub to my left. Then my alarm went off. I must have slept three hours maximum.

It was 2 a.m., the full moon set the scene, and we could pack up our tents without a head torch. I pulled on my disgusting long sleeved shirt, reeking from nine days of sweat and effort, and boiled water for big bowls of oats and honey washed down with strong coffee. It was 51 kilometres to the Old Telegraph Station in Alice Springs and ten kilometres to our next water point at Mulga Camp. Every ounce would count, so we only carried the bare minimum of water to arrive at the next fill point. One blog writer described Mulga Camp as a place of flies and depression, but as we walked in, still shrouded in darkness and creeping passed campers, it seemed hospitable. We filled four litres of water each, and while trying not to disturb the other trekkers, we crept back onto the trail like ninjas behind enemy lines, 41 kilometres to go.

Elise led the way, trying to collect every spider web on her face as she went. We maintained a steady pace of four kilometres per hour until dawn and into the morning, slowing ever so slightly as the heat began to take a toll before lunch. I could tell her knee was giving her grief, but she didn't complain. Only a slight limp hinted at her condition. Simpsons Gap welcomed us in at three kilometres per hour, we had covered 26.2 kilometres and fatigue was setting in. We sat under the camp shelter and removed our boots to give our feet some respite.

'How are you feeling?' I asked.

'My feet are on fire, my knee is not the best, but I'm ok. You?'

'Not too bad, but my feet will give me grief later. Twenty five kilometres to go, what do you think?'

'We will get in late, but I'm keen to keep going.'

'Ok sweet, we will crack on.'

Resilience is a word mentioned a lot in today's world. I often hear it at corporate events relating to business and team dynamics. The challenging thing was, how do you build resilience in yourself, which would then flow into all aspects of your life? I often suggested executing something like what Elise and I were doing on the last day of our Larapinta trek. Push your physical and mental boundaries, and stand your ground when suffering sets in. Doing this makes a small deposit into your resilience bank, a stockpile of past experiences to be drawn on later in life. For some people, a challenge could be a day hike, a paddle trip on a kayak, or sleeping in the backyard for a night. For others, it will be a solo ascent of K2 in Pakistan. It doesn't matter what it is. If you contribute to your resilience bank as often as possible, you will be ready when life throws you an ultimate challenge.

We sat and gulped down coffee, ate copious calories, and topped it off with some Panadol. At the camp there was a particular spot for phone coverage, and once connected to the outside world I phoned the G'day Mate Tourist Park in Alice and told them what we were up to. After hearing we would be rocking up very late, the manager offered to leave out a key for a cabin and told me the combination for the lock on the front gate. They couldn't be more accommodating, and I thanked them before hanging up. We now had a bed waiting for us, comfort, hot showers, and fresh food. We shouldered our loads and stepped off.

There was often an easy way out from discomfort in our everyday lives. When you commit yourself into the wild, however, options become limited. The battle was having the mental stamina to go on when all you want to do is quit and run for comfort. This close to the end, we could easily hitch a ride from Simpsons Gap with one of the caravans driving past on the highway and arrive in town within the hour. I could conjure up a story to justify it and make myself feel better; Elise's knee was a perfect excuse. But if we did that, we would miss an opportunity to test ourselves and see what we really had left in the tank. Feeling sorry for yourself was easy, and to keep moving forward through pain and discomfort is tough, but it's in those moments beyond where you thought your limit was that you discover who you really are and what you are made of. A poem titled 'Self Pity' from the great DH Lawrence often comes to mind during these difficult times.

'I never saw a wild thing sorry for itself.
A small bird will drop frozen dead from a bough
without ever having felt sorry for itself.'

The heat beat down, sweat dripped from my nose, and my shirt was soaked through again. Wallaby Gap campground lay vacant, and we found a shaded shelter to rest. It was 3.20 p.m. with 14 kilometres to go. Such a short distance in the overall length of the trail, but at that moment, it almost felt insurmountable. My feet were on fire, throbbing with a deep ache like bruised bone, a pain that felt like it could leave some long-term damage if I pushed it too far. We rested for 40 minutes, dried our feet, and brewed coffee. Caffeine is an essential teammate during endurance expeditions and could often be the morale boost needed to carry us through to the end.

I didn't drink coffee until I was 17, and I remember my first sip vividly. It was the last week of Infantry School. We had been through ten weeks of hell, and it was the final five days. We were deep in the bush outside Singleton in New South Wales, it was frigid cold, and we had been digging pits and trenches with tiny shovels for days on end with no sleep. My morale was low, I was freezing and starting to throw myself a pity party. A fellow soldier and future best friend, Liam, came over with a steaming cup. We were both soaked to the core, but he seemed to be enjoying himself. He noticed how dishevelled and down I was and offered me the cup. It was a hot, sweet, strong cup of coffee, most likely instant with sweetened condensed milk, but it changed my world. It lit a fire inside me, which carried me through the day, the following week, and into the ranks of the Royal Australian Regiment. From then on, I was a coffee drinker.

We pulled our boots on and tentatively started the next leg and the final push. The last section looked flat on the map, but we quickly realised it was undulated with constant ups and downs, torturing Elise's knee, and our battered feet with every incline. We followed the trail to Euro viewpoint, which offered a clear line of sight to Alice Springs in the distance, close enough to touch but still hours away in our current condition. As we descended, a giant fully grown male kangaroo broke from concealment and bounded away.

His fur was deep red, and he easily stood five feet high; he was impressive. We both stopped and watched him escape with ease through the scrub. It was the first kangaroo we had seen on the entire trip. He was very skittish and had obviously encountered humans before but had survived, unlike most of his species which had been hunted to near extinction around townships in the Northern Territory.

The sun set, and we were engulfed by night again, donning our head torches and pushing forward at an ever decreasing pace. We ascended a rise leading up and over a railway line, then down under a bridge, and we could finally see the glow from streetlights on the horizon. We were getting close. The last five kilometres seemed to pass by in slow motion, with every step sending a lightning rod of pain from my foot to my brain, and all I wanted to do was lie down. Elise was in a similar state but never voiced her emotions.

I was on high alert while walking through the bush on the outskirts of Alice late in the evening, remembering all the stories Neil had mentioned about the crime rates and what I had witnessed while travelling through the Territory. I picked up a rock as a weapon in case we were ambushed, most likely unjustified, and it could have been sleep deprived paranoia driving my delusions, but better to be safe than sorry. The trail looped around, and in the glow of my head torch, the dirt path evolved into a black tar road. A small sign to our right read, 'Old Telegraph Station.' We had made it.

Have you ever seen great tennis stars when they nail the game winning shot? Or a premier league soccer player score a goal to win the match? They clench their fists, flex their biceps, while pumping their arms, and screaming with a raw uninhibited display of emotion. Sadly, that feeling is one many people in the world will never experience, but it is within everyone's reach. We dropped our packs to the curb, and I hugged Elise. We were too shattered to pump our fists and scream, but inside, the feeling of accomplishment and winning was the same. We had set ourselves a task over a distance we had never travelled, 51 kilometres in 15 hours, battling the demons in our minds along the way, and we had done it.

I phoned a taxi and then sat down on the side of the road. I already knew our post expedition recovery plan, straight to Woolworths to stock up on salmon, eggs, avocado, and bacon. Shower first, then gorge on fat and nutrients. Wash it all down with a few painkillers and sleep for 12 hours. Tomorrow, I would wake feeling half refreshed and free of regret. I looked up at the stars, then back to Elise. With pain pulsing through my limbs I said,

'How good is this? I think we are ready for Nepal again.'
She turned to me with that knowing look and replied,
'Absolutely.'

Paddling an inflatable kayak on the Franklin River in Tasmania.

Rafting the mighty Franklin River, a must-do whitewater adventure.

Aboard Stormbreaker heading to Strahan on the final day of our Rafting the Franklin adventure.

Visiting Uluru during our cycle journey through the Outback.

Fixing flat tyres was a daily ritual when cycling across Australia.

Burnt cars were a common feature near Outback communities.

Our team standing on the summit of Island Peak in Nepal.

Taking a moment to myself on the summit of Island Peak before starting the descent.

Our farewell from Phuket inside Grants pedal powered Little Donkey.

Jean Andre Quemener, aka the Beer Barron. He died doing what he loved, rest in peace brother.

Starting our summit attempt on Ama Dablam.

Mum and Dad in their caravan were our road crew during Outback adventures.

Elise, Dad, and I on a treasure hunt in the Northern Territory.

Taking a break next to a waterhole on the Larapinta Trail.

Hiking the Larapinta Trail in the West MacDonnell National Park near Alice Springs.

Descending from Mera Peak after a successful summit bid.

Our tent at Camp 2 while climbing Ama Dablam. One of the most exposed camps in Nepal.

Descending towards Camp 2 on Ama Dablam, one of the toughest climbs I had ever attempted.

High on Mera Peak in Nepal, a perfect weather day.

On shift pedalling our boat while attempting to cross the Bay of Bengal.

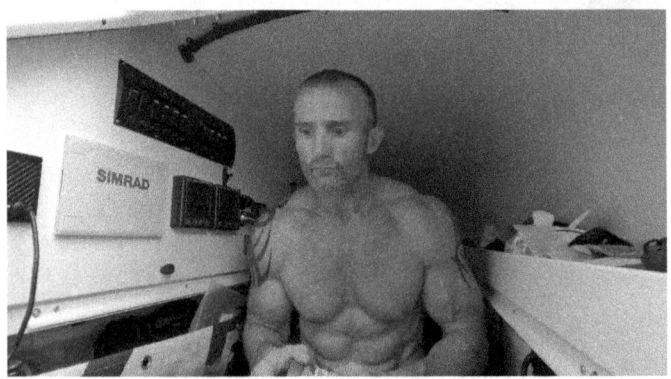

Contemplating life inside the tiny cabin before I devoured a tub of peanut butter.

The end of surf camp, with the legend Craig Edmunds on the right.

CHAPTER 7
Point Break

Have humans ever been in harmony with the raw power of Mother Nature? I don't mean by harvesting it for energy by damming rivers for hydroelectricity or building wind farms. I mean working hand in hand with the chaotic power of the environment to achieve an objective. It's possible a canoe could have been Homo Sapiens first attempt at this symbiotic relationship. Riding the surface of a river's currents and using an oar to steer and explore down streams. Sailing would have come next. The wind's energy deflected off a canvas sheet, held tight with human hands, propelling a ship across oceans, and expanding the known horizons of a magnificent world. But was this an accurate representation of seamlessly living and working with nature? Unlike birds or fish, which seemed to glide effortlessly during the most brutal conditions, we were constantly poised on the brink of tragedy, with reefs, breaking waves, and hurricane winds able to easily sink our floating creations, absorbing our bodies into the sand.

What about planes? The modern jet engine could lift hundreds of tonnes of humans and cargo off the ground in seconds and carry it halfway around the world before needing to touch down. Is this harmony? Or just another example of technology raging against the elements? I journeyed down this rabbit warren of thought until I concluded that we had never genuinely blended with our natural environment, we were always separate from it. I held firm in this belief until the day I sat on a jagged outcrop of rock at an iconic location on Tasmania's Southeast coastline called Shipsterns Bluff.

An omnipotent southerly swell had collided with the shallow rock shelf, lifting it skyward to create one of the heaviest waves on Earth. 'Shippies,' as it was known in the local vernacular, is 25 feet (11 metres) of barrelling wave, breaking in only a few feet of water, encased in a great white shark breeding ground, and in the southern hypothermic ocean of Van Diemen's Land. A Red Bull big wave surfing event had been planned to coincide with the swell, but due to COVID-19, it was cancelled. This didn't stop the local surfers from paddling and being towed into the tsunami. I had never witnessed anything like it up close. I had seen plenty like it on YouTube and social media, but in the flesh, to the naked eye, it created a cascade of hormones and emotions that left me speechless. Awestruck would be an appropriate term. In the movie Gladiator, starring Russel Crowe, upon seeing the Roman Colosseum for the first time, one of the slaves breathlessly utters, 'I didn't know men could build such things.' While sitting on that frigid rock at Shippies, I had no idea humans could ride such things. I wanted to learn how.

Looking back throughout human history, the first surfing references were found in Polynesia, where 12th century cave paintings depict people riding on waves. The Polynesians are well known for their seafaring and navigation. For thousands of years, they crossed vast distances of the Pacific Ocean in outrigger and double hulled canoes. Amongst the goods they undoubtedly carried to trade, they also took their unique ability to ride waves. Upon reaching Hawaii, this board riding seed was firmly planted. It became ingrained in Hawaiian culture and grew into what surfing is thought of today. From a lush tropical paradise in the middle of the Pacific Ocean, the sport spread to the United States and then to every corner of the globe, even to the frigid southern waters of Tasmania. According to the Surf Industry Manufacturer's

Association, in 2022, between 17 million and 35 million people actively pursued surfing as a hobby. Some are lucky enough to make lucrative careers on the professional surfing world stage.

I have friends in my network who are avid surfers, yet when I approached them about the best way to learn how to surf as an adult with a Rugby player's physique, they all replied, 'You should speak to Edo.' Craig Edmunds, known as Edo, served alongside me in the Army. We were posted to Townsville in North Queensland and deployed on operations overseas with the 1st Infantry Battalion of the Royal Australian Regiment (1 RAR). We had worked in different sections of the same company and didn't know each other well. I had no idea Edo was a hard charging big wave surfer before and after his time in the military. I reached out via social media, where even on his Facebook page, there were no images of waves or hints of greatness. He replied immediately via messenger, and before I could respond, his name popped up on a video call.

'Richo, how the hell are you mate? Long time.'

'I'm great mate, how are you? It's nice to connect again.'

'Brothers for life Richo, 13 Alpha all the way. I'm good. What's happening in the land of adventures?'

I had forgotten our old call sign of 13 Alpha, the memory had faded or been suppressed after all these years, and it brought back memories of our time together in the green machine; the good, the bad, and the ugly.

'Adventures are coming thick and fast mate, that's why I'm reaching out. A little birdie told me you're a bit of a surfer. I'm looking for a coach for Elise and I, and somewhere to do a surf camp.'

'Richo,' he replied with a chuckle.

'Welcome into my world. We have a lot to talk about. You are coming to my place. I'm in Pottsville, north coast New South Wales, get up here. Some of the best swell in Australia is on my doorstep, and you two have a lot to learn.'

And just like that, we were off on our next adventure.

We planned to commit to a month of solid surfing and see what happened. With only raw enthusiasm, no wetsuits, no boards, or any idea about what we were doing, we flew up to the

Gold Coast in Queensland. Another good mate, Ken Ware, the NeuroPhysics Therapy founder, loaned us his spare work vehicle for the month, and we pulled onto the highway heading south. Pottsville was located 60 kilometres away, over the border inside New South Wales. We stopped at one of the numerous surf shops on the coast and bought some Rip Curl wetsuits, so we would at least look the part.

The highway followed the coast intersecting some of Australia's most iconic surf locations. Burleigh Heads, Kirra, Snapper Rocks, and Cabarita, endless pristine beaches and breaks, with countless surfers dotted amongst the swell. We had come to the right place. Pottsville, a small town with a population of 7000, welcomed us with a relaxed atmosphere and a cool coastal vibe. Potty, as it was nicknamed, was like the chilled surfer uncle to the trendy aunty of Byron Bay, half an hour's drive further south. We pulled into Edo's driveway, who appeared with arms wide open and embraced us like family at an airport arrivals hall.

'Welcome legends, get in here and have a coffee, lots to catch up on, then we are going surfing.'

Over an afternoon brew of Nescafe's Blend 43, the cheap coffee brand being the lifeblood of infantry soldiers, we got to understand who Edo was outside of a camouflaged uniform.

Born in northern Western Australia, he grew up in the remote mining town of Karratha. His father was a police officer specialising in domestic violence and worked closely with Aboriginal communities. Like any remote country kid, he grew up fishing, hunting, and playing Australian Rules Football. He saw his first barrelling wave while fishing with his dad off the coast and was instantly drawn to it like a miner to flecks of gold. Through his footy club, he met some older guys who surfed, and he started to learn at the ripe old age of 13. The harsh, unforgiving coastline of the west became his proving ground. Travelling in the boot of a car, sometimes for hours, and riding a donated surfboard missing a fin, Edo embraced waves he thought were normal. They were far from it.

'My first surf as a kid, I spent eight days in five to ten foot swell getting slapped and thrashed constantly. On the last day, I caught one, pulled in under the lip and into the barrel, and then came out the other end. From then on, I was obsessed.'

He got his boat licence at 15 to venture out alone. Five foot waves grew to ten and 15 as he began to fine tune his new obsession.

'It felt natural; I had no information, no fear, I knew I had to do it, knew there was power to be harnessed. I didn't know it then, but I had ADHD, so I was comfortable with the speed; it felt slow. Normal street life was chaos, and I'd get wound up. The intense situations in the ocean slowed me down.'

He joined the Army to serve his country and left his surfboard at home. North Queensland, where we were posted, is sheltered by the Great Barrier Reef, which meant no more of his precious waves. His ability in the water led him to water polo, where he represented the Army and Australia as Team Captain.

'I was strong in the pool. We would tread water in training with 20 kilogram vests and a plastic chair above our heads. It was great conditioning for surfing as well.'

Edo and I served together on operations overseas, and the barbarity of human nature left a scar on both of us. Every soldier had a different journey after discharge, especially those who had been involved in war and seen its atrocities. Without direction and unbeknown to each other, Edo and I found alcohol and drugs to help us deal with our experiences. We had both danced with the devil of drug addiction. I spent three years in the ballroom of the beast, and Edo stayed much longer.

'I was fried after the Army; my head was in bits.' Edo explained.

'For eight years after we discharged Richo, I was addicted to methamphetamine. I injected twice every day, but I was a high-functioning addict. I thought of it as my medicine. I was working on the gas and oil rigs off the West Australian coast, technical and dangerous work, but huge money.'

'Wow, I didn't know. Could you sleep?' I asked Edo, remembering my battle with sleep during the drug years.

'Yeah, I could sleep, ate well, and in my weeks off work, I would figure out online where the biggest swell was, anywhere in the world, and fly there. Charge hard for a week, then come back to work. I surfed most of the biggest breaks on Earth. Life was intense.'

'How did you hide your drug use at work?'

'I didn't. I had my needles and 'medicine' in the fridge of the medical room. I didn't know meth was bad. Until my life started to unravel, that is. I lost my wife, access to my son, lost my job, had to sell my houses, everything mate. Life crashed down, and I checked into rehab.'

Edo's story was not uncommon. Many combat and regular soldiers who have seen the darker side of conflict while serving struggled to transition back into civilian life. He was diagnosed with PTSD. During his recovery, he spent multiple stints in rehab, countless sessions with psychologists and psychiatrists, and made amends with his family and friends impacted by his addiction.

'Life is all good now brother.' Edo says with a smile.

'Got my son back, I get to surf every day, and now I help other veterans struggling with addiction.'

Edo donated his time in critical care for veterans. He was on call, 24/7, for the police and ambulance officers in his community to come and help with any ex-military personnel. Over the previous three years, he was called out over 100 times.

'We saved a lot of guys. Lost a heap as well. It's a tough job mate.'

'What do you do when you get called out?' I asked.

'Well, here is a story from the last callout. The guy was sitting in his car, passed out and naked. Needles were everywhere, he was overdosed but alive. His car keys were on the windscreen wiper outside. Police arrived, he woke up and went mental. I was called and arrived on the scene before they arrested him. I calmed him down, got him into my van, gave him a beer, and took him fishing while he came down off the meth. Once he was lucid, I could drive him to the rehab centre and check him in. That was a good result. Other times I was called to scenes, and they had already killed themselves.'

After everything Edo had been through, wanting to give back to other veterans was a true testament to his character. His unique life experiences were a gift to those struggling with PTSD, or addictions, and to our first responders who had to deal with its consequences on the street level. He was an asset to the community.

'Alright, enough of this gloomy past.' Edo says as he stood and dropped his coffee cup into the sink. 'Let's work on the future, it's time to get wet. Get your wetsuits on; we are going surfing.'

We climbed into Edo's van, which was already stacked full of surfboards of various shapes and sizes, and then drove ten minutes north. We pulled into a parking lot overlooking the sheltered beach and point break of Cabarita. 'Welcome to Fat Caba, this will do us for today.'

'Why is it called Fat Caba?' I asked.

'It's the way the wave is formed; the sand and rock here create a thickness in the swell, really fat and rolling, instead of a steep faced dumper.'

The three of us, and a few other locals, stood on the hill and watched the swell. Edo rattled off a million facts about wind, storms, waves, and the seafloor dynamics. He was like an economist explaining inflation in detail to a 3 year old; I nodded along in ignorance. He then took us through a brief lesson on how to paddle, lay on a board and pop up into a standing position.

Edo had vast experience in the surfing world and he knew the theory behind everything by heart, but he had never taught the basics to anyone before. He was battling with the correct way to go about it. I have seen similar struggles many times over the years in the fitness industry. A phenomenal athlete with all the talent could not teach a beginner how to perform basic lifts safely. Alternatively, someone who might not be in the greatest shape could be one of the best coaches. It was a skill like any other. He watched me fumble around like a newborn giraffe for a few minutes before his impatience kicked in, and the gravity of the waiting swell drew him to the water.

'That will do, you will get it. Let's get in there.' Edo said. He then chuckled, 'You have to learn to dance on a wave Richo, or you're going to get smashed.'

We walked to the end of the beach towards the rocks, where a waiting entry point offered a small rip. A rip is a path water will take back into the ocean once it has been pushed onto the beach by the waves. Often it will show up darker and smooth on the surface. It can be dangerous to swimmers because it will drag them out into the deeper water. As kids, we were taught that if you ever got caught in a rip, swim parallel to the beach until it lets you go and then swim back in. Or let it take you all the way out, where it will dissipate, then calmly swim back to the beach. One thing to never do was to swim against a rip. It will tire you out rapidly, and this is when people drowned.

To a surfer though, a rip was a gift, a conveyor belt allowing easier entry when venturing 'out the back,' a term referring to getting behind the breaking waves. We had waxed up the boards near the van, and before we started paddling, Edo said,

'Wet the wax to get it hard and grippy, then dive under and wet yourself. You are a dolphin now Richo.'

In reality, I was a recently evolved gorilla with tight fascia and no balance, as far from a dolphin as possible, but I followed Edo's instructions and got wet. The frigid winter water, although an improvement from Tasmania, shocked my system. We followed Edo into the shallows, waited for a break in the white water, and launched onto the rip. I struggled to lie on my board and slipped off from side to side as I frantically paddled. My heart rate was jacked, and my shoulders burned with lactic acid. Edo glided effortlessly on his tiny board, calm paddles producing maximum thrust. He was peacefully waiting out the back when we arrived.

While I recovered and tried to sit on my board, which was no easy feat, I noticed Edo's body structure. His upper back was large and overdeveloped from a lifetime of paddling, and his neck and shoulders were out of proportion to the rest of his physique. His body had adapted to surfing, and he looked at home, sitting on his board and watching the horizon.

Elise and I were in the very early stages of adaptation. I was constantly falling off my board, much to everyone's amusement. Then, when I managed to stay upright for any brief period, Edo would spin my board, pointing me back at the beach and yell, 'You are on Richo; paddle hard.' With his cue I paddled full throttle while hearing the building wave behind me, sensing its power. I would love to say I felt the board start to glide, popped to my feet, angled along the smooth shoulder, and rode the wave like a Kelly Slater prodigy, but this was not a Hollywood script. Real life delivered an enormous crashing wave directly onto my head; I was spun and thrown, held under for a lifetime and lost all sense of which way was up. In this script, I was smashed.

Elise had a similar experience and was then more selective with her wave choices than I was. Even with Edo's cues, she would pull back before annihilation, whereas once I was committed, there was no turning back. The session was one of full frontal emersion and desensitisation. Getting smashed didn't injure me, and I didn't drown. It became normal and allowed my initial fears to dissolve. The highlight of our first session was when Elise and I caught the same wave and rode it on our bellies long enough to smile at each other and cheer. We both wiped out when we tried to stand, and I ended up back on the beach, exhausted but ecstatic. Lesson one was done.

I woke up the next morning stiff and sore like I had fallen from the world's tallest pine tree and struck every branch on the way down. Something was going on with my rear deltoid, my neck couldn't turn properly, and my back was a furnace. Nothing that some aspirin, a mobility ball and a big feed of bacon and eggs couldn't remedy. Edo arrived in the kitchen for some coffee and said we would go back to Cabarita.

'The swell is much nicer today. Yesterday was a rough intermediate wave, it will be simple beginner stuff this morning.'

'Intermediate, you say,' I said with a smile. 'Thanks for the easy introduction bro. I thought it was big yesterday.'

'I wanted to get you both comfortable out there first, and now we will work on the skills.'

We pulled into a packed car park at Cabarita. Edo waved to the locals he knew while he nudged the van into a free spot. He swung open the back door and unloaded the boards, pulling out a giant ten foot plank for me. I looked out at the break and counted at least 20 surfers dotted along the lineup. My first thought on seeing so many surfers was that I would kill someone with this enormous board. With zero ability to stand or turn, I was like an unguided North Korean missile; once launched, I could strike anywhere.

'What decides who gets the wave?' I asked.

'The rule is you always give way to your left on this right handed swell. The surfer closest to the white water has the right of way. If they catch the wave, you pull off the back.'

'Easier said than done when riding Noah's Ark over here.' I said as I picked up the board. 'I'll kill someone out here today mate.'

'Don't worry. I'll be hanging on your inside and will block anyone trying to get on your wave. You will be fine.'

It was starting to shape up like a movie plot. If we ended up in a fight with a guy named War Child by the end of the session, I wouldn't be surprised.

The swell and shape of the waves had changed entirely since the afternoon before. It was a more extended period, which meant the time between waves was greater. The longer the period, the cleaner/smoother the face of the waves usually were. I arrived out the back and had barely recovered when Edo told me to get ready. He stayed on my inside and blocked the other surfers as I kicked into gear and paddled hard. To everyone's surprise, mostly my own, I popped up and rode the wave on an angle for a few seconds. I was pumped. My first stand and the first time feeling the transition from moving under my own power, to the wave pushing me along. Surrendering control to nature was what I needed to get used to before I could harness it.

On the next dozen waves, my confidence and excitement from beginner's luck were thrashed to pieces by the ocean. I was overthinking everything, moving too fast, frantic in my paddling, and hard on myself for not being better. I nosed dived the board, went over the lip sideways, tumbled along the sea floor and swallowed enough salt water to never cramp again. We called it a morning and rode the white water back to the beach. I licked my wounds, swallowed some aspirin, and vowed to do better.

Back in the water for an afternoon session, Elise had stepped up her game, achieving her first stand and a short ride. The swell was blown out on the point, meaning the waves had been rendered choppy by a strong onshore wind, and we found ourselves a small, sheltered break close to the beach. I noticed very few surfers ventured out when surf conditions were not ideal, yet acceptable for beginners. Then, when the swell was decent, every person with a board, plank, or piece of flotsam was paddling out to catch a wave. I had vastly underestimated the popularity of surfing. It didn't matter if it was Saturday morning or mid-week during work hours; if the swell was pumping, employment took a back seat.

Frustration was building as I wiped out for the millionth time at the end of day five. My body was beaten, and the tiny gains we had made were barely keeping my morale buoyant. We had more sessions at Cabarita and a white water session in the mouth of the Pottsville River, where I had nosedived at speed and impacted the sand. The fibreglass fin on the back of my board sliced open the top of my head. I paddled back out, blood seeping from my skull, to then watch a five year old kid ripping down the face of a swell twice as big as him. Unlike any other training or sport where you could measure progress in a linear way, when dealing with the chaotic variation of the ocean, it was sometimes hard to see any progress at all. I had to maintain a military mission focus, or like many others who tried to learn to surf as an adult, I would throw in the towel and take up fishing or golf.

We enjoyed a much needed rest day to let our bodies recover and gain some contrast to the new stimulus we had bombarded them with. Contrast in our nervous system, no matter the skillset or task we try to achieve, is a similar process at all scales. When we fail ten times to thread fine cotton through the eye of a needle, we often need to take a break and rest for a moment. Then when we try again, we nail it the first time. This is gaining contrast and adaption through the visual cortex. We had been trying to learn a new and complicated skill for five full days. Over our rest day, I hoped to gain a higher level of adaption and then wake up with Mick Fanning's skills.

Edo arrived for coffee early the following day with an extra bounce in his step. He sat down, took a drink, and said,

'We are off to Byron Bay to a break called The Pass. It's time to change things up, get ready.'

The iconic Byron Bay is home to hippies, surfers, and Hollywood megastars. It boasts some of Australia's most expensive properties, yet the streets are often filled with bearded environmentalists living in rainbow coloured vans. Buskers crowded the village corners after dark, and Hare Krishna disciples belted drums and sang profound monotone mantras. Over two million tourists flock to its pristine beaches each year, filling restaurants, bars, and festivals during the holiday season.

We pulled up at an elevated car park close to the beach above 'The Pass', Byron's most popular break. Through the trees, I saw an impressive swell peeling off a rocky point. It developed into a long smooth wave that seemed to go on forever, and I watched one talented surfer ride from the point to the beach over several hundred metres. It was an aesthetic step up from Cabarita; the postcard beach and palm trees gave the scene a historic feel. I was like an English explorer witnessing a Pacific Islander ride a wave for the first time. The excitement was palpable. We waxed our boards rapidly and double-timed it to the beach.

As we paddled out, I noticed the swell was a decent size, three or four feet from the back of the wave. It should have been intimidating, but after the punishments I had taken over the previous few days, I felt calm and in control. It was starting to make sense. Where to enter the water, how to get into position, and then finding the breaking point where the sandy bottom forced the wave up and it began to peel. I could work out the distance I needed to paddle to be near that point at the right moment.

'This wave is mechanical Richo. Once you find your spot, it will always be the same every time.'

The first wave I paddled for grabbed my board, and I recognised the moment of transition. I slid to my feet, forced my toes into the right side, and turned. Angled along the wave, I stayed low to maintain a solid balance. I flew down the face and remained on my feet. The speed was phenomenal, like my first freefall in B.A.S.E Jumping, a feeling of total freedom. I let out a childish scream without embarrassment, oblivious to the surfers I passed; they knew what I was feeling. Time slowed down, the flow state, pure focus and living in the moment. Each second felt like a minute while every tiny detail was embedded into my consciousness. I rode the wave and the euphoria to the beach, where the white water cradled me into the shallows. I was overwhelmed and took a second to reflect. 'Holy shit, that was amazing.' I said with wild excitement to no one.

My emotions calmed, and I caught my breath as the adrenalin was absorbed into my system. The euphoria slowly subsided, and I looked towards the point. Another surfer was carving a line of his own, and a twinkle of envy emerged. I slid onto my board, turned towards the ocean, and paddled hard; I wanted that feeling back. I was now a surfer.

It took one wave to erase a week of frustration, pain, and mental beatings. One experience of 30 seconds to delete hours of misery. Was it so powerful because the skill was much harder to acquire than other skills, such as climbing or paddling? Or was it powerful because it required skills to align in harmony with Mother Nature? I think it was the latter. When B.A.S.E Jumping or climbing, I needed nature to play ball and keep the sun shining and the wind away. However, riding a wave required much more to come together, almost like winning the lottery.

Living systems, like human beings and nature, are unique because they are complex and adaptive, therefore linear thinking will never work. One plus one won't always equal two. For example, surely if I get good at popping up onto a board on the beach, I will be perfect when I enter the water. I can tell you from experience that this is not the case. The same is true when working with injured humans. A client might present with a sprained back, and we could take the reductionist approach and only strengthen the back muscles believing this was the cause. Or we take a systems approach and look at the whole mind and body; stress levels, fatigue, and sympathetic hyperarousal as the primary cause. Injury is rarely a muscle issue; it's often an entire system issue. Everything is non-linear when dealing with a human, which is why most fitness programs fail after a short time frame. Following a linear performance trajectory within a non-linear system is doomed.

I had to remind myself of these scientific facts after I had paddled back to the lineup, where I tried to catch my next three waves, and was subsequently smashed. I caught wave number four, rode it to the beach, and then ate sand ten more times. My ego had expected me to continue riding every wave I went for; however, a non-linear Mother Nature re-educated me for the remainder of the morning. Elise was also making improvements but was yet to gain a long ride. Close to the end of the session, Edo could see I was frustrated after a particularly vicious wipe-out. He paddled over. 'Get off your board, dive down to the sea floor and bring me back some sand.'

I followed his instruction and slid off my board. The cold water was refreshing and crystal clear, allowing me to see with bare eyes to the bottom. I held my breath and swam to the sand, pausing briefly as I noticed the wave like pattern on the sea floor, replicating the pattern on the surface above. I carried up a hand full of sand and showed my coach.

'Nice one, now how do you feel?'

'Better bro, thanks. I was getting a little wild.'

'All good mate, just relax a minute, then get back into it.' Edo said with a smile before paddling back to the point.

Edo might not have fully understood what he had asked me to do, but he knew it worked. By getting off my board, I was breaking symmetry. Then, while diving down and focusing on a new task, I changed my environment and became grounded. This tool is often used in psychology when dealing with patients suffering from anxiety disorder and PTSD. During an anxiety attack, patients could begin searching for three red objects and naming them; it had the same effect as collecting sand in the surf. By doing this, the feedback loop of the attack or emotion is broken, and the symptoms will begin to recede. By having a short swim to the bottom, I felt relieved of my perceived burden and frustration. I paddled back into the lineup and scored another ride.

Our second week progressed very slowly, much like the first. Elise was yet to bag a long ride, but I could see her improving every session. We spent a lot of time at The Pass, and on day ten, the ocean delivered a swell that had me pause on the sand and re-evaluate my skills.

Edo turned to me, 'There is some nice nine foot swell out there bro, biggest day yet. You ready?'

'Mate, I will try and get out the back with you, but I don't think I'll be riding one of those.'

'I'm going to wait on the beach boys.' Elise said, placing her board down on the sand. 'This swell isn't for me.'

'No problem Elise, just rest, and we will go have a look.'

It was high tide, and as soon as we entered the water, the undercurrent pulled me off my feet. The loss of control was intimidating, but I knew the worst that could happen was getting smashed, tumbled, and then riding some white water to safety. I followed Edo and gave myself over to the power of the currents. We waited for a break in the sets and then launched into the churning mess. Edo duck dived under the waves like he must have had feathers and a beak in a former life. With my enormous board, diving wasn't possible, and I had to roll over and let the swell skim across the top, losing hard-earned ground each time. I copped one more breaker straight on the head before I was out the back with a heart rate hammering like a blacksmith.

Edo paddled off to the point to slay a giant, and I hung out deep to recover and watch surfers getting eaten by the monsters. One guy almost lost his head when the peeling lip of the barrel he was trying to enter nearly decapitated him. The power and weight of the water went through him like a runaway train through mist. I was sure he was knocked unconscious, but moments later, he surfaced, shook it off and went back out. Another surfer snapped his board in half and swam back in. Meanwhile, guys and girls like Edo made it look effortless like they were born on the water.

After 30 minutes of immersion, I was calm and ready to try and bag one for myself. It was a big perfect swell, which meant that every surfer with the cojones living within a 50 kilometre radius had turned up and paddled out. I counted 70 in the lineup, which made me more anxious than the swell.

Edo blocked and called me in on a wave. It roared to life as I popped up and made the turn, but then almost collided with a short boarder. I wiped out and apologised for the near collision. I hadn't noticed him take off late on my inside. I needed a ten metre run up at the take-off point, whereas skilled surfers could make three quick strokes and catch the wave. I was out of my league. For the following hour, every time I turned to paddle, I was confronted with four or five other surfers waiting for the same wave. I was outclassed and out of my depth. I decided to hang back, watch the professionals, and bag any leftover scraps that snuck through.

Back on the beach after the session, I wasn't disappointed. I went from being initially fearful and intimidated, to getting out the back and trying to catch a few waves. It was the biggest day I had been out in so far and a big step in my progression. Back at the car park, I looked down at the peeling giants coming around the point. I wanted to ride them the way Edo does. I had some serious work to do.

Elise had a tumultuous second week and struggled to find a rhythm after changing boards a few times. On one session out at Cabarita, she managed to snap a board in half while I almost killed a lady on a longboard. On another day at The Pass, there were 150 surfers in the lineup; it was total carnage. Yet progress was made despite the wipeouts, snapped boards, frustration, and chaos. Ever so slowly, I gained more skill, control, and comfort in the water until Mother Nature tried to kill us.

Like a Venus flytrap, Elise and I were lured into the water at Cabarita on a day Edo had to work. It was one of our rare solo surfs, and what looked like a big, yet achievable day was anything but. We could only see two other surfers from the car park, the first unseen red flag. The swell looked big, yet through our inexperienced eyes, it looked no bigger than what we had surfed already. The car park wasn't busy, and plenty of people were sitting on the hill watching the swell, drinking coffee; the second red flag. We stood on the beach and felt a slight grumble of uncertainty. The third red flag; always trust your gut.

'It looks pretty hectic out there.' Elise voiced her concern.

'Yeah, it does, let's just get out the back, and then have a look. If it's too big, we can drift down and come in on the white water.' I replied with buoyed enthusiasm.

We waited for a lull in the sets, launched onto our boards and paddled hard. The first white wall that hit me checked my reality. The power was a step up from anything I had felt before, and I was shoved back towards the beach. I copped the next two dumpers on the head and knew that if my waning energy depleted, I would be in a terrible situation. I doubled down, chopping at the water with intensity, desperate to avoid the next breaker. I popped over the top of a wave split seconds before it broke; my freefall on the other side jolted my sternum and chin into the fibreglass. I was semi-concussed, exhausted, with borderline cardiac arrest, but I was out the back. I turned, hoping to watch Elise pop over the next wave, but she was nowhere to be seen.

I immediately went into a panic. I scanned the boiling white water, then the beach, but nothing. I scanned further down the shoreline. Minutes passed as I drifted with the currents searching. Then I noticed a small figure waving frantically from the shore. Elise had crawled up on a jagged rock and was signalling me. I waved back with relief that she was okay. She had been pushed a long way down and driven into the rocks, but she was alive. I knew I had to get in quickly and check on her, but the swell made getting into the beach desperate.

The safest thing to do was surf in. 'Stuff it; I'm having a go.' I said aloud, trying to buoy my confidence. I moved into position and paddled for the next wave. It rose behind me like a waking giant, and the second before it arrived, I realised I had made a huge mistake. The board was picked up, and the velocity caught me off guard. I popped up, but only got to my knees, stuck in an awkward praying position as I skimmed down the face. I had a brief second where I thought, 'Holy hell, this is a monster wave,' before the demon gobbled me up. The water pressure held me down on the sand for an aeon before releasing me into the land of the living. The pummelling wasn't as bad as I thought it would be, just a standard smashing. I was motivated by this new realisation. Wiping out on big swell did not equal death, and after checking to make sure Elise was still on the rocks, I paddled back out to try a few more.

I should have retired after the first wave, but I was drawn in like a moth to the flame. I caught two more waves before I was caught off guard, lifted up, and went over the falls of a giant. 'Over the falls' in surfing is when you have missed the take-off and go over with the lip of the wave at the exact breaking point. This entails the biggest free fall, with the entire weight of the wave crashing down upon you. I came down hard, sideways on my board, and speared my elbow through the fibreglass slashing my skin. I was held down for probably 15 seconds, which in wipe out time equals about five minutes, before bursting through the surface, desperate for air. I was then thrashed onto the beach by a vengeful force who was tired of my antics. It was like the ocean had decided I didn't belong and cast me out.

Elise walked towards me and burst into tears.

'I'm alright, don't worry,' I said. It was then I realised she wasn't crying for me.

'Are you ok?' I asked. She wasn't.

'I was smashed onto the rocks and nearly drowned, I was so scared,' she replied through tears. 'You are bleeding,' she said, looking at my arm.

'Yeah, I had a little dance with a devil out there. Got hammered.' I gave her a big hug, and we walked back to the car together. People were still watching the swell, enjoying their coffees; no surfers were heading out. Lesson learned.

Elise had endured near drowning, which for most people would have been quickly followed by the surfboard being up for sale. That was not her style; she persevered and came out at The Pass after a weekend of rest. The big swell had dissipated, but a panic attack gripped her when she hit the first wall of white water. After retreating to the shore, she stood on the sand looking out at the break, heart racing and told herself.

'If you don't go back out now, you will never go out again.'

She forced herself into the water, paddled out to the back and sat there until her fears were conquered. She was in the game again, and I was proud of her for overcoming her demons.

The crowds along the coast at the most famous surf breaks, which happened to be all the beginner ones we needed, grew exponentially in the third week of our surf camp. I was becoming increasingly frustrated in the surf with so many other people, and I took a walk one afternoon to mull over why it was getting to me so much. I realised that surfing's popularity, and subsequent crowds, created a roadblock for me to enjoy the natural environment in the way I was used to. When I went out hiking, climbing, paddling, rowing, or cycling, there was rarely anyone inhibiting me from enjoying the outdoors, especially where we lived in remote southern Tasmania.

With surfing, because of its finite options for ridable waves, and an acute spot to take off on those waves, many more people accumulated. This increased the need for rules, etiquette, and patience, ultimately leading to frustration. Apart from a few traffic jams while summiting big mountains in Nepal, I had never had to overcome this obstacle in the outdoors before. I also realised most of the environments I entered were remote and full of challenging conditions, keeping the average weekend warrior and outdoorsman away. Whereas to access some of the most beautiful surf breaks in the world, all you had to do was drive to them with a coffee in hand, and then paddle out. I doubted surfing would lose its appeal anytime soon, and I would need to adjust my expectations and adapt.

Surfing a wave felt amazing and euphoric. It was a moment of calm in a tense world full of hypervigilance and stress. During our final week, however, the barriers to getting to that moment were grating on me. I could instantly see why surfers ventured to remote islands in Indonesia, to find a place to themselves where these barriers didn't exist. Yet to reach those waves and ride them the way they deserved, I needed to get back to work.

On a rare day at Cabarita, around mid-morning, we were the last few people still out. It was a lumpy day, but with no one crowding the take-off it was perfect. While sitting on my board, I realised I had been out there for almost three hours. How was I able to stay motivated throughout the session when I was only catching a handful of waves? It was that cheeky neurotransmitter dopamine at work again, just like when metal detecting.

While hanging out the back and watching the horizon for the next wave, my dopamine levels would spike when I thought one was approaching. If I missed the wave it didn't matter to my nervous system, it was bathed in sweet dopamine anyway, and it gave me the extra motivation to wait even longer for the next one.

The following morning, Edo took us to meet his board shaper and pick up his new custom made board. We pulled into a bush block off the highway near Crabs Creek south of Pottsville, and at the end of a long driveway was a derelict house. Old surfboards were piled up in every corner of the yard, and stacks of building materials, bikes, some old cars, engines, and rubbish were strewn about.

'Ra, where you at?' Edo called out at the front door.

No reply was heard, so we walked around to the back, where a few old sheds covered with more surfboards and debris were located.

'Raaaaaa... you in there bro?'

A big man wearing a gas mask appeared in the doorway of one of the shanties. He was overweight, pouring sweat, had bloodshot eyes, and looked like a backyard illegal drugs chemist. He removed his mask to reveal a beaming smile.

'Edo, how are you bra?'

This was Ra. A local legend to the surfing community, he had been shaping boards for over 30 years and was considered a master of the craft. Edo introduced us, and Ra motioned for us to enter his workshop. Tiny particles of foam covered the floor and were knee deep in places. Piles of materials, rolls of fibreglass, and barrels of toxic resin were stacked and strewn about. Fumes began to burn my eyes and scorch my lungs the deeper we went inside. I knew artists were supposed to be messy creatures, but Ra had taken it to another level.

In an adjoining shed, amongst the garbage, rubbish, and uninspiring mess, held up above the chaos on a small table was one of the most incredible surfboards I had ever laid eyes on. It was not Edo's board, but he seemed just as excited as I was to see it. A deep blue colour, clean and shining under the light above, nine feet long and shaped like a medieval sword, this foam and fibreglass creation was a thing of beauty.

Edo broke the silence, 'There you go Richo, that's what you need to ride big waves. That's called a GUN.'

Images of me riding this blue weapon down the face of a giant swell flashed before my eyes, and my heart rate quickened with excitement.

'Wow, that is amazing Ra.' I told him while admiring his work.

'Thanks mate, it came out nice that one.' he replied. 'Yours is out here Edo.'

We followed Ra to another small workshop, where he handed Edo his new board. This one was short, gold coloured, and looked like a rocket. Custom built to what he desired; Edo was like a kid at Christmas going over every detail. Over the following hour, Ra taught us the basics of building surfboards and answered hundreds of my questions. He was lovely and more than happy to share his knowledge and stories. We talked over the intricacies and frustrations of surfing, and he told us to persevere with it. 'Once you get it, you will never give it up.'

He told us the billionaire magnate James Packer had visited the coast back in the day. James' mates were out surfing, and he wanted to try it himself. There were no surfboard shops back then, so he tracked down a local shaper and a friend of Ra's to make him a board. In typical billionaire style, James asked for a board to be ready for him by the following morning. Considering it was late afternoon, the shaper replied no way, that it was impossible. James pulled out his money and laid out note after note until the impossible became possible.

By morning the shaper was tired, but the board was ready. James went to the beach with his mates, entered the water and received what all newbies to the ocean received, a massive flogging. He walked back onto the beach, threw the board on the sand, and never surfed again. Ra asked us if we would continue with it. I replied yes immediately. As tough as the sport was to learn, I wasn't going to quit.

For our final surf session, we journeyed back to Byron Bay to see what The Pass had in store. We loaded up with coffee and burgers at 6 a.m. and arrived at the car park shortly after. The swell conditions were not ideal, but we knew this would keep the hoards away. We stared out from the beach; the swell was two to three feet and slightly chopped up by an onshore wind. Few surfers were out; the usually perfect conditions had spoiled the locals. We entered the water, and I had the cleanest line while getting out the back. I felt comfortable and in control.

With no crowds hogging the point, we could attempt almost every wave. I could wipe out, learn from my mistakes, and try again on the next set to come along. Previously, we would get six waves in a session when it was busy. This time within the first hour I had tried to paddle on ten and ridden three all the way. I had downsized my board and was learning all over again how to surf, and the speed increase had caught me by surprise. Elise caught her first long ride and was ecstatic. She went on to catch plenty more that morning, and had found her flow. Edo was doing his usual thing, and I rode right into the beach on my last wave of the session. I was exhausted and euphoric. It was the perfect last surf of the camp.

Edo was pumped for us back on the sand. We had arrived total beginners and were leaving semi-competent beginners who could stand and hold a straight line. It didn't sound like a huge progression, but trust me, it took a hell of a lot of effort. It was the most challenging skill I had ever tried to learn by far, and after B.A.S.E Jumping, the most addictive. Over a cold beer that night, before our early flight home with surfboards and wetsuits, Edo asked me, 'So where do you want to go with your surfing bro?'

Images of Ra's blue board and videos of famous big wave breaks flashed in my mind. I took a swig of my beer, looked at Edo, and replied,

'I want to do what you do mate. I want to ride giants.'

Edo's face broke into a knowing smile, we clinked bottles, and before drinking he said,

'Well alright then, we better get to work.'

CHAPTER 8
Three Peaks

At the end of 2019, we were licking our wounds at Mt Ama Dablam base camp after our failed summit bid. If someone had told me then that I wouldn't be back in the mountains for almost three years, I would have laughed it off as an impossibility. Three years without climbing would have felt like an eternity. Then without warning the COVID-19 pandemic swept the world and changed everything overnight.

After two years of enforced domestic exploration, international airports were finally allowed to reopen. Elise and I hopped online to book flights immediately with one destination on our minds: the Himalayas. We had plenty of time to plan our comeback climb, yet we knew our abilities would have depleted over the previous three years. We needed an objective that would wet our mountaineering appetite and challenge us without undue risk. It also needed to be a multi-peak objective. After a long period of cooling our heels, one mountain would not cut it.

Mera Peak came to mind first. At 6476 metres in altitude, it is considered a trekking peak in Nepal but would be a cold beast judging by the blogs I was reading. It was non-technical in its approach and would be a great first climb to ease back into it. Afterwards, we planned to trek across a remote valley and over the Amphu Labtsa pass to drop in on Island Peak at 6160 metres. Imja Tse, as it was known to the locals, required slightly more technical climbing and was a popular mountain boasting incredible views of the surrounding 8000 metre peaks. If all went well, we would finish the trip with Lobuche East at 6119 metres, which I had climbed as acclimatisation for Ama Dablam, but Elise had missed out due to sickness. I emailed Mingma Chirri Sherpa in Nepal, booked him and his Sherpa team to act as our guides, and the Three Peaks Expedition was ready to execute.

Before the pandemic, travelling internationally had become like riding public transport for me, with little fanfare. Post-COVID, I felt the excitement again when we were dropped off at the airport for our flight. I was like a little kid at Christmas, and I almost did something I had never done before: pay five dollars for a trolley to shuttle our bags into the terminal. Of course, I didn't; airport trolleys are daylight robbery. Instead, Elise and I shouldered two duffel bags each to get the job done.

I had butterflies checking in and fumbled around looking for paperwork like a total newbie. Mask mandates were still in force, and looking around, I noticed all types. Cloth ones covered in colourful artwork, neoprene types with fancy ear loops, builders dust masks, plastic face shields, and the N95 professionals, supposed to stop even the most ambitious COVID microbe from getting through.

We had heard news reports of chaos at Sydney Airport and long wait times, so we arrived 3.5 hours before our flight. However, the reports were false; it was the calmest I had ever seen in the usually bustling terminals, with a seamless flow of people due to new technology upgrades designed to limit face to face contact with staff. We were through customs and immigration in record time.

While walking through the terminal, Elise and I always opted for the stairs, especially when they were bordered on both sides by packed escalators. Whenever I walk upstairs before a mountaineering expedition, I visualise myself taking the final steps onto the summit. I focused on my exact foot placement, weighting each leg evenly as I progressed slowly upwards step by step. Passers-by could consider me mentally diminished while slowly slogging up the stairs with my eyes partially shut in a state of Zen. Little did they know I was on the cutting edge of optimal human performance. Visualisation is a tried and tested method to increase the likelihood of success.

As Einstein's saying goes, 'Thought creates biology.' Which is an easy way of remembering some complicated human chemistry. Let's experiment with it. First, imagine you have sliced a piece of lemon; then, imagine placing the slice in your mouth, biting it, and rolling the juice around on your tongue. Most likely, you have begun to salivate while reading these words. This is thought giving rise to matter; the act of thinking about something causes a cascade of reactions in the human system. The neurotransmitters released while visualising an action are the same that are released on game day. The challenge is to remain calm, composed, and focused while using these visualisation techniques to prompt positive adaptions. Like a tennis star practising their serve or F1 drivers practising corners before a race. If there were no benefits in doing these drills, they wouldn't bother. So be aware that every thought you have causes a chemical reaction. So, just like Peter Pan, it's best to think happy thoughts.

Due to limited flight options, we were routed through Singapore on the way to Kathmandu. We boarded, took our seats, and settled in. When the Singapore Airlines video started to play in that soft polite foreign language I couldn't understand, I began to get emotional. It had been so long since I heard the unintelligible Asian safety briefing that it choked me up. It was an auditory cue for freedom, and when the jet engines kicked in and the wheels lifted off, I was euphoric.

In Singapore, we met up with three amigos joining us on the expedition. Yok, our friend from Phuket who had climbed with us on two other Himalayan projects, joined us first. He had solid climbing ability, knew what he was getting into, and had learned valuable lessons on Ama Dablam, where he almost lost some fingertips to frostbite. Kelly, who arrived next, was from the Northern Beaches of Sydney and has been a friend of Elise's since childhood. She works as an intensive care nurse and has spent the last two years doing 12 hour shifts caring for other humans during one of the most intense periods of our medical system's history. Although she had zero climbing experience, her job required a calm mind, limitless empathy, and a love of life. She sported a wicked sense of humour and a high pitched laugh I could hear across the terminal.

'My last night shift was a shit show,' she explained as we waited to board our connecting flight.

'I have been nocturnal all week with patients that continue to want to ascend towards the light. I'm excited for this relaxing holiday.'

Harriet is a partner in crime of Kelly's and our third teammate. She is a CrossFit athlete and coach from Queensland who, like Kelly, was a first time climber. Her strength is her supreme fitness and calmness under duress. With a cool head and solid physical ability, the skills of the mountains could be taught.

We touched down in Kathmandu, shuffled off the plane and onto a waiting bus. The aircraft had taxied within 50 metres of the terminal entrance, but this short distance was apparently too much of a safety hazard to walk. Once full, the bus pulled away from the terminal and took a ten minute circuitous route to bring us back, passed our plane, to stop in front of the doors I had been staring at the whole time. We were back in the developing world, where mystifying bureaucracy was common.

Even though the transport system had remained the same outside the terminal, inside modern technology had arrived. We were through customs and immigration in under an hour, a feat I thought impossible for Nepal. Our last visit entailed 2.5 hours of cues, paperwork, cash, and a cheeky bribe; this was a breath of fresh air. Leaving the terminal, the fresh air remained inside, and we were hit with the humid, dusty scent of noisy streets, and the great unwashed. It was good to be back.

Over the years, we learned it was best to spend as little time in Kathmandu as possible to avoid getting sick before we flew up into the mountains. We had one day to buy last minute equipment, collect snacks, and sort out team paperwork. We also had a stray

Canadian climber named Stéphane join our team, hoping to climb Ama Dablam. He had asked Mingma and me if he could join us to acclimatise on Mera Peak before going his own way. We were happy to have him tag along. He was 61 years old, worked as a commercial pilot for Air Canada, and brought a wealth of experience to the team.

We devoured some boiled eggs at dawn and returned to the airport for our short flight to Lukla. Kathmandu was peaceful in the mornings before the traffic noise dominated; it had a frontier sense of mystery about it. The city has been here since 167 BC and will still be a gateway to adventure for many years to come.

The scent of burnt rubbish and sewage poured in through the car window, and heavy dust tempered the brightness of the rising sun. On the roadside, I noticed a guy squatting low with a rolled cigarette hanging from his mouth. He wore cheap thongs, rough clothing, and was surrounded by mountains of bagged rubbish. One by one, he opened them, sifted through them, and removed any plastic he could recycle. This was the way he earned his living.

Further on, we passed a small river coloured black with putrid pollution, it was flowing fast and cascaded over a concrete causeway. The bubbling froth had built up at the base of the falls, not the kind you imagine at the bottom of a tropical waterfall, but more like something following a chemical spill. The detergents mixed with the rubbish, filth, and rancid water showcased humanity at its worst. Was I looking at a symptom of a developing nation, or was this a glimpse into the future for all of us?

This chain of thought persisted while we waited in another bus on the tarmac for our small plane to be fuelled and made ready to depart. I noticed a tiny bird sitting alone in a skeletal tree, with only the timber remaining, void of anything green. The busy airport bordered on one side with thick diesel fumes filling the air, and on the other side, an old river was being bulldozed into more tarmac. The bird was surrounded by civilisation and progress. All that remained of his natural home was squeezed into a patch of dying grass the size of a basketball court. I was staring at a snapshot of our global climate crisis and short sightedness, although in this moment I was lost for ideas on how to halt the spread. The pessimist in me believed we had come too far and will follow our chosen path to its species ending conclusion. The optimist in me hoped we could turn it around before it was too late.

I turned to Harriet sitting beside me; her face had gone pasty white. She had a visceral fear of planes after a near crash in China a few years before. As her plane was going down, everyone was screaming and in brace positions, then at the last minute, it pulled out of the dive and landed safely. From that moment, she had been consumed with a fear of flight. Not an ideal phobia to have when we were about to land at the world's most dangerous airport, wedged onto the side of a mountain.

We boarded the plane and were airborne in minutes. I watched the chaos of Kathmandu fall away, and the upper valleys come into view. The past few years have seen vast agricultural development. Almost every mountainside in the lower valleys had been ploughed and tiered to support crops. Contour lines filled the slopes as we flew higher into the mountains and the aerial view of the farms had a beauty to it. It was an earthly artwork from our altitude, sustaining life and securing a future for thousands living off the land.

The turbulence kicked in as our tiny craft weaved through the mountains. The underpowered aircraft dropped, bucked, and shuddered through air pockets and updrafts. Harriet's tears flowed as she gripped my arm. With headphones on, she tried to separate herself from the ordeal, but the music seemed to have little effect. Her peaking anxiety was easy to read. She was folding her boarding pass into smaller and smaller squares, trying to shrink it enough for it to disappear. Or maybe she hoped she could disappear from the flight altogether. The plane descended rapidly towards the short runway, and the experienced pilot easily landed it, immediately braking and turning sharply into the ramshackle terminal building. Much to Harriet's relief, the engines powered down, and the doors opened.

We collected our bags and met our team of guides and porters at a restaurant opposite the runway. Elise, Kelly, and Mingma were on another plane that landed shortly after ours. The look on Elise's face when she entered the restaurant told me it was not a pleasant experience.

'That was the worst flight I have ever been on,' she said with red eyes. 'We were screaming and thought it was going down,' she added.

Elise was not one for drama; if she said it was bad, it was most likely terrible. Mingma came in next, 'Worst flight I ever had, I take jeep next time.'

If Mingma was willing to endure a 15 hour jeep ride along the worst dirt road in Nepal instead of a 30 minute flight, it must have been a shocker. All I could think was, lucky Harriet was not on their plane.

We shouldered our packs with little fuss, the porters bent into their loads, and we all set off down the hill from Lukla. The standard Everest Base Camp trail departed north, but Mera Peak was in a different valley, one I had never trekked through before. Its remoteness away from the tourist trail meant we enjoyed the scenery all to ourselves. The first day's hike reminded me of my first visit to Nepal in the early 2000s; it was still an obscure destination back then and not as easy to access. This southern trail still seemed to be at the beginning of its development, and 4.5 hours after leaving Lukla we arrived at Paiya, to a recently built tea house and our bed for the night.

I feasted on deep fried vegetable momos, sherpa stew and dhal bhat while Kelly entertained us with a hilarious story about her sleepwalking.

'It's true I sleepwalk all the time,' she said. 'It is always the same dream as well. I'm at home having a party and entertaining people. Then in my dream, I go off to bed and fall asleep. I wake up, remember I have guests, quickly make my bed, and then rush down the hallway to announce to everyone, don't worry, I'm here. Then I wake up.'

We were all in stitches, and then she added.

'That's nothing. I did it once when I had a one night stand and when I made the bed, he was still in it!'

Kelly was a great addition to the team. Her good banter and humour would keep team morale high, especially when the climbing gets tough or things go wrong. I was shattered after a big day and chose to skip the card game the team were settling in for. I snuggled into my down sleeping bag, high up in the crisp mountain air and slept for nine hours straight.

On day two, our six feet five inch tall Canadian teammate Stèphane led the way out of Paiya. Stéphane had been to Nepal 15 times during his climbing career but was humble about his achievements. It took many conversations over the following week to draw out some of his history, including his many 7000 metre ascents, multiple ski descents off well known peaks and countless failures along the way. His stride was enormous, and he was always well ahead of us throughout the day. He moved like a fit 45 year old, not someone in their 60s who had punished their body in the mountains. Over the years, I have learned that rehabilitation of joints and muscles after trips and preparing well before expeditions would be a key to longevity.

I walked with Harriet for the morning and quickly realised that she had a love for dogs that I hadn't witnessed before. Nepal was littered with canines in various forms of breed, health, and ownership. Harriet seemed drawn to the most decrepit, malnourished, abandoned mutts that clung to the trail.

'Ohhhh puppy hello!' was her vocal reaction upon seeing a dog. She would then pat them, play with them, and feed them whatever she had on hand. I warned her about rabies in Nepal, but to no avail; she would cradle the most hideous frothing example of a dog and then invite it along on our journey.

During one of our conversations, Harriet started listing off all the injuries she had suffered from. The elite CrossFit competition world and intense training regime had battered her body, especially her joints and feet. Before coming on the expedition, she had two cortisone injections into her feet to help with the pain.

'I'm glad I got these big boots,' she began to tell me. 'Because I have no tendon strength left, and if I roll my ankles, I'll go down like a sack of shit. I often black out from the acute pain.'

'Are you serious? You pass out?' I asked, a little alarmed, picturing this happening on an icy slope.

'Yeah, but don't worry, Kelly has been with me when it happens, so she knows what to do.'

I was a little concerned, but she was adamant she would be fine and could handle the day to day misery. I made a mental note to keep a closer eye on her once we got higher and onto the ice.

After seven hours and twenty minutes of knee-trembling muscle activation, full of ascents and descents, we arrived in Panggom. A large tea house made of shaped and stacked natural stone finished with a whitewash of clay would be our home for the night. The amount of manpower it took to erect one of these buildings on an inaccessible slope in the mountains was baffling. Back home in Australia, it would probably entail a two million dollar budget for labour alone.

Our bodies were slowly adapting to the new environment. The trembling I was experiencing in my legs on the acute descents was the dormant muscle tissue being activated again. There was only so much training you could do to prepare yourself for mountaineering, and nothing would ever compare to the real deal.

Harriet and Kelly were the life of the tea house at dinner. As I sat down, Harriet turned and asked a question.

'Kell, I haven't seen you do a drive-by shooting in a while; where have you been?'

'What do you mean a drive-by?' I asked, shocked. Southwest Sydney had made the news recently for gang crime and shootings, but these two fitness girls did not match the profiles.

Kelly laughed and explained. 'So, whenever I see Harriet at a café on a date or with friends, I roll up slowly, wind down my window, make a gun with my fingers and yell, drive-by motherfuckers and make shooting noises.'

'It always gets shocked looks from everyone.' Harriet added while laughing.

'I bet it does, you nutter. You will get locked up one day Kelly.' I told her.

'Yeah, probably.' She replied with a grin.

Pangomm Monastery was our first stop after breakfast the following day. I happily accepted all blessings and prayers when entering the mountains, anything to keep the mountain gods happy and luck on our side. The iconic structure was detailed with elaborate colours and sculptures, its entire perimeter surrounded with prayer wheels. After a small donation inside to pay respects, I circled the building three times, spinning the wheels and saying the most common prayer in Nepal.

'Om mani padme hum,' is a six syllable Sanskrit mantra on repeat in every temple and place of worship throughout the nation. It is carved into countless boulders in the Himalayas and becomes a soundtrack to expedition life.

The young monks, all teenage boys dressed in bright orange robes and sporting shaved heads, congregated around us and took a liking to Harriet's most recent dog, who had followed us from the previous day. They fed the scruffy beast biscuits, and in a blink of its mucus-filled eye, it swapped Harriet for the kids, choosing to stay at the monastery as we pushed on.

A porter carrying eight pieces of timber on his back, each four metres long and as thick as my thigh, walked slowly uphill along the trail. I asked Mingma, 'How heavy is that load?'

'One hundred kilogram,' he replied.

'Wow, and how much will that job earn him?'

'If he is going to Namche, that's two days walk up and one day home. He will be paid one dollar per kilogram for the job.'

'Ok, so $50 a day, that's not terrible, but bloody hard work.'

'Yes, very hard, but he must pay for his food and accommodation for the three days it will take him.'

I crunched some numbers and realised his monumental effort would earn $20 USD daily when factoring in the return journey. $60 USD to feed and care for his family through completing tasks that took a huge toll on the body. I asked more questions, and Mingma gave me the lay of the land for porters.

'Up in the Khumbu region, for all Everest expeditions, the porter price is set, and it is not good. The local Government controls the price. When boys' porter for me, I always pay them extra. That's why they like working on our expeditions.'

It sounded like unions were non-existent in the Himalayas. I knew Mingma paid his team well; that's one of the reasons we kept coming back to climb with him.

Our first glimpses of Mera Peak appeared at the top of a steep ascent shortly after lunch. The intimidating southern face was sheer rock and hanging ice, an impossible climb from this angle and terrifying in its beauty. Our goal was its snowy central summit, but we would be approaching from the northwestern side where a gradually sloping face, fixed with safety lines, hopefully, awaited us.

Travelling to remote corners of our world can enlighten us with a perspective that is often impossible to gain anywhere else. On our third night, we shuffled into a tiny tea house perched atop a ridgeline with drop-offs on three sides. It had the most incredible view from the toilet, and in the corner of the dining area, we noticed a one month old baby, sleeping. The infant's mother was in the kitchen preparing our evening meals. I watched as she raced outside, chopped wood, started the fire for us, and then returned to the kitchen to fetch boiling water. The baby slept through a cacophony of noises, oblivious to it all.

Kelly couldn't help herself and started to nurture the tiny future Sherpa. Whenever he stirred and started to cry, his mum appeared with a bamboo basket and straps. The baby was placed inside, and the homemade portable crib was pulled onto her back before she returned to the kitchen without missing a beat. I watched her bend over dozens of times, almost flinging the baby to the floor, but it slept on as if through a lullaby.

Australia is a progressive nation with countless benefits to help our citizens live happy and healthy lives. One of the policies our government and companies support is six months of paid maternity leave for all mothers. Six months to settle into life with a baby without worrying about work or income. Some companies offered this to the father as well. Yet, here in Nepal there was a woman who couldn't imagine such luxuries; days after delivering a baby, she was back working in the kitchen by night and most likely in the fields during the day. Elise and the girls were blown away.

I've had similar reality checks while travelling through Africa in my youth. I often thought I worked hard until I watched a man shovel river sand through wire mesh to sift out the rocks before shovelling it further into a truck. Sunrise to sunset he endured his task for $2 per day in wages. I have never worked that hard in my life. I think as a man born into a civilised Western democracy, sometimes I forget how good we have it, and travelling allowed me to re-discover this truth.

Our small team traversed the lower valleys gaining and losing altitude with each ridgeline. We threaded our way through misty medieval forests covered in a thick veneer of green moss, where ancient trees stood beside our trail in full bloom of pink and red flowers. They reminded me of trees I would see at my grandma's house, old, strong, and the keepers of secrets. The dense lowland had a primitive Jurassic feel, and as we slowly ascended, the forests and scrub gave way to scree slopes and sparse land covered in short tufts of hardy grass.

An enormous waterfall peeled off the mountains parallel to the trail. It rolled over an edge 1000 metres above us, fell through tiers of boulders, and down sheer rock cliffs, and dissected our path before being guided by gravity along the valley. The water was freshly melted snow, crystal clear, and freezing. I soaked my shirt in one of the many rock pools before we pushed on through the afternoon sun.

We left the tree line behind us by day five, hour by hour, metre by metre, gaining altitude, and with every step we breathed ever thinning air. Kothe was our home for the evening, the most built up village we had seen since leaving Lukla. Stacked stone structures blended in with modern timber designs and corrugated tin roofs. Satellite dishes and solar panels were mounted on most buildings, where bright signs offered hot showers and Wi-Fi to weary trekkers. It seemed the modern world had finally penetrated even the most inaccessible valleys.

When we arrived, the tea house had two other small teams resting in the common room. The conversation generally orbited around a few similar themes when meeting other parties. Where are you from? What are you climbing? If the discussion lasted longer than the cursory length, we sometimes delved into more meaningful topics. Why go through this misery? What motivates you?

Motivation was an interesting topic and a constantly evolving one. In my early years of adventure-seeking, I was driven by records, ego, anger, and anxiety. I was trying to prove something to the world. These were not the best drivers for long term health and happiness, but as a goal orientated, fit as a fiddle young man, it was more than enough fuel to get the job done. My motivation changed as I grew older and worked on my psychophysical health through NeuroPhysics Therapy training, reading, and writing. I'm now calm, composed, and in control during situations where I used to be the opposite. I learned patience and gratefulness along the way, and my current motivation is to make the most out of the finite time I have left. I have developed a hunger to explore for no other reason than to see what is over the horizon.

A late afternoon rain settled in, forcing us all indoors around the yak dung fire for warmth. Kelly was nauseous and couldn't eat; she sat with us in the tea house but soon retreated to the comfort of a movie on her iPhone. Two small boys, children of the tea house owner, were playing inside with a water bottle tied to a string. They were chasing each other around and having a hell of a time with the most basic toy. Upon seeing Kelly and her phone, they ditched the plastic poodle and climbed into her lap, planting their faces inches from the bright light and moving images.

The device's power over their behaviour and attention was clear. It's a power these incredible inventions have over all of us. I watched the kids and felt guilty for robbing them of a natural youth, while at the same time, I logged into Wi-Fi to send pictures and videos to my sponsors. The saying that modern technology is a double-edged weapon rang true for me that evening.

Our team was nestled inside small rooms and shared a communal squat toilet. We returned to our frosty sleeping bags from the warmth of the tea house, and upon entering the toilet, Elise yelled out, 'What the hell guys, who did this?'

On inspection of our squatter, I concluded we must have had a silent assassin visit our abode while we were having dinner. The inconsiderate guest had exploded onto the back wall and deposited a generous portion onto the floor, missing the toilet by half a foot. The physics of it baffled me more than the rudeness of not trying to clean it up. For anyone wishing to visit the Himalayas, India, Africa, or other developing nations, amongst the unique natural beauty, scenes like this, which the girls cleaned up before bed, were guaranteed.

We finally poked our heads above 5000 metres of altitude at the end of our first week as we walked into the village of Thungnuk. This height was considered the trekker's death zone in climbing circles, borrowing a term from mountaineering. The 'death zone' was originally allocated to a point above 8000 metres on Mt Everest, where the human body slowly consumes itself and cannot survive. For the average trekker, 5000 metres often became their most challenging point, and it was a height most climbers started to feel some effects of altitude. The temperature dropped with the gain in height, and during a necessary rest day, we hiked up a nearby knoll to 5100 metres, where a brief but windy whiteout greeted us and followed us down.

Inside the tea house that evening, whilst warming ourselves with bottomless pots of milk tea, a French team arrived on their way down after a failed summit bid. One of them had severely frostbitten fingers, a common occurrence in mountaineering, but a result I couldn't fathom on a peak like Mera where it was so easy to turn back and get down quickly. I couldn't grasp how someone could knowingly sacrifice their fingers for a summit. It was a harsh reality the girls needed to understand; even humble trekking peaks in Nepal could have severe consequences if you made the wrong decision.

I love early mornings in the upper mountains. The temperature was below freezing as I crawled out of my sleeping bag and went outside while the others still slept. I found a quiet perch all to myself. The dawn arrived, and the sun's rays penetrated the icy wonderland as I watched the first drops of snowmelt fall from the roof of the tea house. The skies were clear, and two small birds flew together seamlessly through the crisp mountain air. My eyes were drawn to a flash of white through a bedroom window above me. I was confronted with Harriet's bare arse as she pulled her pants down and flashed me good morning. I chuckled to myself and turned away as the girls cracked up laughing. Their banter was in line with the altitude, at an all-time high.

I knew I was back in the mountains on day eight when the hardy grass disappeared, and all that remained was rock, scree, ice, and snow. Khare was the next village and was the staging area for most ascents of Mera Peak. The central summit was off to the east, dwarfing us with its intimidating western face. Enormous seracs hung at unusual angles threatening to tear down the mountain at any moment. Though unusual, the scene was not unnatural; it was nature at its rawest and most powerful, with often only luck deciding who lived or died. We were placing our humble bodies of brittle bone and meat up against Mother Nature's ferocious, awe-inspiring weight. We would often come out second best in that battle, and only our preparation, abilities, and decision making could help level the playing field.

I met a father and son duo in the tea house waiting for helicopter evacuation. The teenage boy from the United Kingdom had a decent dose of altitude sickness, and his dad had torn his calf muscle on the summit push. Two older guys, also from Britain, were waiting for another helicopter after their failed attempt. They both openly boasted about being delirious and tripping over while up at high camp, they also seemed relieved to be getting a lift home and avoiding the hike out. They were drinking beers and laughing, and I wondered about the seriousness of their symptoms.

There was an evacuation insurance roundabout operating in Nepal that had been going on for years. It was an open secret that foreigners could claim their evacuation on insurance by first catching the helicopter out and then obtaining a signature from a sympathetic doctor back in Kathmandu. This guaranteed payment from the often foreign owned insurance firms to the helicopter operator, the hospital, and a commission for the guide; everyone became a winner. Except for the multinational company, and who cares about those thieves, right? There is a special place reserved in hell for the necessary evil that are insurance companies, and why not milk it when we can?

The ease at which a person could claim an evacuation flight out on their insurance provider, and the large commissions flowing up and down the valleys, saw a surge in evacuations in recent years. This roundabout became so common that in January 2019, insurers threatened to boycott the entire trekking industry in Nepal if it didn't clamp down.

The biggest downside from what I could see in this flourishing airborne economy was the inflationary pressure it placed on helicopter seat costs. Western climbing operators that utilised them for logistics were now required to pay a premium. This cost was then passed onto their clients, making guided climbs more costly every season. I have also witnessed solo climbers without insurance forgoing the extravagant cost of a flight, preferring to limp out over days at further risk to their frostbitten limbs and health.

The people I worried about the most were locals, like our lead guide Mingma. His wife recently had a baby, and when she went into labour, the closest hospital was in Kathmandu. The choice was a 15 hour jeep ride from his village or to call in a helicopter. He booked a seat for his wife alone, and it cost him $2000 USD to get her to a doctor while he took the jeep. This would equate to 3.5 times the average monthly wage for a Nepali. There was seemingly no difference between westerners and locals regarding the cost of air assets. Every action we took as a foreigner in Nepal had an effect down the line on the locals.

I sat with the British guys and bled them for information about the mountain conditions while they were liquored up and chatty. They confirmed reports I had heard that it was bustling up at high camp. A sizeable Israeli team and an assortment of smaller teams filled every possible tent spot. Besides helicopters arriving to collect climbers, Khare was currently quiet, and I took this as a good sign. The bottleneck of teams would hopefully be clear when we made our summit push in a couple of days.

After lunch, we exchanged the comforts of the Khare common room for a super slow acclimatisation hike up a nearby ridgeline. The process of climbing high and sleeping low was a tried and tested method to help us adjust to the altitude. At 5220 metres, I started to feel a light throbbing headache. I hadn't taken any Diamox so far on the trip, opting to let my body adapt naturally as best it could. We all moved in slow motion on the ascent, with only Stéphane showing minimal signs of fatigue, choosing to push even higher than the rest of us.

Back down at the tea house, my vision started to blur while sipping on a fat and salt-infused Sherpa tea. White shapes began to dance in front of my eyes, and I had an immediate stress response knowing I was feeling the effects of pressure on my brain. After a short period of panic, I entered a moment of weightlessness and delirium but was still cognitively aware of my surroundings and what was happening.

I took some deep, slow breaths and calmed down. I asked Kelly for the Diamox from her med kit, intuitively knowing it was time to let modern medicine do its work. Altitude affected us all differently, and I had never felt what I was feeling that afternoon. I forced down some food and retired early to my sleeping bag, where I dropped into a black hole of sleep for 10 hours. I needed to urinate into my pee bottle a few times throughout the night, and I woke at dawn to three litres of yellow nectar collected. The fluid build up inside my skull had been relieved through Diamox's diuretic power, and I felt like a million dollars. This was fortunate because we were due to push up to base camp on rotation. The climb was officially about to begin.

Mera Peak

A rotation in mountaineering lingo is climbing to a high point on the mountain, then returning for rest and acclimatisation. The bigger the mountain, the more rotations a climber will endure. We only required one rotation, and then we would be ready to push to high camp and line up for a summit attempt. It was day nine, and we departed at 8 a.m. for a slow and steady hike along a worn path winding northeast around Mera. The switchback trail of scree and dirt threaded through boulder fields before reaching the snow line and crampon point. We donned our large mountaineering boots, strapped on crampons, and roped in together as a team. This would be the first time wearing full battle attire for Kelly and Harriet.

The crunch of snow under the metal points of my crampons was music to my ears. I felt solid on the slope as it approached 50 degrees, where a fixed rope section had been set up earlier in the season. I clipped in for safety and plodded up onto Mera's shoulder while taking in the incredible beauty around us. The sun highlighted the contours of the ice and brought out the deep blue in the glacier below. Large crevasses split the icy playground with a black zebra pattern highlighting the imminent danger if we slipped at any moment.

Being roped together with total beginners, who were wearing crampons for the first time, on a steep slope, and with crevasses beckoning below was enough to test any climber's mental fortitude. I contemplated the worst case scenario: What happens if one of the girls fell and dragged the team off their feet? In that situation, once momentum had built up, it would be near impossible to arrest our fall. I was glad to be clipped onto the fixed line. Our whole team made the top of the ridge at over 5400 metres and hung around long enough to feel the effects of a new altitude before beginning a rappel back down.

Harriet's health seemed to deteriorate quickly during the descent. She started to stumble and reported feeling nauseous with a splitting headache. I offered to take her backpack to ease her burden, but she wouldn't hear of it. Her competitive nature and dedication to physical suffering gave her the endurance to make it back down to the crampon point and then to the tea house under her own steam. It was a big day for the girls, lots of new skills were acquired, and if the weather gods were kind, we would make our summit push in the coming days.

Our rotation was followed by a full day of rest, which for me entailed hours inside the common room, drinking tea, eating, reading, and staring out the window at Mera. I ordered every flavour of hot liquid from the lovely Nepalese ladies in the kitchen, who delivered them inside colourfully painted thermoses with cork bungs. Every common room was different and decorated to the family's unique taste. This one had a large iron belly stove as its centrepiece, with a pot full of water on top. The owner told me it cost him 1000 Rupees daily, about $15 AUD to heat the room for travellers each night. Wood was flown in by helicopter due to a shortage of dry animal dung, the most common fuel in the upper Khumbu. The interior had small wooden tables around its edge, with bench seats along the walls. Carpets and cushions of varying colours and designs covered the seats, and bright golden curtains hung from every window, tied back with red satin ropes. The scene reminded me of the Gobi Desert, where the inside of the friendly nomads' yurt was decorated to inspire happiness and life, while the bare exterior bore the brunt of the harsh environment.

The common room filled for dinner as teams arrived down from summit attempts, and other groups arrived heading up. An American team of two couples were on the latter journey and sat opposite us at mealtime. One of the girls caught my eye, not because of her beauty, but due to her pale complexion and sickly weak appearance. She looked terribly ill. Within seconds of sitting down, she began hacking up phlegm and coughing openly into the room.

After two years of health measures and hygiene education, thanks to COVID-19, this young woman thought it acceptable to spew her sickness into a space full of climbers desperate to stay healthy. I was shocked and watched in horror as she started to blow her nose. Like something out of comedy, she unleashed endless mucus through one nostril at a time far longer than socially acceptable. She trumpeted for so long it caused the room to fall silent, and I was sure she was taking the piss; she wasn't. My irritation grew with each passing second as clumps flew from her nose into the reusable hanky in her hands - something I hadn't seen used since my grandfather's snot rags from 30 years ago. I sanitised my hands out of habit, covered my face with a buff and went back to eating awkwardly, unfairly cursing all Americans.

My frustration had cooled later in the evening, and I was caught passing the walking sack of pneumonia in the hallway heading to her room. With awkward hesitancy, we spoke briefly about Mera, and she mentioned she had picked up a chest infection. 'Oh no, really?' She was devastated at not being able to climb higher, and I started to feel sorry for her. I had been in her position several times before, and it was a miserable way to start a big adventure. I collected some cough syrup and lozenges from my personal kit and donated them to her. She was appreciative, wished me luck on the climb, and went off to bark long into the night.

Day 11 dawned, and we were suited and booted, ready to move to high camp. We followed in the footsteps of our rotation day and after reaching the top of the fixed line carried on upwards. The gradient wasn't steep, but our progress was steady. Harriet was nauseous again and moving slowly. As Murphy's Law states, 'If anything can go wrong, it will.' Clouds started to form, followed shortly after by a stiff cold wind blasting us head on. Whiteout conditions settled in, obscuring the way forward, and the temperature plummeted. Snow was being whipped around, and I had to pull the hood of my jacket over my face to protect me from the biting cold.

Mingma led us through the blizzard, following well worn crampon scars in the ice. He knew the route by heart and guided us into a deserted high camp. It consisted of a dozen empty tents surrounding a central cook tent and a few small permanent wooden toilet blocks clinging above a vertical drop. The camp was nestled behind a rocky escarpment protecting it from the wind. The tents were perched atop every available flat surface, with some on the edge of a vertical chasm that plunged thousands of feet to an icy grave below. We were at 5800 metres, and each given our own tent as a luxury. The traffic jam from days prior had cleared, and we were the only team there. Elise, Kelly, and Yok were all feeling fine, Stéphane was on top of the world, and I was feeling strong. Harriet, on the other hand, was not. She crawled into her sleeping bag shortly after arriving and passed out. The altitude was kicking her ass.

Late in the day, the wind speed dropped to zero, and the clouds cleared to reveal a setting sun lighting up the summits of the mountains around us. I unzipped my tent and looked up towards the central high point. I couldn't see much in the way of crevasse danger on the first part of the approach, and from my angle, the slope looked secure. Knowing the snow and ice would be safest under cover of darkness during the deep freeze; we planned to be up at 2 a.m. and set off for the top shortly afterwards. I went inside, slid into my sleeping bag, swallowed some headache tablets, and drifted off.

I was surprised I had slept for four hours when my alarm started to beep at 1.30 a.m. Typically the night before a summit bid I was a ball of restless anxiety, and I knew the extra hours of recovery would pay dividends later in the day. I dressed in my summit apparel and crawled outside, greeted by zero wind and stars above. I went to check on Harriet and the team. As I expected, she hadn't improved and was in no condition to go higher. Kelly hadn't slept and was not feeling the best, but she got dressed and wanted to push on. With a slight delay as we reshuffled our guides to ensure Harriet was looked after, we roped in and stepped off at 3 a.m.

The urge to sprint ahead and power to the top was ever present, but experience had taught me to calm my excitement and make sure of every step. Slow is smooth, and smooth is fast, and it would ultimately win the day. Our head torches illuminated a small area in front of each of us as we drifted into our own worlds. The cold was penetrating and clawed at any exposed skin or idle appendage. I had purchased new mountaineering gloves in Kathmandu, a new model from a top brand, but within the first hour, I realised they were not up to the challenge. My fingers throbbed with the cold, and I needed to pound life into them every time we stopped. I knew the dawn would save me, but it was still hours away; we needed to keep the pace up.

Three hours after leaving high camp, the angle of the slope kicked to 50 degrees, and Kelly seemingly hit a wall. She was trying to keep to our pace but struggled and needed to stop and rest constantly. This caused the remainder of us to get cold, so we would race to warm up when we started again. This tug of war for warmth and rest continued for an hour until Kelly was exhausted, and my fingers were blocks of ice. She made the tough but wise call to turn back with Mingma and slowly made her way down. Our other climbing Sherpa, Ang Phurba, took the lead, and we continued the ascent as the sun's first glow lit the horizon. Mera is not a technical climb. It is a hard slog up a high altitude slope in freezing conditions and was more of a mental battle than physically taxing.

Crevasses sliced through the upper slope like delicate ribbons, but we could jump or step over them without breaking stride, except Elise, who decided to fall into one up to her waist to see what was down there. She extracted herself quickly and carried on unphased. The sun finally arrived in force and in the nick of time. I had lost sensation in my fingers, and as I warmed them, the pain of the nerves returning to life was a relief. If there was no pain I could have frostbite, and I thought back to the French team member we met who had lost his fingertips. I had almost committed the same critical error.

Firing on all cylinders with the sun's warmth, we continued and reached the South Summit an hour after dawn. The Central Summit was a further 30 minutes and 50 metres of vertical ascent, which at sea level was nothing. However, at 6400 metres of altitude, when feeling depleted, and four hours into a summit push, it's a battle of will. Yok chose to stay at the South Summit and shoot video while Elise, Stéphane, and I moved off with Ang Phurba. The steep finish burnt my lungs and legs with every step, but there was no way we weren't going to make it. The skies were blue, not a cloud on the horizon or a whisper of wind, perfect conditions.

One final crunch under our boots and we had made it to the top of Mera Peak and were surrounded by 360 degree views of pristine mountains. I could see dozens of peaks, including Lhotse, Makalu, Ama Dablam, and the mighty Mt Everest watching over the top of them all. It was crystal clear, and I couldn't remember ever seeing a better view. It was a rare gift from the weather gods. We took photos, downed some snacks, and enjoyed a brief fifteen minutes on the top. Good weather could be like sirens from ancient Greek mythology, calling sailors to their deaths on jagged rocks with enchanting music. It was tempting to stay on top for hours in the sunshine, but it could all change and snatch our lives away in a hiccup. We were only halfway and needed to stay focused and get back down safely.

The sun blazed upon a softening slope as we descended on snow that now had a slushy consistency, increasing the danger of crevasse falls. I removed layer after layer of clothing as the snow reflected the sunlight and scorched us from every angle. It took five hours to reach the summit and two hours to descend, stumbling back into high camp in a dehydrated euphoria.

With high fives and handshakes, Mingma congratulated us, then said, 'Rest now, one hour, and we go down.'

'You are a tough man Mingma; I'm tired,' I joked to him.

'Ok, 1.5 hours, then we must go.' The day was nowhere near done.

I checked on Harriet and Kelly, who were both feeling rough but were stable. I then inhaled hot noodle soup and passed out wearing my boots. Woken by Mingma barking commands at the porters, I slowly packed up in a daze. Coming up is always undertaken in baby steps, with light loads, utilising all available assets to get the team into position on the mountain. Once the mission was achieved, the next goal was to get down to safety, which for us was a camp situated in an opposite valley over 1000 metres below. My pack was overloaded with climbing gear, rubbish, and excess fuel we had brought up with us. I pulled it on, straining the straps and buckling my knees, then roped up in the lead and led the team out of high camp.

An hour of descent took us to a steep glacier traverse, nothing too sketchy but we had to pay attention in our battered states. Dropping below the snow line allowed us to ditch the cumbersome mountain boots and crampons, pull on our soft hiking shoes, and follow the dirt trail. We travelled a further two hours through an afternoon that seemed to never end, and just as rain started to fall, we arrived at Konge Dingma camp. One large shelter of roughly stacked stone covered with scrap timber and large blue tarps made up our home for the night.

The valley we had dropped into was off the main tourist trail, which meant these remote camps were seldom used. It was a picturesque setting, situated next to a flowing river, in a small flat field of grass and surrounded by cliffs. If I wasn't so shattered I would have appreciated it more, but in my current state, all I wanted to do was devour bowl after bowl of soup, rice, and dhal before disappearing into my tent. The last thing I remembered was a sprinkling of snow on the roof, and as I relaxed and let the tension in my body fall away, I thought; mission one accomplished.

Island Peak

Over three days we hiked our way up one of the most beautiful valleys in Nepal. Our next objective was to cross the Amphu Labtsa Pass, a formidable barrier between us and the next valley where Island Peak was located. It was the shortest way to get there, but wasn't for the faint hearted. Its technical aspects and crumbling icefall prevented any yaks, donkeys, or horses from being used to ferry loads. It was up to us and our cheerful porters to carry everything. With less foot traffic from tourists, the trail and surrounding scenery were pristine. The use of animals and tens of thousands of hikers on the Everest Base Camp route gave it a unique scent and vibe. I preferred this remote valley.

One of the nights we stayed in a newly built structure with an actual roof and 12-volt lighting. I asked Mingma, 'This one is nice, was it built this year?'

'Yes, a family lived here last winter, but it was a bad season and it snowed heavily for four days. The snow built up, and the whole house collapsed killing all ten people inside.'

I was shocked. The way Mingma spoke about the tragic deaths of an entire family was nonchalant. Living in these remote high altitudes carried real risk, and stories like this were sadly widespread.

I walked with Ang Phurba the following morning as we slowly ascended towards Amphu Labtsa base camp. He was 26 years old and weighed 58 kilograms wringing wet but had the strength of a buffalo.

'Have you been involved in any mountain rescues lately?' I asked him.

'Oh yes one last season, my hiking client from Canada to Everest Base Camp got very sick and had no insurance. He was 92 kilograms and I carry him on my back, swapping with another Sherpa all day and night to get him down fast.'

'Bloody hell mate, that's incredible. I bet you got a nice tip for that. Well done.'

'No, no tip, but he was sick, it's ok.'

'No tip, that's horseshit!' I said incredulously. 'He should have tipped you big time mate.'

'It is no problem.' Ang Phurba said with a smile and a shrug of his shoulders.

The humble nature of these mountain men and women will never cease to amaze me. Nor will the selfish and arrogant nature of some foreigners. If anyone reading this ever gets rescued by another human who physically carries you on their back for 24 hours and is paid cents on the dollar compared to the average Australian, I hope you tip them, and tip them well.

Our final camp before the pass was at 5500 metres and was no more than a cluster of tents nestled next to a half frozen lake. Above us was a wall of rock and ice, seeming more like an impenetrable border than the way forward. The pass topped out at 5845 metres, but we needed to navigate an icefall that looked spicy. We had no idea what to expect. Mingma had scheduled this as a trekking day, and I hadn't investigated much further. It was shaping up to be much more than a simple hike. We settled in for a rough altitude sleep, with snow falling and wind drowning out conversations. It was feeling like another pre-summit night.

Ang Phurba and Mingma set out at dawn breaking trail. The snowfall overnight added an extra challenge to the day ahead. For the first hour, we followed their fresh path through snowfields, rocky ridges, and flat ice sections. Then the fun started. The pass had been secured by steel fixed cable in years past; those were mostly buried in ice or had been torn off in an avalanche. Our ropes were retrieved, and one of the most fun and sketchy climbing days shortly followed. Over four hours we climbed up steep rock faces, ice chutes, and through areas of frozen white fingers where gale-force winds had whittled away the snow and ice. Mountain boots and crampons were now necessary, and as the altitude took its toll, I paused at a critical point.

At the top of the icefall, an enormous hanging block of ice had tilted at an acute angle, ready to tumble down the slope at any second. Its weight and impact would be like that of an asteroid, and anything in its path would be obliterated. The trail hugged a steep edge passing directly beneath this behemoth for 40 metres. Stopping underneath for a rest was not going to happen for obvious reasons, so I paused at its edge, caught my breath, and then double-timed it underneath. I was leaving fate to decide the rest. The team all made it through unscathed, and with heaving lungs, I arrived at the pass and celebrated with snacks.

Shortly after reaching the top, we realised the fixed lines on the opposite side had been torn away or rendered useless. This required a 50 metre rappel down the vertical rock to a sketchy scree ledge before traversing across to the end of a fixed steel cable. Fifty metres doesn't sound like much, but with exposure of probably a thousand feet below it was enough to make even the most experienced climber's legs quiver. For Harriet and Kelly, it would be their first serious rappel, and to add to the flavour, a snowstorm arrived.

What followed next was two hours of arranging the porters one by one into a rope harness and lowering them down. Our duffel bags were next, and then the climbers. With poor communication due to the storm, the process had all of us on high alert, and miraculously, we all made it to the secured cable. Wet and muddy switchbacks welcomed us, and I was exhausted when I reached the valley floor an hour later. Looking back up to where we had come from, it looked impenetrable. Mingma walked up beside me with a smile on his face,

'That was the second most dangerous pass in Nepal,' he said proudly. Then followed up with, 'But I would never do the other one; it's too dangerous.'

Our 12 hour day concluded as we walked into Chuukung, the last village before Island Peak. We would enjoy a rest day to prep gear, then head up again for mission number two. Stéphane spent one night with us before he broke away for his third attempt on Ama Dablam. Bad luck with the weather had forced him back twice already. We wished him calm winds and clear skies.

Island Peak base camp was three hours from Chuukung and was a permanent tent city for the duration of the season. This mountain was popular for new climbers as a first expedition and experienced climbers hoping to acclimatise safely for other summit bids. Once arriving at base camp, we heard many teams had failed over the previous three days. Wind and snow had held them back from an attempt, and those who tried to push through had failed before reaching the top. It was all up to the weather gods. We knew a window was opening for us, but whether the weather was kind would be left up to fate. We crawled into sleeping bags, ready for our summit push.

Before drifting off to sleep, I remembered a night over 15 years ago when I was at this exact location with two good mates, Shannon and Hal, ready for our first ever mountain climb. I was young and naïve; we broke all the rules regarding acclimatisation and were drunk every second day. We didn't stand a chance at a summit. The wind and cold forced us back before we even departed base camp. I always knew I would be back one day.

Elise woke me before my alarm. She was rustling around searching for a toilet bag. It seemed like time was a critical factor as she zipped herself off into the vestibule, dropped her pants and exploded into the plastic bag designed for the purpose. Our relationship had never been so close.

'You all right?' I asked.

'Sorry babe, I have a crook gut, but I slept well; I'm ready to go.'

Inspired by her resilience, I started to get ready, and after 4.5 hours of solid sleep, I was charged.

With porridge and three cups of super sweet Sherpa tea onboard, we stepped onto the trail with head torches highlighting the way forward. Harriet had remained at base camp; the altitude and nausea were still wreaking havoc on her. I looked up and noticed a long trail of climbers ahead of us, a centipede of stars all heading to the same objective. Switchbacks started to weave their way upwards, quickly turning to scree, then snow, followed by rocks, then ice. We made the crampon point above high camp and stopped to rest and boot up. We crossed our first crevasse field as the sun exposed the upper mountain, and an hour later, we took our first look at the summit and the headwall proceeding it.

A wall of ice rose 150 metres, seemingly straight to the summit. It wasn't precisely vertical, more like 60 degrees at its steepest point, yet it would be a formidable obstacle to anyone if the weather turned bad. Making the vertical section harder was the

27 other climbers already clipped into the fixed line and inching their way upwards.

'This is going to be a shit show, have a look at the traffic.' I said to Elise.

'Yeah, it's not great,' she replied. 'Let's keep going and see what happens.'

Luckily for us, most teams were already on the summit by the time we made the bottom of the wall. We enjoyed a rest in the sunshine before getting ready to head up. I moved to the base, clipped into the newest rope and started climbing behind Mingma. Rope selection was critical on popular peaks like Island. In front of me were three or four ropes going up, with two others off to the side for rappelling down. Some had been in place for years and were dangerous to use, and others were new but not fixed correctly to the ice. It was paramount to take it slow, make the right choice, test it, and then climb confidently, utilising the ropes sparingly. Many experienced climbers had perished due to clipping the wrong rope which quickly turned to paper under tension.

The general rule in climbing is that those coming up have the right of way. However, in my experience this was not always the reality. Most teams had summited and were coming back down when the inevitable bottleneck occurred, and the right of way rule went right out the window. Two Russian teams descending barrelled down, oblivious to anyone else who was coming up. We chose to pull off to one side and let the traffic clear. Eventually, the masses passed, and a friendly American team above called out.

'You guys have right of way, come on up,' one of the team yelled.

I thanked them on our way through, and moments later, I pulled myself up onto the ridgeline with the path ahead all to ourselves. Sheer drop-offs on both sides of the narrow ridge made the final 50 metres an exciting finish. With clear blue skies and not a sparrow fart of wind, this was the second time we had the best conditions imaginable in as many weeks.

Along the ridge, I was moving in slow motion, but eventually there was nowhere else to go. I took my last step onto the summit where Elise and Mingma already waited. We had the entire tabletop sized summit to ourselves. Yok arrived next, followed shortly by Kelly. This was her first summit, and we cheered her on after missing out on Mera. Her breathless words on arriving were classic Kelly.

'What's my name?' she panted.

To which we all yelled, 'Kelly!'

After the usual celebrations, some snacks, and photos for the sponsors, my attention shifted to the descent. We tentatively picked our way down through the labyrinth of ropes and dangers. I held onto three ropes at once and rappelled down the most intimidating spots with grip strength. I trusted my grip more than these weathered ropes. I watched with horror as the sun's heat melted the ice around the anchors and allowed them to slip in and out of their fixed position. It wasn't until we were all safely down at the crampon point, below the ice and crevasses, that I could finally relax. All that remained was two hours of knee buckling switchbacks to the valley floor, then another two hour descent from base camp carrying a full load before our fantastic 11 hour excursion in the mountains would come to an end.

Inside my warm sleeping bag that night, I wrote some quick notes in my journal, with the final line concluding, 'Mission two accomplished.'

Lobuche East

I sat on a rock by the river at the village of Pheriche, situated on the Everest Base Camp trail and our launching point for Lobuche East. A cold wind was ripping along the valley floor where the large flat river wound between boulders and farmland. The flowing glacial melt had been diverted in places with walls of rocks to allow farming and the grazing of yaks. I noticed five recently born, tiny woolly yaks playing together amongst the herd, oblivious to the freezing temperatures and noise from the helicopters.

Choppers were busily coming in and out of the landing area. Some ferrying teams down from the mountains, while others shuttled local families or climbers back to Lukla. Pheriche was midway on the flight path and was always a busy transition point.

We arrived the day before from Chukkung, where I had picked up a microbial hitchhiker from one of the French climbers coughing the virus into the cramped confines of the common room. The fevers set in that night and increased during the hike to Pheriche. By the time I arrived, I was coughing and spluttering, and Elise also started to have fevers.

We isolated ourselves to shield the rest of the team but knew we were going no further. My theory of pretending it wasn't there to help recovery was doing little to stifle the spreading infection. Barely able to breathe while sitting still, moving to our next high camp was out of the question. The rest of the team pushed higher, but from where I sat, I looked up at Lobuche's summit engulfed in clouds and knew they would be having a rough time with the weather. I hobbled back inside, stopping to cough my misery into the Khumbu before covering my face and settling by the yak dung fire.

The following morning, I stared out of the tea house's upper window towards the mountains. I noticed a trekker coming down the trail with speed. As the figure got closer, I realised it was Yok. My first thought was tragedy had struck. Then I checked the time and realised that for him to be down so soon, they mustn't have tried for the summit. He arrived and placed down his pack.

'No summit attempt guys; weather was too bad so Mingma called it off. They are all coming down behind me.'

Such is the way of mountaineering. Sometimes you get perfect weather and clear skies. Other times you get sick and smashed with storms. It's the gamble we took when venturing into the wild. We had achieved two of our three objectives with the best possible weather days, and I was more than happy with that.

The others arrived back, somewhat deflated but understanding. Mingma told us to pack up. It was time to head down to warmer climates and our waiting flight home in a few days. The dusty and crowded Everest trail was our exit route, and as we descended, I took time to reflect and spent time chatting with the team.

'Hey Kelly, I wanted to ask why you decided to be a nurse? It's a tough job, especially these days.'

'That's an easy question to answer, but it's not a nice story.' She started to reply.

'I was a teenager with my family in the Similan Islands, Thailand. It was boxing day 2004, and we had to decide what to do for the day. Our options were to relax in a lovely hotel or head out on a boat for snorkelling. We chose the boat. Whilst snorkelling, whirlpools appeared, and strong currents separated our family and dragged us out into the open ocean. Our boat captain was able to rescue our entire group. He had heard on the radio that a tsunami had hit the mainland because of an earthquake. He wanted to head to land and find higher ground. As we were motoring back towards land, we witnessed the astronomical destruction from the tsunami just hours prior. That was the first time I saw a dead body.'

'On the way in we passed by the resort we were supposed to be relaxing at and it was destroyed. We made it to higher ground, where there were lots of people in a panic, and many were injured. I was just in my swimmers and couldn't do much, but I found a small first aid kit, and I started going around and helping anyone I could. It was on that day I knew I wanted to be a nurse.'

Kelly's story was incredible, not just about how she found her passion in life but about that horrific day unfolding like a black swan event. While mulling over the fragility of life and death, Mingma came up from behind us.

'I just got a message; Stéphane didn't make the summit. He tried for 18 hours on summit day but had to turn back.'

I felt for him. Ama Dablam is no joke; even having the guts to try three times earns my deepest respect. Mingma softened his tone and spoke again.

'Also, my Sherpa friend is missing on the Lhotse South Face. They have been searching, but he is dead, I know it.'

'No way mate, how did it happen?'

'He was part of a big Korean team, five climbers and 14 Sherpas. He was setting up camp one, fixing ropes up high and went missing.'

'I'm so sorry. How do you feel about it? Will the team all come down?' I asked.

'This is very dangerous mountain and a hard route, my friend knew this. I would never climb it, too risky. The team won't come down, the Koreans will keep climbing.'

The harsh reality of most high altitude mountaineering in Nepal is that the Sherpas took bigger risks so foreign climbers could reach the summit. Everyone signing up for these expeditions understood the game, and the lure of money would draw more climbing Sherpas to the mountains every season.

Mingma turned to me.

'That's why we should just have fun and make the right calls to turn back when we have to.' He said with a smile.

I couldn't agree more.

Three days after leaving the shadow of Lobuche behind, we arrived at Lukla for our flight back to the comforts of Kathmandu. Yok filmed one of the small planes accelerating down the steep runway, reaching the drop-off point at the end and lifting off into the sky, clearing the tops of the surrounding mountain peaks. We entered the terminal, checked in, and boarded our little bird back to hot showers, salads, and the comforts of home. Mission accomplished.

◆ ◆ ◆

I was sitting on my couch at home in Tasmania two weeks later, when I received a message from Yok. He had sent through two pictures. One was of the plane that had taken off before our own flight out of Lukla on our final day. The other was an article about a plane going down and killing all 22 people on board. I looked in disbelief before it all clicked; it was the same plane, the tail numbers matched. Twenty two people like us, on the adventures of their lives, died in an instant. A freak occurrence had cut their lives short in a black swan event, just like the tsunami. Sadly, these events occurred every single day, often multiple times. People started their day thinking they would live forever, only to be dead by the evening.

I don't share this accident to be grim, and I didn't want it to taint an expedition that was one the best I've been on; but this was a reality of life we must accept. Whenever something like this happened, I used it as an opportunity to dig deep, and to figure out if I needed to change anything in my life. I asked myself some meaningful questions: Am I happy? If I was dying, would I be filled with regret? Would people remember me as a good guy? Have I left a legacy? What do I need to change in my life?

After asking this last question, the answer was nothing. I'm on the path I want to be on with the people I choose to be on it with. I know death could be waiting for me at any moment, but I am comfortable with that.

I messaged Yok back, 'Let's keep living brother, onwards to the next adventure, and let the chips fall where they may.'

CHAPTER 9

The Deer Hunter

'Guns don't kill people. People kill people.'

The phrase above is often quoted following the latest mass shooting in the United States. It has been adopted and popularised by the National Rifle Association of America for the gun control debate. On the surface, the words sound correct. A piece of metal cannot kill a person. A physical trigger must be pulled to fire a weapon, which, if intended, could kill someone. However, the rebuttal was that a person intending to kill would not be able to if they didn't have access to the gun in the first place. It's the chicken or the egg dilemma.

My past experiences have allowed me to add a few extra layers to the debate around firearms and human behaviour. I grew up a hunter, learning to shoot at a young age and lived in Outback Australia where the rifle was simply another tool utilised in operating a cattle station. I then joined the Infantry, into the 1st Battalion of the Royal Australian Regiment, where I learned the specific skills to, as quoted from the rifleman's handbook:

'Seek out and close with the enemy, to kill or capture them, to seize and hold ground, and to repel attack, by day or by night, regardless of season, weather, or terrain.'

Killing our own kind for the defence of our tribe is as old as our species and, dare I say it, a naturally evolved human behaviour; we have gotten very good at it. I also live in Port Arthur Tasmania, a place when mentioned, would often remind people of Australia's largest mass shooting which took place here in 1996.

The final factor allowing me to tackle the gun debate better than most is that I hunt and harvest meat from my property to eat. There is a vast difference between selecting a choice cut of meat from the supermarket shelves versus watching an animal take its last steps through a scope before pulling the trigger and taking its life. The process of harvesting the warm meat, which moments ago was part of an animal oblivious of your desire to eat it, is also as old as our species. Over time we have removed the public from the harvesting process, separating them from the bloodshed, and the emotional burden.

Emotion is an excellent place to start this chapter. When the firing pin strikes the primer of a bullet casing, it causes a small explosion. The explosion from the primer ignites gunpowder causing hot gasses to rapidly expand inside the cartridge and propel a projectile down the barrel. The metal projectile leaves the barrel and accelerates towards its target. Does it decide where it lands? Does it have an emotional response to what it's about to do? Will it alter its trajectory if aimed at a child soldier but stay true at a paper target? The answer to all these questions is no. The bullet will go wherever the operator intends for it to go, factoring in human error, environmental inputs, and the behaviour of the target. So do guns kill people, or do people kill people?

This chapter is not a pro-gun piece, I want it to be a journey for you as the reader, along the emotional landscape of a hunt, but it seems today we cannot talk or mention hunting without the gun debate taking over. So before moving on, let me clarify my position. Australia is not America; we have different cultures, populations, and histories that lay the belief systems towards gun ownership. Inside Australia's enormous land, there are people inside states and territories who need firearms to survive. Australia's strict gun rules for one part of our society can severely impact the productive capacity of others. I do not believe I need an AK47 with a 30 round magazine to harvest my dinner; but disarming our entire population and making gun ownership a convoluted, tiring, and bureaucratic process will come back and haunt us if our country ever needs to repel an enemy. As with most issues, it's not black or white; it's grey. And it's in the grey where our leaders and citizens struggle to agree on solutions.

Before I take you with me on my first deer hunt, let's get in the grey and state openly that the death of an animal is attached to everything we put in our mouths, wear on our bodies, or use in our lives. Every vegetable or salad grown would not be here if a mammal, reptile, insect, or bird hadn't died first. Every acre of land, cleared to grow organic insecticide free vegetables involved killing animals. Every piece of rubber on our feet, minerals in our phones, timber in our houses, or water in our cups would not exist if some creature, great and small, hadn't died.

A perfect example is a farmer who asked me recently to harvest wallaby, rabbit, and bush turkey from his back paddock. Knowing I ate wallaby, he told me, 'Take as many as you want; the buggers are smashing my plants.' He had recently planted rows of new seedlings, and had built expensive fences to keep wildlife out, but they were not 100 per cent effective. Tasmania is famous for its organic world class food but I wondered how many people who enjoyed its natural flavour and taste, knew the death count attached to each mouthful.

This example is not a criticism of farming at all, simply an example of the cost of production. Similar numbers could be tallied for every single product we utilise in our lives. Textiles for clothing, every source of electricity, growing soybeans for tofu, and even the paper used for the flyers on animal welfare carried a toll from the land cleared to produce the trees. I'm sure you are getting the idea.

So, if we first accept this fact, the debate shifts to the value of life. Are the lives of the lizards, ants, bugs and grubs I displaced and killed for my rainwater tank less valuable than the wallaby I shot to harvest as food? Are the animals displaced and killed by land clearing to mine and process silicon for my 12-volt off grid solar panel less valuable than the cow I slaughtered to feed my family for a year? Were the birds displaced and killed for the phone towers, which allowed my friends to protest on social media about gun control, less valuable than the fish I caught to eat?

One could argue that there was a difference, and one animal's life is not as valuable as another; a species of threatened giraffe is more valuable than an abundant feral pig, for example. However, this could lead us down a slippery path. Does the life of one cute wombat outweigh 50 wallabies? Or is one majestic wedge-tailed eagle more important than 20 lizards? One frog or one million ants? The life of one law abiding citizen or five hardened murderers?

I believe there is no difference; all creatures' lives are valuable, great and small. We are all part of the natural environment. Some species will die by the thousands daily and become extinct, while others will thrive and spread unchecked. Over 150,000 humans die each day in our world, and this is without any known predators. Once I understood this cycle of life and death and that humans are the apex predators in the food chain, I gave up on debating the issue. I calmly came to terms with my place in the world and learned to harvest what I needed to survive and flourish, while limiting the damage to the environment around me. I wouldn't drive fast cars, wear fancy clothes, live in a big house utilising every modern appliance, or clear bushland because I liked the look of grass. I decided to live simply, harvest wisely, and give back to my environment, knowing that my actions were causing death.

Now that we have waded through the grey, I'd like to take you with me into the wild and utilise a unique set of skills to find, kill, and harvest one of the best game meats in nature's supermarket. This next journey won't be as easy as picking up a shrink-wrapped packet. Achieving our mission will take days of searching, physical hardship, whisky, and two nervous shots. Let's go hunting.

◆◆◆

I didn't wake up one morning as a middle aged man and decide I wanted to be a hunter. Inception started at a much younger age. As a little kid living and growing up on cattle stations, I witnessed my parents shoot poisonous snakes with shotguns, harvest bullocks for food with rifles, and shoot clay targets for fun at the local gun club, I grew up around firearms. At age 10 when I was old enough and strong enough to hold one, Dad bought me an air rifle.

The first air powered guns were designed in the 16th century, and modern versions are still widely utilised. They fire a tiny slug or pellet using compressed air potential stored inside the rifle once it is cocked. Cocking my rifle back then involved bending it in half to compress a cylinder before releasing it back to a straight position. The effective range of air rifles today is 20 to 30 metres, mine was 10, and even then, I would miss half the shots I took. Cane toads, rats, feral cats, and stray pigeons docile enough to come within my kill range were open targets. Starting young with a relatively harmless weapon allowed me to learn the principles of safe firearms handling before I graduated to the adult world of lethal rim fire and centre fire weapons.

Rim fire rifles are small calibre and operate when the firing pin strikes the outside of the bullet shell casing, igniting the internal gunpowder and firing the projectile. Centrefire rifles utilise a primer in the centre of the shell casing; this mechanism is common for all big calibre weapons. Calibre is a term used to describe the internal diameter of a gun barrel bore. It is most commonly measured in fractions of an inch and can confuse a beginner shooter.

An easy way to think about it is that the smaller the number, the smaller the internal barrel diameter a bullet can be inserted into. After my air rifle, I moved up to .22 calibre rim fire, then onto the slightly bigger .22 magnum, before finally having the shoulder girth to handle the larger recoil from a .303 and shotgun. We have all watched war movies with the big military machine guns mounted on Humvees. Those are typically 50 calibre or .50 denoting a big bore size and large projectile. While serving with the Army I fired the 50 calibre sniper rifle which kicked like a stallion.

Hunting is in our genes as Homo Sapiens. Our weapons to harvest have evolved from rocks, deadfalls, and sharp sticks. To bows, arrows, and swords. Next came the accurate and lethal cannons, rifles, and handguns. The Chinese invented the crude versions of gunpowder in 142 AD, and the black powder's explosive potential changed hunting and war forever. One more piece of theory before we move on. If you read the side of an ammo box, there will always be a grain weight amount; '.308 calibre 155 grain,' for example. This second number refers to the weight of the projectile that will be fired through the barrel and go on to hit the target. A heavier projectile could be a better option depending on the target and if you needed more stopping power. If a shooter hoped for greater accuracy at a long distance, a smaller weight projectile with higher gunpowder loads would be better. Ballistics and accuracy theory is a world unto itself, and I will now back away from the conversation before I provoke the marksman aficionados with my common understanding.

There are two different processes when harvesting meat from the wild, shooting and hunting. Shooting I could describe as driving along in a 4x4 truck, spotting the animal you want, taking aim, and shooting it from a distance. The requirement for this harvest is good shooting skills and a vehicle. Then there is hunting; walking out into the wild backcountry and living in the bush for days while learning the land's topography and your prey's behaviour. Stalking up on your target to within 100 metres and then placing one perfect shot through the heart and lungs to bring the animal down humanely. The two differing styles had the same outcome, but I would soon learn that the latter carried ethics and a sense of achievement I had never experienced before. I had also never eaten a deer before which every other hunter I'd spoken to raved was the best meat around. With all this in mind I needed some guidance, and I had one buddy in my network who lived and breathed the warrior's life.

Al Kidner was a section commander of 3 Platoon Alpha Company, and I had served under him while on operations in Australia and East Timor. Some soldiers in the Army were good at their job, handling the hardships of living in the bush easily and rarely whining about even the most miserable conditions. Then there were soldiers who loved the job, couldn't wait to spend weeks in the jungle soaking wet and tired, and who were what I would label as the warrior class. This was Corporal Kidner. He was the soldier's soldier and had been an avid hunter before and remained one after his time in the military.

In the same way that there are different types of soldiers, there are also different types of hunters. Rifle hunters can be successful with basic skills and good shooting capability; the longer range and damage inflicted by bullets is an equaliser in the wild. Bow hunters utilising modern compound bows required a higher level of skill. They must be able to track and stalk their prey to within 40 to 50 metres and deliver an arrow into vital organs with the aid of modern sights. Then there are traditional bow hunters. Imagine Robin Hood; a simple wooden bow, one string, and a quiver of arrows. No sights, no modern technology, just bushcraft and training. These purists needed to get even closer and still be able to deliver the arrow to its target with the naked eye. Al is a traditional bow hunter and a very successful one. Without blowing his head up anymore, this soldier's soldier and hunter's hunter is also a good bloke.

Al and I served overseas with the Army in 2003, conducting war fighting patrols and peacekeeping missions in East Timor. After spending a few weeks in the deep jungle, wet, filthy, and living off bare rations, returning to base was a joyous time. Especially when, after our first shower in nearly a month, there was a pile of letters and care packages waiting for us from family and friends back home. The morale boost was enormous, except not all of us were in the same boat.

While most of us ripped open parcels and devoured cakes and words of love from home, one section scout, a young Aboriginal kid named Ned, didn't have a single letter waiting for him. Nothing. Zero. Corporal Kidner was the section leader, and part of that responsibility was caring for the men and managing their morale. Upon seeing Ned's situation, he immediately called home to his own mother on the satellite phone, telling her to fill up a big box with all sorts of goodies and address it to Ned. When that package arrived, Ned broke down in tears, as did many of the hardened young soldiers.

Attitude reflects leadership, especially in the harsh environments of war. Small acts like what Corporal Kidner had done for Ned created a determined fighting force, willing to follow their leader, as Shakespeare once said, 'Once more unto the breach, dear friends.'

Corporal Al Kidner was discharged from the Army following a sterling career and will now be known as Al for ease of storytelling. Al and I had been back and forth via email for a few weeks, and then I gave him a call.

'Al, how are you mate?'

'All is well Richo, no complaints. Are we going bush?'

'I would love to. You let me know a date, time, and location, and I'll be there.'

'Come up to Queensland, I have access to some big properties full of Red deer, it's outside of stag season but I can show you the ropes and we can hopefully get some dinner.'

'Sounds perfect, I'm picking up a new rifle this week. A Lithgow .308.'

'That will work nicely. Get it zeroed in, remember your marksmanship principles, and I'll see you soon.'

'Copy that.'

Buying a weapon in the United States is as easy as walking into a Walmart, showing your ID for a quick security check, and then taking it home. However, in Australia, it is a little more challenging. There is just enough paperwork and time lag to dissuade any of the wrong types of characters from owning firearms.

First, to gain a firearms licence, you must have permission from a landowner to shoot on their property or be a member of a gun club. We already owned land big enough to qualify, so didn't need permission. The next step was to complete a safety course and be signed off by an instructor. Then you can find the rifle you want, within the limits of your licence, and purchase it. The weapon remains at the store for 28 days until the police complete background checks and only then can you be issued a permit to acquire it. This permit can be taken in and exchanged for your rifle. The system worked well, and after going through the process I walked into the store, picked up my new rifle, attached a scope, and took it home.

As I do with all my projects I dove in headfirst. I devoured books on ballistics and shooting techniques, read blogs, and built two large targets out of plastic pipes and cardboard to practice on. I'm fortunate to have a friend named Mick close to home who owns a large sheep property, perfect for shooting safely out to 200 metres. With his permission I spent a few days there relearning how to shoot accurately and preparing my new rifle for the hunt.

I drove through Mick's property on a sunny Tasmanian day. The dirt road was bordered by beautiful green fields dotted with native gum trees and filled with fat healthy sheep. Amongst the flocks I saw alpacas and one giant wombat pretending to be part of the family. I pulled up at Mick's large workshop, where he operates a mechanical business, to say hi and get directions.

'Hey Mick, I saw a big fat wombat down in your paddock on the way in; he your pet?'

'Hey Luke, nah mate, I'll have to scare him out of there if he doesn't move along; he is eating all the feed, ripping up the fences and leaving big holes through the fields.'

'What about those alpacas, what are they for?'

'They protect the sheep and keep the wild dogs away; they are vicious when they need to be.'

Being a farmer carried both a weight and moral balance that could often be hard to bear. A wombat needed to be moved away from feeding grounds so thousands of lambs would have enough feed to eat and be delivered to the market. I knew farmers in the area who often killed 200 wallabies in two hours to keep their numbers under control and ensure their animals had enough grass to eat. In Queensland the latest estimates for the feral pig population were between 20 and 30 million. With an abundance of food, the herds were impossible to control and devastated farmlands. Until a larger market for game meat opened in Australia or for export overseas, these wild herds would continue to be culled and wasted. Every year hundreds of thousands of tonnes of meat are left to rot in the sun, while half the world doesn't have enough to eat; it's hard to make sense of it.

I got directions to an empty paddock, jumped in Mick's all-terrain vehicle and set off. While I was in the military, I had no concept of the financial cost of war. We would spend days and weeks at the rifle and explosive ranges shooting thousands of rounds and detonating tonnes of material that went boom. While buying the first box of ammunition for my rifle I realised very quickly that it was not going to be a free for all anymore. A small case of ammo containing 20 rounds cost me $69, working out to $3.45 per shot. I didn't have an unlimited Government budget for this hunt, so I needed to relearn to shoot a tight group at 100 metres in as few rounds as possible. While hunting amongst the thick bush in the backcountry I was unlikely to take long-range shots out to 200 or 300 metres. Those skills could come later.

It took me four sessions at Mick's and $345 worth of trigger time to shoot a consistent 30 millimetre group at 100 metres. The recoil from the rifle, while I was lying in the prone position, had battered my shoulder; but it felt amazing to be back shooting and relearning the skills I had buried deep for many years. In my youth I could comfortably hit targets at 400 metres and beyond; however, accurate shooting at longer distances took years to master. There is a lot to take into consideration for a bullet to land where the marksman wants it to, at ranges of 500, 600, or 1200 metres. Your body position, trigger pressure, breathing, wind, rain, sloping ground, gravity, the movement of the target, and even your hemispherical place on the Earth, (known as the Coriolis effect) comes into play at long range.

Like every profession there are masters of the craft and the distances a human can kill another in today's world are scary. An unnamed Australian sniper recorded a kill during operations overseas at 2815 metres. This record stood for many years until an unidentified Canadian sniper, during operations in Iraq, acquired a confirmed kill at 3540 metres. The benefit of practice and mastery of the shooting craft for war operations is obvious, but we also spend time on a range to zero a rifle before a hunting trip to ensure a clean kill. To shoot an animal in the wrong spot, causing it to run off and bleed out in the bush over a more extended period, hinders the harvesting of the meat and is a worst case scenario. My goal was one shot and a quick kill; anything less than that was unacceptable in my mind.

I boarded my flight to sunny Queensland after checking in my rifle and ammunition. It was a strange feeling walking through a public place with a firearm. If anyone asked, I would tell them the case carried an expensive trombone. I touched down in Brisbane and was picked up by another Army buddy Alex, whom I also served with overseas on operations in East Timor. After sharing stories over dumplings, he dropped me off at a large timber home on the edge of town. From the outside it didn't seem like the home of a great hunter, but upon crossing the threshold, it was a step back in time.

'Come on in mate, welcome to Brisbane.' Al held open the door and welcomed me.

I stepped inside and into a Wilbur Smith novel. The floors were covered with exotic skins, and beautifully mounted animal heads adorned the walls. White skulls with protruding tusks sat on shelves, and in every nook were books on hunting, bushcraft, and the warrior life. I had entered the realm of a master, and I knew I had come to the right place for my apprenticeship.

Over a glass of whisky, we caught up on the past and planned the next few days. Al was still in great shape. At 47 years old he trained daily with the goal of being mountain fit for hunting and, in his words, 'To keep the old man out.' His wife, Karen, was also a hunter and had served a long career in the police force before retiring and taking up leadership roles with the Department of Education. Al also had a son and daughter who were both currently serving in the military; I was among a family of patriots and sound operators.

Al finished his glass and stood up, 'Get your head down mate; we will prep gear early tomorrow and get on the road. It's a bit of a drive to the insertion point.'

'Sounds good, sleep well, see you at 5 a.m.'

◆ ◆ ◆

By the middle of the following day, we pulled up at a small ramp entering a freshwater dam. We unloaded the large canoe from the roof of Al's truck, followed by the rest of our gear. We had spent the early hours prepping, just like in the old days; running through contingencies, emergency procedures, actions on, and standard operating procedures. The final check before departure was a bottom up mental checklist. Boots, laces, socks, pants, belt, shirt, wet weather gear, hat, sunscreen, pack, food, cooking kit, and on it went until everything had been ticked off.

The water was calm, and the sun shone; it was a perfect Queensland day. Around the edges skeletons of trees protruded up through the surface. The large timbers had been pickled in water when this valley was dammed and flooded. The valley was surrounded by hills thick with bush. Al had hunted this rough country many times and knew every contour like the wrinkles on his hand.

We attached a small electric outboard to the back of the canoe before I loaded our rifles and stowed them out of sight. With our backpacks placed on top, to anyone watching, we were a couple of blokes heading out for a fish and a bush walk. As we were about to shove off, an old guy in an even older truck pulled up.

'I thought that was you. How are you mate?' Al said as the old timer killed the engine.

'I'm all right mate, what you blokes doin, chasing dinner you mad bastards?'

'Yeah Greg, need to fill up the freezer mate. Any hunters around?'

Al had met Greg a few times over the years. He was a local and kept a sharp eye on the comings and goings of the dam. He had mustered cattle through this rugged country his entire life and had seen it all. He was too old to ride horses like he once did, and now spent his afternoons catching yabbies and drinking a few beers instead.

'Not many blokes around, couple of pig hunters in trucks but they won't bother you, no roads where you're going I'm guessing.'

We chatted with Greg and watched a young family fresh out of the city struggle to get their expensive wake boat into the water. Greg led the commentary and made us laugh the more they battled.

'Have a go at these dumb bastards. You know one time I watched this bloke who couldn't get his boat started and had to use an anchor and rope to pull back into the ramp. As he was throwing the anchor, it hooked on some wreckage not far out. Turned out it was an old car. The council pulled the bugger out, and you know what they found?'

'What mate?'

'A dead bloke in it, been there for years as well,' he said while chuckling at the memory.

'Bloody hell, you wouldn't know what is out in that water hey,' Al replied.

Greg went quiet, nodded, and looked at the picturesque scene, his face carrying the lines and burden of years in the bush. He spoke again.

'Lots of problems disappeared out there over the years.' Al and I both looked at each other, thinking the same thing.

'Anyway lads, have fun. I'll keep an eye on your car while you're out.'

'Thanks Greg, much appreciated,' Al replied before he drove away.

'He's a funny old bugger isn't he,' Al remarked as we slid the canoe into the water.

'Sure is mate, he's the real deal. I like him.'

We skirted the bank and chatted while the electric engine provided the renewable thrust, it's quiet hum was a perfect fit for the natural world around us. I constantly scanned the bush for movement, searching for my first deer. An hour later we nudged a muddy bank, and Al killed the engine.

'We will stash the canoe here, load up packs and start walking.'

'Sounds good, let's do it.'

We had filled our water bottles before leaving the house. This allowed us a few days without returning to the dam to refill. I shouldered my pack, its familiar weight causing me to bend slightly forward, and started walking uphill following Al. With my rifle in hand, I was transported back 15 years to the jungles of Timor, on patrol, searching for the enemy. Only this time we were the apex predators, and there was no threat of being hunted back. It had been many years since I held a weapon in the open and it felt illegal or wrong somehow. The time spent apart from hunting, Australia's strict gun laws, and society's conditioning influenced me feeling this way.

This feeling wouldn't last; it slowly dissipated the further we walked into the bush, and the more comfortable I became. By the time we made the top of the knoll, dropped our packs, and started to set up a base camp, it felt natural again. Two men out hunting for meat was as authentic as it gets, and as I slung my hammock between two trees, it felt like returning home.

With a fixed position on the high ground, we pulled out our patrol packs. These were much smaller, and only carried a litre of water, a poncho, butchering knives, and meat bags. With a few hours before dark, we set off on our first hunt to get a feel for the area. We walked out of base camp at a casual speed along a ridge cleared of thick vegetation from a bushfire the year before. Green grass sprouting from the blackened earth is like chocolate to a deer.

Once we were a few hundred metres away from camp we both fell into the rhythm of patrolling. The conversation ended, our pace slowed, our senses heightened, and each foot placement was considered. The ground was dry and littered with sticks and twigs. Stepping on one would produce a loud crack that pierced the natural silence and act as an alarm bell to any deer in the area. As prey, they had evolved in a world of predators; and any unnatural sound, like a noisy human stepping on a branch, sent them galloping. This flighty behaviour is a genetic trait strengthened in the animals with each generation. The deer that were the most skittish and ran away at any foreign noise or smell would be the ones to survive and reproduce. Hunters and other predators picked off the deer who were inquisitive and not so nervous; so over time, the deer became harder to hunt.

Animals, in continents like Africa, where they have been hunted by lions, cheetahs, leopards, and every human throughout history, have evolved to be extremely hard to stalk and kill. Al told me one species of antelope he hunted had such an acute radar that they would hear the release of his bowstring and jump out of the way before the arrow could strike its mark, which was travelling at 70 metres per second. Natural selection at its finest.

I was trying my best not to embarrass myself on our first patrol (hunt). I scanned every centimetre of ground before placing my foot down, which was tiring at first, and I saw nothing else but the ground in front of me, but slowly my senses adjusted. After 30 minutes I could walk silently with my head up and scan the bush around me for movement. Al held up his hand and stopped. He then gestured for me to come closer.

'Smell that?' I sniffed the air and smelt a musty animal aroma, a wet, dusty dog scent.

'Yeah mate, what's that?'

'Deer. We have the wind in our favour, they are below us somewhere.'

Fifteen minutes later we heard crashing through the bush in front of us. A group of five deer were spooked and bounded away at full charge. They had either heard or smelt our approach before we could see them.

Smell is a unique sense. It's the fastest way to trigger a memory because unlike other sensory stimuli it bypasses the thalamus and goes straight to the brain's smell centre, the olfactory bulb. This is connected directly to the amygdala and hippocampus, explaining why a smell like grandmas' scones or gunpowder, can often evoke a detailed memory or intense emotion. Our scent evoked the fight or flight stress response in a group of deer, and they bolted.

'That's what we were smelling, a group of hinds.' Al explained. 'We will keep moving, we might be able to get up on them again before dark.'

Hinds is the name given to female Red Deer, the species we were hunting. Bucks or stags are the males, and most sought after by hunters for their impressive antlers. We descended the ridge and found a shallow wallow with fresh deer and pig tracks in the mud. It was late afternoon, and most animals would be heading for water before bedding down for the night.

'It could be a good time to lay an ambush.' Al said as we assessed the ground around the muddy water.

'Sounds good, where?'

'Let's move back up the ridge, gain some height, and find a spot with eyes on this wallow. Something will come and drink soon.'

We sat with our backs against an ancient blue gum tree for cover at a range of 100 metres from the wallow. The sun was setting, and the bush was a soft symphony of birds and insects. We sat for an hour whispering in conversation with my rifle at the ready and a round in the chamber. We heard hooves striking dirt behind us, growing louder and approaching fast. Before we could pivot and see what was coming, the same group of hinds we had startled earlier galloped down upon us. They didn't see us until the last second and halted 10 metres away, staring at the two strange figures before them, not yet processing what we were. They were large healthy females of varying ages and were much bigger than I thought they would be. It was impossible to miss a shot at this range. I could have hit one with the butt of my rifle.

We sat staring at them. They stood staring at us. Their brains rolled back through centuries of evolution to make sense of what was in front of them. Our brains held back the primitive urge to charge at them with clubs and spears. There was no point attempting to turn around for the kill, any movement and they would scatter. Instead, we relished the moment. A few seconds later a breath of wind carried our foreign scent and the head of the oldest female perked up; then, she instantly spun on her hooves and bolted back up the hill with the others in hot pursuit. They disappeared over the ridge.

'There you go, your first red deer,' Al said, breaking the silence.

'That was awesome, this is a good area.'

'Yeah, it is, we are on to them now. It's getting dark. Let's get back to camp and get out again at first light.'

We sat around a roaring fire that night catching up on years of stories. Eventually, the conversation settled on hunting, and we dove into the moral landscape of it all, especially trophy hunting in Africa, where most criticisms were often focused.

'How do you justify a bow hunt, especially big game?' I asked.

'Well, over in Africa once humans had carved up the land and built fences, roads, and country borders, the large herds of migratory species could no longer wander and feed over thousands of kilometres like they used to. The populations grew rapidly in smaller areas and destroyed the land from overuse. The countries' Governments and private landowners then had to cull. It's no different to us culling kangaroos, horses, or camels here in Australia. It's just that the animals over there are bigger and iconic. The choice for the landowner was to either kill the animals and often waste all that meat or they could offer a certain number of animals each year for sale to hunters. This created income, jobs, and a massive economic boost to the area. So that's what evolved. A system of animal and land management that grew their economies, created employment opportunities for the poor, fed communities and helped stop the poaching.'

'Sounds like a good system. How did it stop poaching?'

'A lot of the poaching was by impoverished locals who needed food and income from the meat and ivory. But it's a very dangerous occupation. Not just from trying to hunt these animals without the right tools, but if the locals were caught by the authorities, they were either killed during arrest or thrown in prison. Given the choice between life as a poacher or life as a hunting guide, tracker, driver, or safari camp cook for international hunters, the locals would choose the safer option every time. All the meat harvested was shared with local villagers, and no ivory was ever allowed to be taken or sold into the market.'

I hadn't heard the breakdown of the hunting business before, and I peppered Al with questions as he fed more wood into the flames. The economics made total sense to me, and the animal numbers management system was sound. So where was the problem? The critics got caught up in the weeds and backed themselves into a corner by saying all hunting was morally wrong, disregarding the information and reality in front of them. Ultimately, as a hunter, I would struggle to kill certain animals but not others. I had the power to take the life of a kangaroo, an enormous buffalo, or a bull elephant, but should I?

My gut answer would be no way. I could never shoot a wild elephant. However, if a manager of a National Park said to me, we have an old bull elephant at the end of his life who is destroying the crops of local villages. The elephant numbers are big this year, and we will cull five of the oldest males. The animals will be shot regardless of whether we sell these hunting tags. The price is $25,000 each which will go to the whole industry and help the conservation programs. First, we must pretend I had that sort of money, and then what would my answer be? What would you decide?

The next time you see a picture on social media featuring a smiling hunter next to a trophy animal, please fight the urge to drop into the comments and attack them. Think about the reality of the world and our roles in it. After learning from Al, I concluded that the hunters often did more for local communities in Africa, injecting hundreds of thousands of dollars into regional pockets, than many non-government organisations or charities. Who knows, maybe some hunters deserve a pat on the back for this philanthropy. Sadly, however, I don't think that will come anytime soon.

I slept soundly in my airborne nest, woken only once by a bellowing male koala who sounded like he was inches from my eardrum. After a hot brew and a quick feed of oats, we stepped off into the bush for a morning hunt. Al and I moved through the scrub in silence, and I was being extra diligent with my foot placement, when out of nowhere and with no time to muffle the noise, I erupted, 'ACHOOO.' The early morning silence of the bush was shattered, and if there were any animals to hunt nearby, they were gone. I was embarrassed and looked over at Al, who turned to me with a severe look. We made eye contact and his frown morphed into a grin as we laughed. We weren't patrolling in the jungles of Timor looking for armed militia anymore, we were on a fun hunt in Queensland, and it didn't matter.

This sneeze, while embarrassing, became a good reminder for me; of how we can relive past events from simple activities and triggers. On reflection, I realised I also have the opportunity and the power to change old narratives, to rewire my mind and generate positive associations. In an instant, one simple sneeze had transported me back from patrolling the jungles of East Timor at high alert, to being present on a hunt in Queensland with a good mate.

We had planned a three day hunt and over the following day and a half Al passed on his knowledge about hunting and bushcraft. He taught me how to see into the landscape and pick out lines and movement of our prey. I learned about the straight back of a deer, its angled front leg while feeding, a flick of an ear in the thick bush, and the tell-tale musty smell when we were downwind. He would pause during our patrols and point, using hand signals, at pig wallows, hoof prints in the dirt, or scarred trees from stags thrashing their antlers; details I would have missed if I had been on my own. My predator senses had been dampened from being in towns and surrounded by constant technology, but they were slowly returning to life.

We had laid a few ambushes and bumped two more small groups of deer but had yet to see them before they saw us. We needed to find them while they were feeding so we could stalk in close enough for a clean kill. On the morning of day three I started to think we should have dropped the hammer on one of those hinds on day one. Then I realised that would've been too easy and wouldn't have felt like I'd earned it. I would've also missed out on three days of education from Al.

'If you ever think you hear something and want to dial in on it, open your mouth and push your jaw forward. It opens the eardrum, and you will pick up a higher definition.'

Another one of Al's pearls of wisdom during our lunch break on our final day.

'I don't remember that gem from the unit mate. Where did you learn this stuff?' I asked.

'This was on a reconnaissance course later on.'

'Roger that. So, it's the last hunt this afternoon. What's your gut telling you.'

'We will find 'em, we have put in the work and it's time to reap.' He replied before carrying on with his theory lesson.

'As you know mate movement is the easiest way to pick up game or for them to see us. If we get lucky and we start a stalk on a deer, always go straight at them. If we move laterally, they will pick up our movement easier. Keep the trees in between you and your prey and go straight. If we must get around them, we will drop back out of sight, circle around, then go straight again.'

'Roger that Al, what was that saying from infantry school about why things are seen?'

'Six sluts and a mole,' Al said without hesitation.'

I laughed, 'That's it.'

We weren't being vulgar. This well known line helped recruits remember why things were seen to avoid making mistakes that could allow the enemy to see us first. It stands for size, shape, silhouette, spacing, shadow, surface, and movement.

'It's always important to remember and apply this stuff, especially hunting areas where there could be other hunters.' Al said before continuing.

'Two brothers were out hunting this area not long ago and they split up to circle around a knoll. One brother saw movement and took a shot at what he thought was a big buck. When he walked up to where he had seen it, he saw his brother in the grass. He shot and killed him by mistake. Your eyes and desires will trick you out here. For this reason, whenever I shoot a stag, and I'm carrying out his antlers on my back through thick bush, I wrap them in a high visibility vest to ensure I don't get shot by some inexperienced weekend hunter.'

'Wow, poor bloke, that's brutal.'

'Sure is mate. This isn't a game, it's the art of killing. Now let's get back to it.'

I stood up and tipped the last of my brew into the dirt. Time seemed to have sped up out here. Three days had zipped passed in a blur, and this was the final patrol. We departed camp chambering a round in the barrel of our rifles, and then fell into a silent march. The hunt was on.

We patrolled for two hours, two highly tuned predators silently scanning every inch of the country for our prey. Three days of effort, slim rations, and camping had increased our desire for fresh meat. We traversed the same ridge we explored on our first day and by the late afternoon we stumbled upon the small wallow. On closer inspection of the mud bank surrounding it, it had been receiving a lot of traffic. We decided to set up another ambush. We pushed back up the ridge and I sat down with my back against the same ancient blue gum tree. I felt different from when I last sat in this position. It had only been 48 hours, but I had become part of my environment, in tune with nature. I was comfortable and didn't feel like an outsider anymore.

We waited in total silence as seconds ticked into minutes and an hour had passed. The sun was on its final path to setting and I was coming to terms with the reality that I would most likely not get a deer on my first hunt. This was more common than not. Each season many tags sold to hunters go unfilled, especially in the bow and backcountry hunting domains. I was disappointed but grateful to be out in the bush developing new skills. My mind wandered towards the philosophical landscape of hunting until my reverie was abruptly interrupted.

'There, see 'em?' Al said in a rushed excited whisper, breaking the silence. He had been scanning off to our left flank and was pointing up onto sloping ground towards a ridge. It took my eyes a few seconds to spot them. Two deer feeding in the recently burnt country, greedily feasting on the freshly sprouted grass shoots.

'I see them mate. Nice work. I was looking that way before and didn't pick them up,' I whispered back as my heart rate increased with excitement.

'We are on them now. How are we going to kill these bastards?' Al asked rhetorically. He looked around, his mind already calculating distance, daylight remaining, wind direction, and analysing the bush separating us from our dinner, some 200 metres away.

I lifted my rifle and put my eye to the scope, gaining a clear image of the two deer. One was big, the other about half the size, but I couldn't make out any antlers.

Al had formed a plan.

'We are going to drop down to the wallow, get out of their line of sight, circle around, then start our stalk up the slope towards them. Silent movements now. Let's go.'

Using the cover of the bush to move at a steady walking pace we descended the slope, skirted the wallow, and peeled around behind some thick lantana scrub directly below where we had last seen the deer. Slowly we began to inch our way upward. The thick dry grass underfoot was making a racket and there was no way we could get close enough with this much noise. Al led the way, pushing through a chest high barrier of lantana and, on the other side, a stroke of luck; a bushfire had cleared the path ahead. Nothing but scorched earth and fresh grass shoots remained. This meant silence.

'There they are, see?' Al asked.

'Yep got 'em mate.'

'Right, you come to the lead, I'll be right behind you. Let's start the stalk.'

I moved to the front carefully placing each foot down even though it was mainly ash. My heart was thumping like a war drum announcing the arrival of an army. I kept the deer directly ahead of me and with Al whispering directions, we leap frogged from tree to tree. Metre by metre we closed the distance between us and our prize.

'One hundred and ten metres, can you get a shot?' Al whispered after using his range finder to check the distance.

Leaning against a burnt tree for support I lifted the rifle and looked through the scope. The image bounced around with my rapid heartbeat and shaking hands. I hadn't expected to be this nervous. Hanging branches blocked a clear shot.

'No good, branches.'

'Roger, move up to the next tree.' I stepped forward, diverting my eyes to the ground for a brief second to make sure it was clear.

'Stop.' Al commanded from behind. He hadn't taken his eyes off the deer, and they looked straight at us. 'Don't move, she is watching us.'

The seconds ticked by while my heart pounded. I took a few slow deep breaths to calm myself down.

'They are feeding again, but just wait.'

I would find out later that deer were very clever. Often if they felt threatened, they would pretend to feed, then quickly look up to detect any movement. Years of evolution created behaviours to help keep them alive in a world of predators. However, I had Al, and he knew their tricks.

'Ok we are good. Keep moving mate.'

We were 35 minutes into the stalk, each slow silent step getting us closer to our prey. I felt like a starving lion creeping across the Serengeti moments from savouring a taste.

At the next tree I paused and lifted the rifle.

'Seventy yards,' Al whispered into my ear.

This was it. I clicked off the safety, ready to fire. The rifle was shaking in my hands; I wasn't calm. I tried to lock on with the scope but could not hold it steady. I brought the rifle down, clicked the safety back on and breathed deeply.

'Take your time, calm down mate.' Al whispered.

I lifted again, safety off, it's go time. I took aim, settled the crosshairs, and the deer stepped behind a big tree. I held the rifle up for a minute, waiting, but fatigue set it. I brought it down and put the safety back on.

'Wait for him to step out, follow the front leg up and place the round at the top of the shoulder and a tiny bit back.' Al's guidance had a calming influence. I lifted the rifle again, safety off.

The deer was clear in the scope, and I watched him nibble the grass, inching his way out from behind the tree. I waited. He took one step, then another; his front leg was held before him. Up from the ground, I followed the line of his lower leg with the crosshairs, found the shoulder, and then let out a slow breath as I eased pressure onto the trigger. At the bottom of my breath, at a point of calm, I pulled the trigger.

The explosion of noise hauled nature into the modern world shattering the silence. Dirt kicked up behind the deer and I watched them bolt down the slope at full gallop. I thought instantly that I had missed it. I must have been shaking too much and botched the shot. Al thought the same.

The deer stopped directly in front of us, only 30 metres away. We were still shielded from view by a few smaller trees, and they didn't quite know where or what we were. We had seconds to make a call.

'Go again mate, pick either one,' Al's command from behind me confirmed my missed shot. I aimed again, this time at the bigger one, an impossible shot to miss. I pulled the trigger. The round struck hard and on the mark. The big hind trotted 10 metres before dropping dead. The bullet had ripped through her lungs and heart, causing a quick kill. As the cloud of dust puffed up from where she fell, the first deer I had shot at also dropped dead. I was confused. Then it all dawned on me. The first bullet I fired hit the deer, but it struck low in the lungs and missed the heart. This was why he hadn't dropped by the time I chose to take the second shot.

'Shit mate, I didn't miss the first one, I have killed them both.' I turned to Al.

'That's alright mate, good job.'

The magnitude of the moment had caught me off guard, or maybe I had dust in my eye, and tears began to form. The adrenalin was pumping through my veins and mixed emotions of joy and devastation took over. On the one hand we succeeded and earned our kill the hard way. On the other I had taken two lives when we only required one. I removed the magazine, unloaded my rifle, then turned to Al and grabbed him by the shoulder.

'That's one of the most exciting things I have ever done mate. Thank you so much.'

'My pleasure mate, that was great.'

Al knew exactly how I was feeling. He had been in my position many times before. His misty eyes gave away his own emotions. Here we were, two hard army blokes deep in the wilderness sharing a special moment.

We walked over to the deer. I knelt beside them and patted their dusty fur. The smaller one was a male, maybe 18 months old.

'He will be great eating.' Al spoke at full volume again.

The bigger one was an old hind around four or five years old.

'She won't be as good, but we should get as much meat off her as we can. The easy part is done and because you shot two, we have some bloody work to do.' Al looked at me with a grin.

'Yeah, I was feeling hungry so thought we better get them both,' I replied.

'Not much daylight left so let's get a couple of photos and get to it, it's time to harvest.'

A wild animal's life could end in a few different ways. It could reach old age, lose all its teeth, and then slowly starve to death, dying alone in the bush a withered shell of its former self. It could be cornered and torn up by dingos, or it could be injured fighting and be set upon by wild boars, dying a horrendous death of being eaten alive. Or while feeding one perfect afternoon on fresh grass shoots, out of nowhere, a high-velocity projectile could obliterate its vital organs, and it dies within seconds, to then be respectfully quartered and carried home to feed a village.

We dragged both deer close together, laid out a plastic sheet for the meat, and then Al pulled out his roll of knives and went to work. Step by step he talked me through the process. First, he removed the skin to expose the dark red meat underneath while leaving the stomach intact. He expertly carved off the back legs, handing them to me one by one, followed by the back straps, a choice cut of meat attached to the top of the spine. Then the tenderloins, a smaller cut located inside the body cavity underneath the vertebrae. The last job was to fish out the heart which had been destroyed in one of the deer but was intact in the young male.

Eating the heart of a freshly killed animal was a tradition shared by many Native American tribes. They believed that by eating the heart they would inherit the qualities of the animal – bravery, strength, and agility. Although I didn't ascribe to this belief, I knew the high nutrient value of heart meat and was looking forward to devouring it. I placed the warm flesh inside cotton bags, and we loaded as much as possible into our patrol packs, the back legs to be carried by hand. We estimated we were taking 30 kilograms of prime cuts; the remaining carcass would be consumed by nature over hours, days, and weeks. Eventually, the bones would be absorbed into the soil and disappear. Much like we all would in our final resting place.

That night I had slept the sleep of the content. At dawn the following morning, we humped down from the hill with full loads and upon reaching the canoe, changed into our civilian clothes. We slid into the water, and the purr of the electric outboard sounded our extraction. When we nudged the boat ramp, we were two fishermen returning with no fish, and our old mate Greg awaited us.

'What the bloody hell have you blokes been eating the last three days?' he asked with a big smile. Before we could answer, he followed up with, 'Did you get some meat?'

'Yeah mate we got two.' Al replied shaking his hand.

'Good on ya's, I tell ya what ya's do it the hard way, but the right way.'

That night back at Al's home in Brisbane, we had cleaned rifles, sorted gear, enjoyed a much needed shower, and sat around with a glass of whisky. The BBQ smoker beside me was puffing away, smelling incredible, full of freshly harvested deer, heart included. I thought over Greg's parting words. We had done it the hard way, earned it, and in the process, I learned valuable skills and found a new respect for wild animals.

Although methods have changed throughout human evolution, the act of men and women venturing into the wild to harvest meat will forever be part of who we are. Al pulled the heart from the smoker, sliced it on a wooden board in front of me and handed me a juicy morsel. I placed it into my mouth. Whether it was the agility of the deer entering my system or the fat, salt, and richness of the meat, it was delicious. The reviews were correct; deer is by far the best game meat I have ever eaten. Karen and Al's son joined us for the feast of vegetables and wild game, and through a mouthful of backstrap, Al tried to talk.

'So, mate, we are off to Namibia next year for a hunt, a big game reserve managed by good people. They have a cull list every year. Want to tag along?'

I lifted my head while chewing the most tender tenderloin and my newfound hunter's instinct kicked in. In a second my mind flashed back over the last three days, then jumped forward to the imagined possibilities of Africa. Before I could swallow, I smiled, then nodded; I was in.

CHAPTER 10

A River Runs Free

At the bottom of Australia, across a narrow stretch of frigid water, is my island home of Tasmania. On this island's western interior grows an ancient forest where harsh weather and inhospitable wilderness have repelled permanent settlement. A vein winds through this rugged landscape, a river with a unique history. It carries a story of protest, profit, and politics, and one that culminates in a victory allowing one river to run free. Today as I type these words, every sizable river in Tasmania has been dammed for hydroelectricity, except one. How did a single remote stretch of water remain untouched? How did a community come together to halt its destruction, defending the natural world for future generations? I will take you on a raft along this river and through the history books so you can understand the power of this victory. It is much bigger than water, trees, or money; this is the story of the Franklin.

◆◆◆

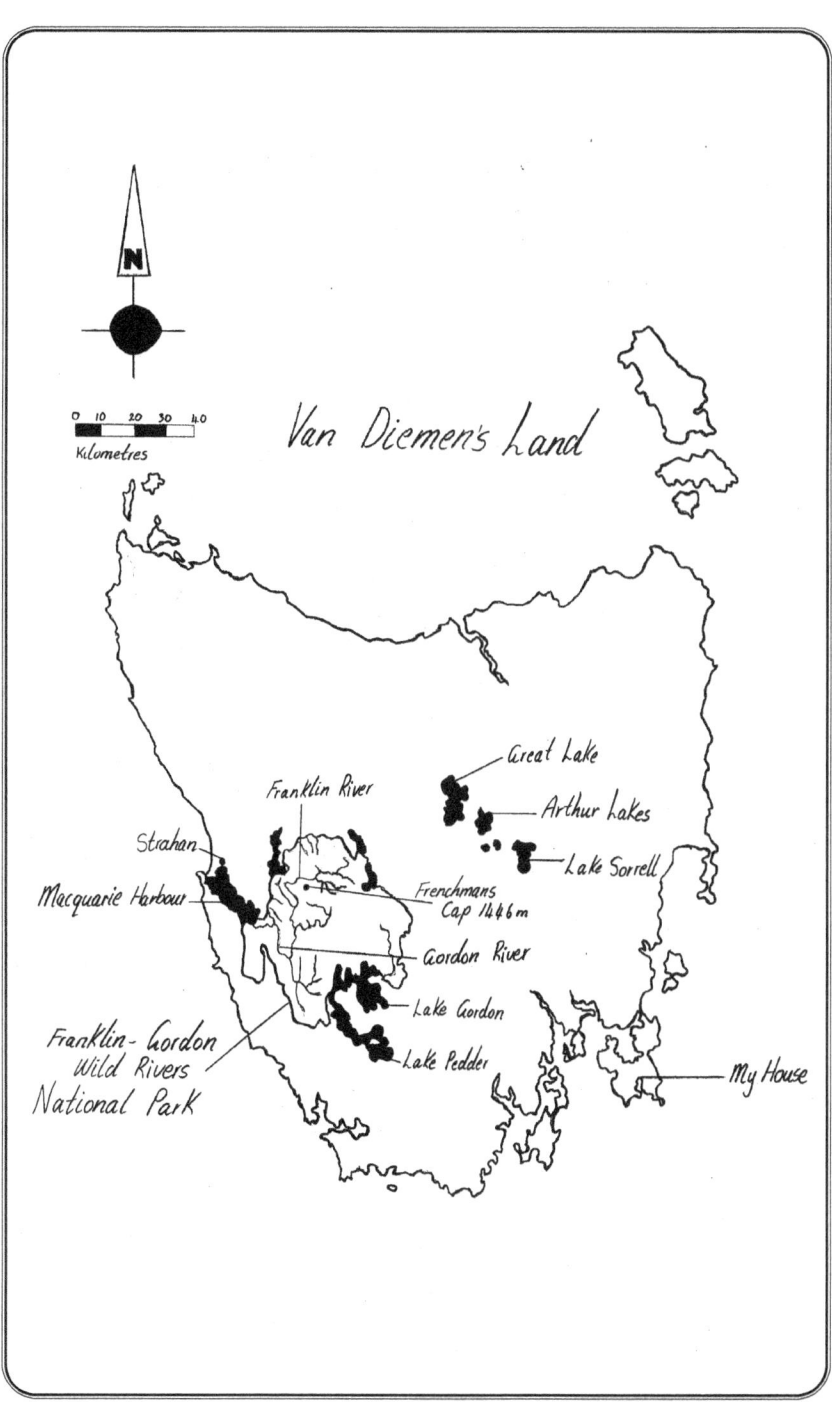

I first read about the Franklin River in a Lonely Planet guidebook that highlighted an activity to do every day of the year from various countries worldwide. On one of the pages under a heading for a must do trip was rafting the Franklin River. I immediately logged into Google Earth to find its location.

Stretching for 129 kilometres the river has its catchments in Tasmania's Central Highlands and western regions. It is located inside the Franklin-Gordon Wild Rivers National Park and is part of the Tasmanian Wilderness World Heritage Area. It was named after Sir John Franklin, a British Royal Navy officer and Arctic explorer, who, after serving in wars against Napoleonic France and the United States, led two expeditions to explore the Arctic Archipelago in 1819 and 1825. He served as Lieutenant-Governor of Van Diemen's Land from 1839 to 1843 before he set off on his third expedition, an attempt to traverse the Northwest Passage in 1845. His ship became trapped in ice off King William Sound, where he tragically died in June of 1847.

During the 1970s and 80s, Tasmania was in a hydroelectricity boom period, with every natural flowing resource seen as an untapped energy stream for the state and an export commodity to the mainland. The Franklin proposal for damming in 1978 was the plan that broke the camel's back. Local Tasmanians had endured enough from the push of progress at the cost of the natural world, and they started to assemble. The Tasmanian Wilderness Society under Bob Brown, initiated the call to action. What at first to the Government must have sounded like a murmur of dissent by a small portion of society quickly turned into an avalanche of opposition. The battle of a generation had begun, one the Tasmanian politicians were unprepared for.

By June 1980, the 'No Dams' movement was gathering steam, and over 10000 people marched through the streets of Hobart in opposition to the proposal. To appease the growing dissent, the State Government under Premier Doug Lowe agreed to place the Franklin River in a new Wild Rivers National Park. The construction plans were altered to move the proposed dam wall further up the Gordon River, preserving the Franklin. However, the impact on the region would still be immense, and the growing opposition moved towards greater interference. The political sleight of hand to appease the protestors in the southern state sparked the interest of Australian Democrats Senator Don Chipp, who called a senate inquiry in 1981 into,

> 'The natural values of South-West Tasmania to Australia and the world,' and 'the federal responsibility in assisting Tasmania to preserve its wilderness areas of national and international importance.'

The rest of the country was beginning to pay attention. I knew next to nothing about the river's history or whitewater rafting. I had dabbled in some tourist paddle days on the Zambezi and Nile rivers in Africa and splashed about in some flat water in Nepal. However, from what I read online, the Franklin was the real deal. It was 90 per cent grade two and three rapids, with ten per cent of the navigable river being grade four. Also, depending on the water level, these could change to grade five, the highest navigable grade. The whitewater grading system outlines grade four rapid as:

> 'Difficult rapids that have powerful irregular waves, broken water, often boiling or strongly recirculating eddies, strong powerful hydraulics, ledges, drops and dangerous exposed rocks. The passage is often difficult to recognise, and precise sequential manoeuvring is required.'

When I read the above words for the first time and didn't understand most of the terms, I knew I would need some assistance. As I often do with my projects, I started researching and contacted local professionals who could show me the way. I found a small family operated rafting company in Hobart called Water by Nature, owned by Brett and Klaudia. Brett had been leading trips down the Franklin for over 20 years and was the specialist I was looking for. I emailed him and booked myself and Elise onto one of their seven day trips; we were in.

We drove up to Hobart from Port Arthur and arrived at Brett's house, on the slope of Mt Wellington (Kunanyi) at around 7 a.m. He was busy loading a trailer as the other team members arrived. Brett was older than I expected; I estimated early 60s, but it was hard to tell. He was lean, tall and void of excess fat. He paused to say a quick hello before returning to the task of loading. I had spoken to him on the phone a few times before the trip to learn more about the river and what to bring, and what he lacked in pleasantries and social banter, he made up for with his eccentric, professor like knowledge of the river. Talking to Brett and watching him operate that morning, I realised we might have found our version of John Nash from the Pulitzer Prize nominated book 'A Beautiful Mind,' but instead of a mathematical genius, we had a master of white water.

The first teammates we met were Jess and Nicko, a young local couple who worked as rangers on the Three Capes Track on the Tasman Peninsula. They were both fit and had prior experience in kayaks and rafts. Sarah and Gill were Jess's sister and mum; I then met Richard and Martin, Nicko's brother and dad. It was turning into quite a family adventure. Along with Brett our expedition leader, Dan and Emily were the two other rafting guides. Both spoke little and fell into a routine with Brett loading the supplies. We would have plenty of time to get to know each other.

A bus arrived, reversed onto the trailer, and it was time to go. We piled in with no departure briefing, team welcome, or pleasantries, and the bus pulled away. This was my first expedition in a long time where I wasn't completely in control of the process, and I was anxious about how it began. We picked up our last three members as we passed through the quiet streets of Hobart. The first was Dushon, a middle-aged tiler from Sydney who had been gifted a rafting trip down the Franklin for his birthday from his wife. He was waiting on the corner as we pulled up. Standing on the next street was Alexis, a young freelance writer who immediately reminded me of Bill Bryson with his big black beard and glasses. He was writing an article for the Guardian about the trip, and I made a mental note to be on my best behaviour. Jarrod, an engineer from Melbourne, was our last pickup who had wanted to raft the

Franklin for most of his adult life and had finally made the time. With the team all aboard, the bus broke free of the city, then the suburbs, and we were off heading northwest towards the river.

Our route followed the Derwent River north from Hobart towards the west coast, where the picturesque countryside evolved from sheep pastures and agriculture to native bushland and rolling hills. Four hours after departing, with 200 kilometres of winding roads and steep inclines behind us, we passed by the Frenchman's Cap trailhead, one of my all time favourite trails. We pulled up shortly afterwards at the Collingwood River. In rafting and paddling vernacular, the 'put in' was where one began their paddle. Our put in was on the Collingwood, a tributary flowing into the upper Franklin.

The bus halted on a gravel road adjacent to the river, and Brett was out the door first and off to the Collingwood to check the water level and make his plan. The rest of us began unloading the gear, which included a half dozen blue barrels full of food, eskies containing cold supplies, two inflatable kayaks, and three rolled up red rafts. We set to work with pumps and inflated our transport for the following week. Once done, we changed into Michelin Man sized wetsuits, lifejackets, and helmets, while Brett prepared a small buffet lunch beside the water. I devoured fresh sandwiches, fruit, and a generous portion of sugar rich pavlova, filling my muscles with glucose for the approaching afternoon of exertion.

After fuelling up, we received a five minute safety briefing from Dan, which from what I could gather, encompassed 'don't fall out or you will die.' From reading between the lines and watching the guides work, I could gather his nonchalant delivery regarding safety was backed up by Brett's behind the scenes planning and years of experience. With little knowledge about what I was getting myself into, Elise and I set off first in the two inflatable kayaks. The rest of the team was divided into three groups, split up with the three guides, and we all shoved off into the flow.

◆◆◆

In 1981, while a senate enquiry into Tasmania's wilderness value was taking place, a paddler named Kevin Keirnan discovered some caves on the lower Franklin that early Aboriginal Australians had utilised. Hand stencils, stone tools, and remnants of campfires were found and were carbon dated 8000 to 24,000 years old. At the same time, concerns about habitat loss for endangered species were raised. However, the new Liberal Government elected in 1982 was all for the Franklin River dam. The new premier Robin Gray declared openly, 'The Franklin River is nothing but a brown ditch, leech ridden, and unattractive to the majority of people.' The fight to save the river was far from over.

◆◆◆

The kayaks were nimble little crafts, and apart from the awkward sitting position, they were fun to paddle. We sat low to the water, increasing the feeling of speed through the shallow river sections. I could feel the water's freezing bite through the kayak's thin skin, and its colour of tea was due to the natural tannins of the button grass plains in the river's catchment. I scooped some into my hand and sloshed it over my face and into my mouth. It was cool and refreshing. I had no concerns about drinking the water; this remote region, void of humans and cattle grazing, was pristine and as pure as it comes. I looked up from the water and into the surrounding forest. It was dense, lush, and primitive. I had done my fair share of challenging treks and jungle work, and while gazing into the sheer thickness and structure of the surrounding wilderness, I was glad to be on the water. Travelling overland and off trail through this country would be near impossible.

My first grade two rapids looked like no more than a trickle of water flowing over a rock formation ahead of me. The calm water channelled into a downriver triangle before disappearing over an edge. I could hear the churning water on the other side, and I looked up to Brett in the leading raft, who was pointing at the line I needed to take. He had guided over 250 trips on this river, and I followed his instruction, positioned myself correctly, and felt the pull of the rapid take over. I was carried over the small drop and spat out on the other side. It was a little disconcerting not to be in total control of my kayak and be at the whim of the powerful water, but after a few more rapids, it felt amazing. Each rapid had an ideal sequence to navigate it efficiently and safely. This didn't mean that's what I did each time, I botched every second one, but the grade two and three rapids were forgiving. Even when I went over completely backwards, I made it through unscathed. However, the higher grades downriver would be a different story.

The rafting crews were having a tough time. The Collingwood's water level was low, and they were forced to get out and drag the boats across shallow sections. The fully loaded rafts weighed a few hundred kilograms each and were not easily shifted when stuck on rocks. On the other hand, our kayaks quickly traversed the low rapids, and at one point, I beached my boat and jumped out to help Brett's crew get over a tough spot. It was apparent early on that we needed to be physically fit to complete this trip. Dragging the boats, paddling, and walking across wet, slippery boulder fields was not for those recently rising from the couch. I instantly respected Martin and Gill, our two oldest members, who were mixing in and doing their share of the work.

I felt lazy by the time we pulled up onto a sandbar for a snack break at the confluence of the Collingwood and Franklin Rivers a few hours after setting off. Elise and I had enjoyed a leisurely paddle through the shallows in the kayaks, and it was time to change and do some work in the rafts. Nicko and Jess took over from us, and we piled in with Brett. 'Forward paddle thanks,' came the command. Brett was sitting in the centre rear of the raft, guiding the direction with his paddle.

'Left paddle, right paddle, stop, left back,' orders from Brett were coming thick and fast as we dropped down through a series of rapids at a place known as Gordian Gate. I was sitting on the front right position, perched on top of the outer tube, with my feet jammed in underneath the front and rear tubes for support. I was slightly twisted, which made it hard to generate bursts of force through the paddles.

Brett stood and scanned the way ahead; I could hear the rumble of white water that was still a fair way off. 'The next one is Boulder Brace, should be enough water to make it through,' announced Brett in a nonchalant manner. 'Forward paddle thanks.' The three of us pulled at the water together and eased into the faster flow. The river narrowed and was squeezed in on both sides by large boulders, earning its name through obvious geology. Our speed increased as we entered the point of no return. 'Get Down!' came the command. We dropped ourselves into the bottom of the raft with oars and helmets clashing together. Brett remained seated in the rear and guided us through using his paddle as a rudder. 'Hold on, bump,' was the last order I heard before we impacted a large boulder in the centre of the flow. The raft was forced up against the sheer western wall, down a narrow sluice, and over a drop where we spun around and stopped in a whirling eddy; we were soaked through yet smiling.

With calm confidence, Brett guided us throughout the afternoon and pulled up alongside a small pebble beach surrounded by rock walls. 'This is us for the night guys; well done.' I looked at the bank where an enormous cliff loomed over the river. Its detail was obscured by thick vegetation. On most expeditions, I searched for a flat section of ground to erect a tent; this was not an option on the Franklin. The ground was steep, dense with trees and undergrowth, and had water seeping down the cliff face. The other two rafts tied up next to us, and Emily spoke up. 'There are plenty of ledges up on the cliff to sleep guys. This is a great spot to be if it rains overnight.'

A light sprinkle started to pepper the river's surface as if on cue, encouraging us to unload the rafts as quickly as possible and find some good shelter. With Emily leading the way, Elise and I climbed up the rock face and around to the north. She showed us two narrow ledges ten metres off the ground that were dry and semi-flat; this would be our bed for the night. 'Welcome to Angel Rain Cavern,' Emily said before turning away to go and help settle the rest of the team. This campsite is a favourite for the rafters due to its shelter from the rain and height above the river.

While on the raft, my feet were constantly submerged in icy Franklin water, and I had lost feeling in them for most of the afternoon. My first action while nestled on my sparrow's ledge was to strip off my helmet, life vest, and wetsuit, hang them in a tree for later and get changed into thick warm socks and dry clothes.

Unlike the high mountains where losing sensation in my feet was a big issue and could set me on a course to frostbite, this time was not as serious, and the feeling returned within 30 minutes. I sat on the cave's ledge with Elise, sipping a hot brew, as the slightly painful sensation of blood flowing back into my toes was a welcome relief. Brett was down below us, already cooking up a storm, and as the rain started to fall, our first day on the Franklin ended. It had been sensory overload in a new environment, and apart from the slight unease about not being in control of everything, I felt grateful for the experience.

◆◆◆

By the end of 1981, the 'No Dams' campaign was gaining national coverage, and the Federal Government under Malcolm Fraser offered Gray's Tasmanian government $500 million to stop the project. Gray refused the offer, and Fraser declined any further action, stating in the press that the dam was a state matter. Protests ramped up in 1982 with people like Bob Brown, David Bellamy and Dick Smith speaking out nationally, and in December of that same year the Democrats 'World Heritage Protection Bill' passed through the Australian Senate. This gave power to the Governor General to issue proclamations for particular places. The same week of the Bill's passing, the World Heritage Commission accepted the nomination of Tasmania's Southwest Wilderness for heritage listing, and a blockade of the dam construction site began. At Warners Corner on the Franklin River, 2500 people from Tasmania, interstate, and overseas arrived, and the time for talk was over.

◆ ◆ ◆

Back on the ledge, the rain increased overnight, and I was woken by the sound of water ricocheting off the thick forest canopy around us. As dawn broke, I opened my eyes to see that our little cave had become a waterfall, and we were sleeping behind the curtain. I was warm and comfortable in my sleeping bag and delayed rising, choosing to lay in silence and watch the natural world come into focus. Eventually I sat up, boiled some water, and on my dry ledge with a cup of coffee in hand I looked around and noticed the river had risen overnight. It was rumbling past below us with more energy than the previous afternoon. I watched cold droplets fall from my treebound wetsuit and clothes and wasn't overly excited about pulling them back on. 'Breakfast,' Brett yelled, his voice echoing along the cliff and caves. If Brett yelled in the forest did anyone hear it? They certainly did; I watched my teammates climb down from the ledges, out of the burrows, and move towards the smell of bacon and eggs.

Emily sat beside me at breakfast. 'How's the river look?' I asked.

'It's come up overnight, and a general rule of river paddling is to never get on a rising river if it's still raining,' she replied.

Brett put another pot of water on the boil before walking out into the rain and checking the river. He returned quickly. 'We will be resting today guys. The rain is forecast to stop this afternoon, and we will carry on tomorrow.'

After breakfast, I needed to complete the rest of my morning routine. Due to strict policies on the river to help maintain the natural environment for everyone and avoid pollution, all human waste except urine was captured and carried out with the rafting teams. This was a similar policy we stuck to in mountaineering. The simple procedure involved using plastic sandwich sized freezer bags to make deposits. This was then bagged into a larger garbage bag and placed inside a blue drum labelled 'toilet.' The target was a thin plastic bullseye, 1/10th the size of your standard home toilet. A small tip for amateurs is to empty your bladder first. This for men, avoids the run-away garden hose effect during a delicate manoeuvre. As with any new task, practice will make perfect, and it was a great habit to get comfortable with because it helped preserve the beauty of these unique places for future generations.

A day of rest entailed reading in the comfort of my sleeping bag and returning to the trough for food whenever Brett rang the bell. The rain eased off by late afternoon, and the forecast for the following day looked good.

During mealtimes, I got to know my teammates a little better. Dan was a quiet guy and had guided professionally for over five years. He bounced around between Australia, Canada, and New Zealand linking up the different rafting seasons, and during the time in between, he was a personal trainer. Emily followed a similar path; she lived in her van to save money while in guiding season and was excited to learn the intricacies of the Franklin River from Brett.

Alexis, our Australian Bill Bryson, was a professional writer and had an inquisitive nature suited to his chosen career; he was busy making notes at every opportunity. Jess and Nicko, our two rangers from the Three Capes Track, were in their element. They could recite from memory the names and history of every plant, creek, or rocky outcrop that surrounded us. Richard and Martin were father and son and both doctors, always a welcome addition on expeditions. Richard was enjoying the journey, and Martin, although much older than us, was handling the conditions well. I watched him fall and take a superb hit from a rock on the first day, which he shook off like a rugby player. Jarrod, the engineer was slightly more reserved than the rest of the team. He had dreamt of this trip for ten years and seemed to be loving every moment. Dushon, our builder from Sydney, had worked hard his whole life to provide for his wife and two daughters, and was proud to own a lovely terraced house in the luxurious Surrey Hills close to the city.

Gill, Jess's mum, kept busy helping Brett by collecting water from the river for dinner, and her daughter Sarah seemed as comfortable as the rest of the family in the outdoors. The two sisters had synchronised high pitched laughter, and it was near impossible not to laugh along with them when they erupted.

'How old is Brett?' I asked Dan during dessert as I watched Brett fuss about in his river kitchen, his long grey hair a tangled mess.

'Who knows mate, the Wizard could be 100 for all we know,' he replied.

'Why do you call him the Wizard?'

'Well apart from looking like Gandalf from Lord of the Rings, he seems to be able to get through the craziest rapids with ease. The rest of us would get pulverised while he used his magic.'

The wizard stood up after dinner, looked up at the sky, and then out to the brown river now hidden in the dark. Its soft thundering could be heard clearly, and Brett seemed to be breathing in its power. His mind no doubt weighing up the conditions against his lifetime of experience.

'Early start tomorrow, big day, get some rest,' he said.

Brett was a man of few words, and usually not knowing all the information myself would concern me; however, I could let it pass if he had his magic while I was with him. We dispersed to our allocated burrows and slept.

My wet suit was cold against my skin as I pulled it on the next morning. It barely dried during our rest day, and it would be soaking again soon. Once dressed, I stepped into the organised chaos of loading the rafts and took orders from Dan as we packed the barrels, bags, and bodies. Once ready, we split into teams and climbed aboard. Elise and I jumped in with Dan, and with his command of 'Push off, forward paddle,' we were away.

The water height was up after the constant rain from the day before, but it was no longer rising. We skimmed across areas of boulders, which Dan told us were a difficult portage if the water was slightly lower; he seemed grateful to avoid the heavy lifting. My feet were cold in minutes and numb shortly after the first small rapids. I had grown accustomed to the feeling, and it no longer concerned me. The wild beauty of the river made up for the discomfort tenfold.

Our first official portage at a rapid named Log Jam arrived shortly after leaving camp. As its title suggested, it is an enormous log wedged across the river's width and is impassable. We slowed the rafts and banked them one at a time on the left side of the river. We were ordered out and tentatively shuffled along the slippery rock bank to the downriver side of the jam. One by one the rafts were floated over the log, down the face of the waterfall, and into the cauldron of whitewater, to be spat out the other side with ease. It didn't look dangerous to my untrained eyes until we climbed back in, and Dan mentioned, 'If a person goes into that mess they are not coming out.' You don't know what you don't know, never felt more relevant.

Stretches of calm slow moving water broke up the excitement of the big rapids and heavy portages. During these quiet periods, I could take in all the incredible detail of my surroundings. The water spiralled and bifurcated off rocks around us, an unseen force creating stunning patterns on the surface. It was squeezed and pressurised through narrow channels amongst the boulders, its anti-fragile structure getting more robust during the process. It could carve through the rocks if it had the patience and time, or it could nourish an infant when consumed.

The malleable yet unyielding composition of the water was an excellent metaphor for life. Should I be more like the water? Or the land on which it travels? Am I the force that flows, impervious to perturbation and the stresses of life, through obstacles or around them, giving life and sometimes claiming it before reaching my chosen destination in the same state? Or am I the land, to be shaped over time, learning to work with the brutality and softness of life, to be left alone and unchanged for many years, then carved up and scarred in others? As the foundation, I would last as long if not longer than water; but which am I? Or is there another option? Could I be human? A freak evolution of the universe, an organism evolved to be the most powerful species in our known history, who could shape the land, and capture the water at whim, and who sometimes chose to float along on its surface and contemplate his place amongst it all. A species easily broken, yet hard to change, a vulnerable bag of meat and bones that could create machines powerful enough to destroy a planet. An organism that loves and kills and could be kind or evil, a complex adaptive nervous system constantly evolving to a changing environment.

The deep rumble of the next rapid brought me back to reality and at that moment, I realised a simple truth. I am human, and I am alive. I could use the metaphors of water and land to help me navigate my inadequacies and perceptions, and in so doing, I would find a new respect and understanding for the power of nature.

'Forward paddle.' It was time to get back to work.

We entered the middle section of the Franklin by late afternoon, close to Frenchman's Cap, a unique Tasmanian mountain with a 400 metre sheer cliff face on one side, and tranquil lakes on the other. The trail from the highway to the mountain and back is one of my favourite multi-day Tasmanian hikes. The last time we visited the peak, we were met by a rafting team who had hiked up from the river. They were all shell shocked and seven of them were extracted via helicopter. They had decided to attempt a rapid that should have been portaged and almost lost their lives. They were escaping with crushed ribs and broken bones. Their equipment was lost, and the remaining crew had chosen to hike back along the Frenchman's Cap trail to the highway.

We pulled over towards the bank at a spot where the rafters most likely camped before they began their hike up to Frenchman's to self-rescue.

'This is Dean and Hawkins Camp, our spot for the night,' Dan called out as he started to untie straps and throw out bags. The bank was supported by fallen logs, becoming a natural staircase as we unloaded the supplies. Further in, the lush rainforest took over, with ferns, mosses and fungi growing in abundance. Small cleared areas between the dense forest were evidence of many seasons of rafters camping here. However, the companies' discipline and methods for protecting the surrounding environment were also evident. There was no rubbish and no unnecessary destruction of surrounding vegetation. We could blend in and set up our tents for the night, to depart again, leaving no further trace.

I tied off our small hiking tent to a tree, and then noticed an old metal plaque had been secured to its trunk. On the plaque were the names of Johnson Dean and John Hawkins, two early pioneers who navigated the entire length of the Franklin in 1958. These early explorers had taken three attempts to conquer the river, the first in 1952, the second in January 1958, and the third at the end of the same year in December 1958. Hawkins couldn't even swim, and their harrowing expeditions are legendary. Dean's book, Shooting the Franklin, highlights this early period of whitewater adventure in Tasmania. Below is a quote from Dean capturing a moment from their last campaign.

> *'In the next few minutes, we lived a lifetime...We began a terrifying race backwards down the rushing rapids of the gorge. We were powerless. All we could do was keep the bow pointing upstream as we raced madly downriver, lurching over waterfalls in sickening swoops...I was in the stern and remember seeing Dean rise several feet above me as we lunged over each fall, the canoe standing almost vertically, as I was engulfed in icy waters. It was a miracle that we weren't smashed at the foot of one of the falls.'*

Reading his words, I could relate in some small way. I have been on other expeditions where life and death had hung in the balance. However, we were on a five star luxury vacation compared to their Franklin adventures.

I woke on day four after a solid sleep and a clear night. No rain meant we would leave after breakfast, and with the first rays of sun reflecting off the misty river, I pulled on my cold soaking wetsuit, ready for another big day. With the spirit of Dean and Hawkins leading the way, we climbed aboard with Emily and pushed off once more.

Almost immediately, grade three and four rapids came thick and fast, dotted together with lower grades and fast flowing sections of water. We had entered an area named the Great Ravine and a rapid known as The Churn. This formidable obstacle was a must portage. Under strict instruction from the guides, we endured a portage over a small peak, transporting every kilogram of gear on our backs, through dense bush and over slippery rocks. At the same time, the rafts were stacked three high atop each other, roped together and sent through the pounding rapids to emerge downstream intact.

It had been our most physical morning of the trip, and by the time our lunch break arrived, I was ready for some calories. My feet were numb again, which no amount of star jumps or running on the spot could bring back to life. After devouring every delicious morsel Brett had laid out for us, we were ready to push on, and Brett seemed motivated to cover as much of the river as possible while the conditions were good. To use Brett's words, the afternoon evolved into, 'One of the best days of rafting anywhere in the world.'

The scenery was primal, with flat river giving way to narrow gorges and violent rapids. From a drop off into a sieve of logs that could drown us in seconds, to a calm back eddy with a sandy beach like the cover of a travel guide. The nature around us was timeless; I could have been a human from any past generation, and this environment would have looked the same, and have been just as unforgiving. A few remaining ancient Huon pines were dotted along the shores. This unique tree had been a sought after commodity; the ones we floated past were overlooked due to their deformities. Their knotted branches and bent trunks were a carpenter's nightmare, which became the trees own saving grace during the early logging periods.

We made it to a grade five rapid and usually another portage. However, this time the guides opted to take the rafts through with just two paddlers each. Emily had never guided this rapid before and looked as nervous as we were. Once on board, she swallowed the nerves, took the lead, and followed Brett's line. Navigating a grade five rapid as a paddler is relatively easy. Once committed, we waited for Emily's command of 'Get down.' Elise and I threw ourselves to the bottom of the raft and hung on for dear life. We dropped over what seemed like the edge of the world, and the boat was filled with water as the roar of the rapid drowned out all else. The raft relieved itself of the burden while Emily corrected our heading and steered us through like a pro. Clear of danger, she let out a scream of excitement and relief, associated with the unbridled joy that only comes after overcoming something you had been afraid of. Full of blissful ignorance of the dangers, I hadn't realised I should have been more terrified.

All day the river had been an adrenaline explosion. I was riding the highs and lows of my hormones as rapids named The Forceit, Side Winder, The Cauldron, Thunderush, The Sanctum, and Deliverance Reach, came at us one after the other. It was a Tolkien novel of names, and each one excited and scared me equally.

'This is Newlands Cascade guys, last big one for the day, forward paddle.' We tightened up and followed Emily's command. With expert precision, she angled us through the beast, where we were slammed against boulders and soaked through to our cores, yet emerged unharmed. As we cleared the carnage, we noticed Brett was swimming back to his boat crew. He alone had fallen out. Even the best in the business can get caught out sometimes. We pulled into an eddy and up against a rock wall.

'Welcome to Newlands camp.' Brett said. 'Well done today, big day.'

With Brett's few words of encouragement, we fell into our roles, unloaded the rafts, and carried the gear over to the cliff. Huge ledges had been created by flood erosion whenever the river had peaked, leaving lovely dry shelves for us to sleep on or under. It had been eight hours of rafting, and 40 kilometres travelled, one of the best days on a river I have ever had.

◆ ◆ ◆

By January 1983, 50 people per day were arriving at the newly erected blockade on the river. The Government made things difficult for the protesters by passing laws and enforcing tight bail conditions for those arrested. This did little to dampen the opposition, and when bulldozers arrived at the dam site, 1217 arrests were made, including prominent local figures David Bellamy and Bob Brown. The following month 20,000 people attended a rally in Hobart against the dam, and in March 231 people were arrested from a flotilla of boats on the Gordon River. Momentum was building, but national traction needed to catch up. It would take the power of a single picture to launch the river into the mind of the greater public.

◆◆◆

I woke up early, staring at the roof of my narrow cave six inches above my face. The ground under my sleeping mat had been compacted by the hundreds of people who had slept here before me. There more than likely could have been a convict or logger from the early days of colonisation who had slept on this very spot. He would have made a small fire, started his day with a billy tea, and then headed off along the wild banks in search of his daily wages or family fortune.

We had covered such a large stretch of river the day before that Brett called a rest day. Newlands camp was safe, dry, and a great place to spend time and recover. I wasn't complaining; my body was stiff and sore from paddling and dragging the rafts. It didn't matter how much training I had put in at the gym; nature's unpredictable demands always took a toll. Twisting and stretching me in ways that were hard to replicate in the gym, nature forced my muscles to work in new ways, tearing the fibres and making me groan as I crawled out of my convict cocoon.

After breakfast, we took a short hike upriver along the shore to stretch our weary legs, bringing us to the iconic Rock Island Bend. This remote corner of the river, where the water forks around an island of rock at its centre was a pivotal tool in winning over the hearts and minds of the nation many years ago. The natural pillar supports a small forest of tree life that clings to its summit and has stood its ground against thousands of years of floods and flow. Deep channels had been carved around its base where the water was halted and rerouted, and the eddies on the surface had collected foam from upstream rapids creating patterns and swirls that are constantly changing like a perpetual work of art.

◆◆◆

Peter Dombrovski, an Australian photographer known for his Tasmanian scenes, took a photo of Rock Island Bend in 1983, which became a front page image in Australian newspapers during the build up to a critical 1983 Federal Election. Saving the river needed a change in the Federal Government, and the caption under the striking picture read, 'Could you vote for a party that would destroy this?' It was nature propaganda in all its beauty, and it worked.

The Australian Labor Party, under Bob Hawke, won the election. One of his first actions was to pass regulations prohibiting Franklin River dam related clearing, excavation, and building activities that the Tasmanian state legislation had authorised. The Tasmanian Government chose to ignore these new regulations and continued to work on the dam prompting the Federal Government to take the case before the high court in May 1983. For two months the lawyers did what lawyers do until finally, the judge ruled in favour of the Federal Government, and the environment.

◆◆◆

I woke at 2 a.m. on day six. My belly was swollen and grumbling, and I had that dreaded realisation that I was about to explode into my pants. I was a long way from the designated toilet area, and I quickly tried to extract myself from my sleeping bag, smashing my head on the rock above me. I grabbed a plastic bag, and with no time to make it to the toilet area, I squatted down hastily, and erupted into the tiny receptacle. I filled one bag, then another, and then I filled three more over the following few hours until dawn. I hadn't had a bout of diarrhoea this bad since India, and I couldn't figure out where it had come from. Most likely the communal water bucket and someone's poor toilet hygiene, but who knows. I felt rough, and when Elise woke to see my depleted self, looking gaunt, drained, and sitting on a rock nearby, she asked:

'You ok? You don't look great.'

'Not the best, been up half the night with the trots, I'll be right though, one more day on the water.'

I couldn't stomach any breakfast, but I was thankful the cramps had passed, and I wouldn't need any more plastic bags once we were in the raft. Brett announced breakfast minutes after dawn, and the camp came alive with activity. I stayed clear of the kitchen, not wanting to share my contagion, and packed my gear for departure. I wasn't feeling too bad, and I was keen to get going and finish off our last day. Elise and I climbed aboard and pushed off into the current with Dan and Gill.

The big rapids were behind us, which meant no more hard portages, but it also meant a full day of paddling along slow moving water. My early burst of energy evaporated a dozen strokes into the day, and I felt like an empty battery. I was letting my team down, and our raft fell further and further behind the rest of the outfit. My ego struggled with this new reality. I was typically the strong one, and often made up for what I lacked in skill with raw output of physical strength. On our final day in the raft, I had neither skill nor strength. The river was incredible, and the scenery more vibrant than any National Geographic magazine; however, my weakness sapped the joy out of the first half of the day.

The Franklin was growing broader and calmer as we descended towards the confluence with the Gordon River, and we stopped for lunch on a sandbar in the centre of the flow. I dropped my lifejacket in the sand and lay down to rest my aching body. Elise handed me sugar lollies, leftover pancakes from breakfast, and fruit, which I slowly nibbled down and felt my energy return. By the late afternoon, we paddled into the confluence, and Dan suggested we hop into the water and float through the junction. 'The water in the Gordon is much colder than the Franklin, and you will feel it, jump in.'

We all did exactly that. It was already refreshingly cold, but the temperature drop was remarkable when we merged with the Gordon. The rest of the boat crews had done the same, and Emily yelled out, 'No peeing in the wetsuits. We have to clean them all tomorrow.'

Once on the Gordon, the guides roped the rafts together like an inflated centipede. We still had a few kilometres remaining to reach the pickup point, and paddling together as a team would speed up the process. This took the pressure off my performance anxiety, and we cruised the flat water until we pulled up onto a large jetty at Sir Johns Falls. We were done. It had been a massive day of paddling, and my internal battery was almost dead, but I was swept up in the excitement of finishing and hooked in with the team to unload, deflate the rafts, and peel off my cold wetsuit one last time.

Brett was already setting up his bush kitchen on the jetty and paused to say, 'Well done everyone; get your camp set up in the trees back there, warm up, and I'll start cooking dinner.'

Our small tent wedged nicely onto a flat section of bank beside the jetty. Once changed into warm clothes, I rested at the edge of the tent. Then I noticed the 60 foot long steel yacht chugging towards the jetty. I had forgotten that our lift out from here through Macquarie Harbour to Strahan, was via a chartered boat. The impressive vessel, Stormbreaker, had been shuttling teams up and down the Gordon and around the west coast of Tasmania for over 30 years, and I was keen to climb aboard in the morning.

I couldn't stomach dinner, trying dismally to force down a few dry crackers before I shuffled away from the team, who were joyfully celebrating with recently delivered beers from the boat. I walked past Sir John's Falls, an enormous body of water cascading out of a rock face in the forest behind us, yet I was oblivious to its beauty. I crawled into my sleeping bag and blacked out immediately.

I woke with a jolt to Elise's alarm at 5 a.m. Our scheduled departure was at 5.30 a.m., and I felt like a million dollars. I had one of those deep nights of sleep where the body shuts down entirely to heal. I didn't wake up once to any noise and hadn't even changed my body's position from where I fell asleep.

'Damn I feel good today,' I announced. 'I needed that.'

'I bet you did. I thought you were dead when I came to bed,' Elise replied. 'Your eyes were open, your hands were folded across your chest, and you weren't breathing.'

'Wow, really, that's wild. I was truly shattered.'

'Yeah, I shined my headtorch straight into your eyes, and you didn't even flinch, but then you breathed softly so I knew you were ok, and I went to bed.'

Strangely, I would often struggle with sleeping in my soft king size bed in a comfortable environment. While out here, I could sleep on rough ground, with abundant noise, lights, and discomforts, and be out for nine hours straight. There was a saying on the cattle station where Dad worked that might hold some truth, 'If you have trouble sleeping, you haven't worked hard enough.'

We were aboard Stormbreaker and making our way down the Gordon for a six hour crossing of Macquarie Harbour to our waiting bus in Strahan. Then we would endure another five hour drive back to Hobart. However, I felt amazing and enjoyed every second on board this steel adventure craft. Boats had been in my blood from a very young age. I had saved up every dollar pushing trolleys at Coles Supermarket as a kid to buy my first fishing tinny when I was 16 years old. Now in adulthood, I saw countless opportunities for adventure if I owned a boat like this.

The skipper was Sean, who had recently bought the business from its original owner. Sean was my age, and we hit it off. As we chatted the hours away behind the wheel, it turned out Sean was also a veteran. He had served with 6 RAR, and deployed overseas many times on operations, we had plenty to talk about. He even offered Elise and I a spot on board as crew, if we ever wanted to learn more about the vessel. I couldn't have asked for a better way to finish an epic adventure.

◆◆◆

The battle for the Franklin had been a battle of the people. It evolved from grassroots organising, to Government legislation, then to protests, a blockade, thousands of arrests, and had its tipping point captured in a beautiful piece of art that helped sway support where it mattered most; in the hearts of the public who had voting power. The High Court ruling ended construction entirely, and thanks to the actions of a few who stood up for what was right, it ignited a chain of events that culminated in one wild river being allowed to run free. Without them, we would not have been able to raft this mighty river 40 years later.

◆◆◆

Whitewater rafting on Tasmania's free river had been an adventure with a unique skill set, in a new environment, and we joined a guiding team with specialist knowledge in their field. With Brett the wizard taking the lead, we had no issues and made it down safely, which was not always the outcome for other teams. Due to inexperience, bad decisions, or bad luck, dozens of rescues occur annually on the Franklin. If you are unsure about an adventure, hire the best in the business to show you the way and learn, especially if there is a severe risk of injury or death when you get it wrong.

I smiled and looked along Stormbreakers steel hull, towards her bow, and then out to a picturesque horizon. Elise walked up behind Sean and me at the wheel,

'How are the boys going?'

'Good.' We replied together.

I turned back from the horizon and looked at Elise,

'We have got to get a boat like this babe; imagine where we could go and the adventures we could get into. This thing could go all the way to Antarctica.'

Elise turned to Sean, 'Thanks mate, here we go again.'

CHAPTER 11

The Bay of Bengal

I was at full speed as the hill's gradient fell away in front of me; with no wind, I needed as much velocity as my legs could create to fill the glider. The wing rose above my head, and I pushed my arms straight back as I bent into the harness. Three more strides and the beauty of physics, flight, and the modern wing lifted me from the slope. I was airborne.

Flying in any form for me induces a sense of freedom, whether taking off in a 737 bound for foreign lands or making a leap off a cliff. Breaking nature's rules and taking flight as a human is a rare gift I have missed since retiring from B.A.S.E Jumping.

Elise and I were on a ten day paragliding course in Tasmania, and I knew from the first moment my feet left the ground that I was hooked. It was a safer sport than my previous parachute pursuits and was cheaper and logistically easier than skydiving. It was day four, and we launched off small hills 120 metres high. I loved the sport's hike up and fly down aspect and was already planning Himalayan flights for the future. With this new skill, I would never walk downhill again if I could fly.

The winds had increased too much by midday, so the instructors called lunch, and we drove over to a nearby roadhouse on the side of the highway. I grabbed my phone to check missed calls, and I had a bunch of messages. We all have that friend who cannot simply send one message containing everything they want to say or ask; they break it down into one or two word deliveries. Grant was that friend for me. The same Grant that I attempted to row across the Tasman Sea with, but we ended up self-rescuing after a capsize. He had been building a new boat for the last three years, this time with pedal power. His message stream arrived like this:

Mate
Just sounding you out
No commitment at this stage
Would you be possibly interested and or available to come on a jaunt across the Bay of Bengal in February with me in the new pedal boat?
The main aim is to collect water samples
And it would be easier with two people
Maybe faster
Boat is small
But for less than a 30-day trip for two people should be ok

Messages like this and friends like Grant were one of the reasons I kept myself physically and mentally ready to take on any adventure at a moment's notice. February was six weeks away, plenty of time to be prepared, but I had to ask one person a question before I replied.

'Elise, come over here for a second and have a read of this.' She sat beside me with her sandwich, and I handed her the phone. After reading, she handed it back with a grin.

'The last trip didn't go so well with Grant. Do you really want to do it?' she asked.

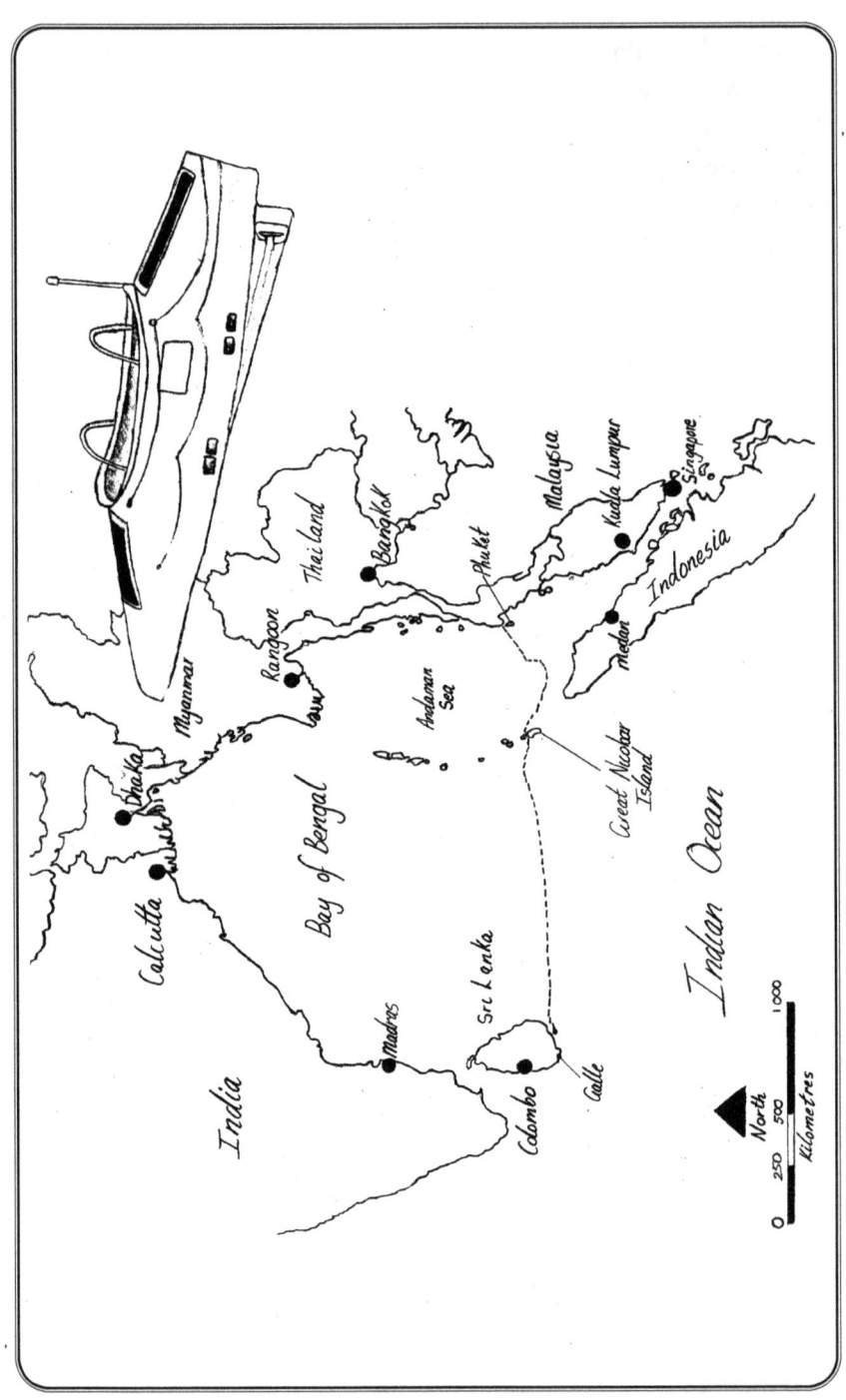

Without hesitation, I replied, 'Yeah I really do.' The gut churn I felt by even thinking about saying no to his request meant I would regret not having a go. This is what my life was all about.

'So, can I go? It will mean we would have to postpone our other trips by a month.'

'If you want to do it, do it. This is what you live for; I'll go to Bali.'

I started typing a reply.

I would be honoured. The boss has given me clearance, and I will book flights tonight. Game on.

For the rest of that afternoon, my mind was in expedition mode, and a million what-if scenarios were rattling around my head. On a call with Grant two days later, I received the full brief. The plan was to pedal from Phuket to Sri Lanka, a route of roughly 2000 kilometres, to take water samples along the shipping lanes, on behalf of a research team in Singapore, while trialling Grant's new prototype pedal boat. The only thing I knew was that it would be an adventure; this was my medicine, my purpose. It gave me a heightened sense and meaning to everything. I was my best self while preparing and executing missions like this, but above all, it is what I loved to do.

◆◆◆

A month had flown by in a whirlwind of paragliding and preparation. I touched down late in the evening onto the tropical paradise of Phuket, Thailand, which I regarded as a second home. Over the previous few weeks, I had tapered back on my intense training regime and increased my calorie intake. It was always a careful balance when trying to put on fat weight. If I devoured too much rubbish food like chocolate, cakes, and ice cream, my immune system would take a hit, and I could get sick. The key was increasing the good calories and dialling the energy output back. I had done this, gained a soft layer of stored energy, and felt fit and ready to go. I also had two weeks in Phuket to inhale as much B.B.Q. Chicken and delicious Thai food as possible before we set off.

After a restless sleep, I hired a scooter and ventured into the chaotic streets to find breakfast and meet Grant. I hadn't been on a scooter in a while, and the traffic on the roads had increased significantly since my last visit. It was high season, post COVID, and Phuket was bursting with tourists. I rode cautiously until I adapted to the traffic flow and remembered that these roads had no rules. I kept a sharp eye on the other vehicles knowing from experience that a truck, food cart, car or scooter could pull out at any moment. The last thing I wanted was to be injured two weeks before a big expedition.

As is often the case, I was drawn to a western café in the tourist areas. There is something comforting in the familiar while travelling, especially when I was fresh off the plane and adapting to a new environment. I devoured bacon and eggs, strong coffee and then messaged Grant that I was in his neighbourhood. He replied, saying he was out on a training ride, but to swing by the villa.

I turned up in the driveway of a white three story house and noticed the expedition gear piled up everywhere. Ropes, dry bags, anchors, bikes, tools, and countless food boxes. Grant poked his head through the door,

'Here he is. How are you mate?' he asked, smiling.

'Great thanks legend, you are looking fit and ready to go.' I replied as we embraced in a bear hug. We hadn't seen each other since our failed attempt to row from Australia to New Zealand.

'Yeah, I'm getting some miles into the legs mate, but honestly, I have been too busy with work for much training. Have you been doing any cycling?'

'Zero,' I replied. We both laughed at the absurdity of our build up training.

'The last time I cycled was across Australia and that was yonks ago, I'm sure I'll get the hang of it on this expedition.'

'That's for sure.' He replied. 'Ok, the first thing I want to do is show you the boat. Hop in the car.'

We drove to the northeast coast of Phuket, close to the Sarasin bridge connecting the island to the mainland. At a picturesque beach area named The Play-yard, sheltered under a tree, was a small, rocket shaped red boat. My first thought was that it's tiny. I climbed up onto the side of the trailer and looked inside. The entire deck was the size of a four person kitchen table and was filled by the pedalling seat and the pedal drive system. Immediately forward of the pedals was the hatch into the main cabin, where we would sleep, eat, and remain outside of our pedalling shifts. There was no room on the deck to relax when not pedalling. This lack of deck space was a significant change from the ocean rowing boats I had used on the Atlantic and Tasman. At least they had a small area to sit and relax if the cabin was too hot, and to stretch after a tough shift.

We planned to pedal for two hours, then rest for two hours, 24 hours daily. This was a standard protocol for ocean rowing in teams, and it can be a brutal schedule. Sleep deprivation was the most challenging component of this style of expedition. Over the years, I have come to realise that I could thrash myself physically to within an inch of my life on any day, but if I could sleep for eight hours that night, I would be able to do it all again the next day and for months at a time. However, when sleep deprivation came into the equation, everything fell apart, and it often became a mental battle for survival, regardless of my fitness.

I climbed aboard and sat in the pedalling seat. It was a reclined position like a recumbent bike in your standard gym, a piece of equipment I had never used before. I often watched people reading newspapers while sitting on the recumbent bikes and brushed them off as gimmicks. Now I was about to embark across the Bay of Bengal in the exact lay back position. The seat was comfortable enough, but from experience, I knew it would be agony within the first few days; I then crawled into the cabin.

The cabin's temperature was cool when shaded under a tree and with a sea breeze. This wouldn't be the case for long. I laid down, and my feet touched the wall towards the boat's bow, while my head almost touched the wall at the hatch opening. About six feet long, I thought, and just wide enough for my shoulders. Next to my right shoulder was our water maker, an essential piece of equipment that could convert 20 litres of salt water into fresh within 30 minutes. Near my left shoulder was our Simrad navigation system, radio, switchboard for lights, charging ports, and the A.I.S, a safety tool that allowed us to see other boats kilometres away on the display screen and for them to see us on theirs.

At my feet was another small hatch that opened into the nose where two large lithium batteries with regulators were strapped in place. Six solar panels sending power into them covered the nose exterior and the back of the boat. At my head was a valve that could be opened or closed. If we ended up inside the cabin together during a storm and had to seal the hatch, this small screw open valve allowed the carbon dioxide out and oxygen in so we wouldn't suffocate.

I sat up and banged my head. 'Fucker,'

'Yeah, watch your head. She is a bit tight in there mate. I had it built for myself to do a Southern Ocean trip. It will be tight and toasty for the two of us.' Grant said, leaning over the side.

I climbed back onto the deck and sat in the seat. Three hatches were underneath me. One hatch opened into the pedal drive gears for easy maintenance. Two more were sealed storage compartments that could be flooded for extra ballast. A significant difference between this boat and other human powered vessels was its high sides. It had walls up to shoulder height on both sides, a new concept, that I liked. While on rowing boats, the constant soaking from the beam on seas was miserable, and I hoped this design would remedy that.

At my back was another hatch to a large compartment. When closed, this space was a critical air pocket to allow the boat to float and self-right during a capsize. It also had a panel on its floor that would open into a moon pool, allowing us to access the rudder and propeller at the end of the drive shaft. While in the pedalling seat, small windows with miniature fold down outriggers were at my left and right shoulders. This simple system was a backup feature allowing us to row the boat in case of a pedal drive failure. The seat could be turned around, and oars lashed to the outside of the vessel could be manoeuvred through the openings allowing us to row ourselves to safety.

I climbed out and kneeled in the sand to see the propeller. It was a thin piece of plastic designed for large model aeroplanes.

'Bloody tiny prop mate,' I said to Grant.

'Yeah it is, but it does the job. One rotation of the pedals will be ten down on the shaft, and the thrust is surprising.'

I walked around, checking out the rudder and safety lines. On the very back was the boat's name, The Little Donkey. The Little part was right. The original Simpsons Donkey was our boat on the Tasman, and this unique prototype vessel was the newer and much smaller donkey. I took in every little detail of this unique craft we would pedal together, and I was excited.

Back at the villa that afternoon, we broke down tasks that needed completing before we set off in two weeks. Grant would oversee filming, safety, communication equipment, logistics for launch, and hopefully, customs arriving in Sri Lanka. My main job was to secure food for both of us. Food was one of our biggest morale boosters on expeditions, but this trip had one element affecting it that stifled most culinary treats, the heat. It was peak summer in Thailand, and the temperatures were in the high thirties, with 90 per cent humidity. This would force the temperature in the boat's storage compartments into the forties, melting chocolate, ruining salamis, destroying cheese in seconds, and welding sugary products into unpalatable masses. I would buy small mountains of these items for cold expeditions, but not this time.

'I bought a heap of dried food from a vegan company.' Grant said over my shoulder as I wrote food lists at the kitchen table.

'You are not a vegan, are they any good?' I asked.

'Yeah I know, but I tried their shakes, and they weren't bad?'

'Ok mate no worries, I'll include one meal per day from them.'

Most vegetarian and vegan options lacked crucial calories, so I would have to be creative to boost the volume. I hit the ground running, which would usually mean riding a scooter while in Phuket; however, with a build-up of traffic I hadn't seen on the island before, I opted for borrowing Grant's car to be safe. Amongst the Australians, Brits and Thais, there was an overwhelming number of Russian tourists. They were possibly escaping the conflict in Europe, opting for safe, sunny beaches instead of a cold battlefront. I couldn't blame them; but it simply meant the roads were chaos.

After three days of traffic jams, grocery stores, and countless stops for roadside chicken to calm my nerves, I had procured 60 days' worth of food. Thirty days each for Grant and me. We estimated a month to cross the Bay of Bengal and couldn't fit in much more. Every little nook and cranny was jammed with food. Every day we each had the following to sustain us.

> Coffee in 3 - 1 pouches x 2 (Nestle, full of sugar and common in Southeast Asia)
> Granola with powdered milk
> Dried mashed potato, with Thai meat pouches
> Nuts, dried fruit, Haribo lollies
> High carbohydrate protein shakes x 2
> Dehydrated meal (vegan)
> Peanut butter to be shared
> Nutella to be shared
> Electrolyte packets x 4
> Protein bar
> Fish oil tablets x 6.

We planned a circumnavigation of Phuket as a trial before setting off for Sri Lanka. The 130 kilometre route would allow us to test not just the boat, but also the communication equipment, food, the navigation system, and ourselves in two hours on and two hours off pedalling cycles. After days of frantic preparation, the sun shone, and the skies were blue as we reversed the Little Donkey on her trailer down into the water at The Play-yard. We had heard that a local kayaker held the record for a circumnavigation, completing it in 21 hours. I backed ourselves to do it faster.

The boat looked tiny beside the yachts and other watercraft moored near the ramp. The Little Donkey weighed only 350 kilograms with all food and equipment, was as wide as a kitchen table, and similar to a canoe in stability. We both needed to start by standing in the water with the rudder and prop clear of the bottom to get two of us on board. Grant would climb up first while I held onto the opposite side, using my body weight to stop the boat from rolling over. Once onboard, Grant would put all his weight to one side while I climbed up and slid into the cabin.

There was no room for me to stay out on the deck while Grant pedalled, and it was so tippy that if I lay anywhere but centre in the cabin, my weight would tilt the boat and make pedalling awkward. Shift changes were a delicate sequence of moves for me to come out on the deck and take over without capsizing.

With the help of an outgoing tide, we drifted west-northwest through the channel separating Phuket from the mainland, passing underneath the Sarasin bridge. We were greeted by the open ocean, where we turned south down the west coast and made significant progress. After completing one two hour shift each, we started to hear a grinding sound from the gearbox, a metal on metal alarm bell. Upon investigation, the bottom of the drive shaft was very hot, and we found a corroded thrust bearing was the cause of the friction. We stripped everything apart using the tools we had on board, which we quickly realised was a challenging process, due to the cramped space, the rocking of the boat, and the risk of losing bolts, tools, and parts overboard.

According to the designers, the drive system needed zero lubrication. However, within the first few hours, this theory didn't stack up to Mother Nature's reality, and we decided to soak the bearing in WD-40 and marine grease. Our speed averaged 2 to 3 knots with the help of light wind and current. Phuket's postcard beaches slowly moved past on our left as we made our way towards the southern tip of the island throughout the afternoon.

By 3 p.m., the sun was beating down, and the two small fans inside the cabin were useless against the rising temperature. The confined space increased to 40 degrees Celsius, and to be inside while not pedalling was torturous. The meagre thrust from the five-volt fans pushed hot air onto my face while sweat poured from my body. The heat made food unappealing and any movement inside the cabin impossible. I tried to lay still, and calm my mind against the negative thoughts starting to manifest. It was dawning on me that this trip would not be the walk in the park we thought it would be.

> *Grants journal: We got a slap in the face as to how tough the living conditions on this tiny boat were going to be. This was to be no 'picnic' and much tougher just to live, eat, rest, and pedal than on the ocean rowing boats we were both used to. Even changing shifts took a coordinated and planned exercise without capsizing the tiny craft.*

I settled in for my first night shift and had forgotten how special yet brutal they could be. On the one hand, I was awake at a time when most slept, taking in the unique beauty of the stars and the ocean at night. On the other hand, my mind and body were exhausted, and I craved sleep. Negative patterns of thought and waves of emotion would bubble up and threaten to overwhelm me. One shift would be bliss and full of positivity while listening to the sounds of the waves splashing against the hull. The next shift would then be a battle for survival, getting thrown around while trying to stay awake and not scream profanity into the night.

I was on shift at 2 a.m. as we were about to round the southern tip of Phuket. The temperature in the cabin had finally dipped into the high twenties making sleep possible, and Grant had passed out. I was steering the donkey around the rocky southern landscape roughly 300 metres from the cliffs to my left. At one point, we were gliding along at 2 knots, then seconds later, the vessel was going backwards at 1 knot and towards jagged rocks. I woke Grant and briefed him on the situation quickly. He was calm and knew exactly what to do. Grant had lived in Singapore for almost 20 years and had spent countless hours rowing boats around its bustling harbour when training for expeditions. He had experience with island currents, and fired off instructions.

'Turn and go with the current mate, then use the speed to head further away from land until you feel the current ease off, then turn back on heading, and you will be fine.' I did as instructed, and it played out as he knew it would. The strong currents forcing their way around the point released us, I could turn east again, and we rounded the southern cape. 'What was going on there?' I asked.

'The tide and current get compressed the closer to land they are, which increases their speed and power. We just needed a few hundred metres of extra ocean room to get out of them.' With a valuable lesson learned, Grant returned to the cabin, and I pedalled on, turning us north up the east coast.

I woke after a one hour sleep; the sun was up, and Grant was working away out on deck. I felt rough; it had been a tough first night back at sea. I knew my body would adapt eventually, but this didn't help me feel better that morning.

'Good morning, how are you feeling bro?' Grant asked, extra chipper.

'So good mate.' I groaned with sarcasm. We both laughed, knowing we felt like shit and had put ourselves in this position again. 'Two minutes mate', Grant called out. He was announcing three words which meant shift change, words that would be shared between us six hundred times in the following weeks.

There was a period on every expedition when I knew my body had adapted and was no longer in survival mode, but instead had started to heal and get stronger. This was usually a few days into mountaineering trips and possibly a week into more arduous ocean rowing voyages. There would be limited adaption on a short lap like the one we were undertaking, and it would be a full day stuck in fight or flight mode for our nervous systems. Perception-wise, we would be under attack and be pumping blood to the legs, with increasing cortisol and adrenalin keeping us going through the hardship. This was a natural evolutionary tool, just as if we were being chased by a lion across the savannah in Africa. When our nervous system is in survival mode, digestion and reproduction systems take a back seat, prioritising our survival.

When I finally adapted to my environment, I would no longer be stuck in fight or flight mode, my nervous system would change to rest and digest, and I would be hungry. This was my cue to know I was finally starting to feel good and adapt to my harsh environment. I was not hungry that first morning.

Throughout the second day, we knew we would finish our lap sometime around sunset, yet this light at the end of the tunnel did little to ease the suffering. We were drinking water by the bucket full, quickly consuming ten litres each the day before; yet still not urinating the day after. We were both severely dehydrated from the constant sweating in the cabin and had to fire up the water maker to refill our barrels. The hours ticked by with steady progress north at 2.5 knots, and as tends to happen when I let the hope of early completion enter my mind, we were buffeted with a headwind that knocked our speed down to a soul destroying .5 knots.

As hard as pedalling on deck was, it was nothing compared to the cabin's heat, and we changed to one hour shifts in the afternoon to combat the risk of heat exhaustion. On my one hour of rest, I chose to stand with my legs in the cabin and my upper body out to gain some respite from the inferno. This eased the suffering slightly but assisted little in helping me recover from the pedalling shifts. Grant's approach was to curl into a ball in the cabin seconds after getting inside, place one fan two centimetres from his face and try to zone out. I watched sweat bead from his back through the open hatch, yet he remained still and endured.

We rounded the northeast tip of the island in the late afternoon, and entered the channel again. Hoping to gain the assistance of the tide, we were disappointed with a neap flow and zero wind. The sun had finally set, giving us some comfort, and we spent the following two hours dodging the moored yachts and pleasure craft harboured in the channel. With the Play-yard's lights now calling to us in the distance, Grant accidentally snagged a rope attached to a vacant buoy, it locked up our propeller, and he needed to open the moon pool and cut it away before we could continue. I spent the remainder of his shift standing and guiding him through the marina to the boat ramp, where we departed from 35 hours earlier.

We hadn't completed the 130 kilometre lap in record time, yet it had served its purpose perfectly. We needed the brutal shakeout to prepare for the crossing to Sri Lanka. On the drive home inside Grant's air-conditioned car that night, we discussed what we had to change. Then at his kitchen table after a hot shower, and in-between devouring chicken and sipping on a cold drink, I was logging mental notes of things to buy the following day to make the coming journey bearable. Bigger fans were a must, extra padding in the cabin to lay on, lubricants for the drive system, simpler foods to eat during hot periods of the day, more electrolytes for dehydration, and many more minor alterations in our critical systems.

Laying my head on a soft pillow, with a belly full of chicken, and the air-conditioner belting out frosty air; I had already started to forget the pain and suffering from the previous day and a half. However, I knew that this trip would be the most brutal expedition I had ever done. If the test lap was anything to go by, it would take all our combined experience and resilience to pull this one off and make it to our destination intact. I let the thought fade away as the aircon hummed, and I passed out.

◆ ◆ ◆

The week following our test lap was a blur of preparation. I had moved in with Grant and his young family, where his twin daughters Kate and Rachel, aged seven, became my little helpers before and after school. The normalcy and routine of family life with them and his wife Stephanie was a nice respite amongst the chaos of preparing for a unique ocean crossing. The last few days before any big expedition was always madness with never ending to do lists. We also squeezed in a talk at Kate and Rachel's school, who would be following our expedition from their classroom. The teachers took an active role in the crossing and developed learning activities around what we were trying to achieve.

Another big part of this trip was the water sampling Grant had agreed to do for Professor Federico M Lauro, from Nanyang Technological University in Singapore, who had pioneered this type of research conducted from small pleasure crafts. Although our vessel didn't qualify as a pleasure craft in my book, the sampling kit was packed down into two pelican cases and could be stored in the back hatch. The goal was to sample water inside and outside the busy shipping lanes that sliced through the Bay of Bengal, testing the health of the microbes to see how the starting point of the global food chain is faring. Federico flew up from Singapore two days before departure to teach us the correct procedures for avoiding contamination and storing the samples for later use.

The day of departure arrived, and the shores of The Play-yard were bustling with school kids, locals, and family who were there to see us off. We squeezed 60 days' worth of food into the boat, 30 days each, and the two new 12-volt fans were humming away in the cabin. We launched the Little Donkey at high tide, and the elements lined up in our favour, with the tide turning at 10.30 a.m. to help push us out.

There was a 15 kilometre breeze from the northeast, rippling the surface of the channel and softly nudging the yachts moored offshore. The sun's glare reflected off the water, and I put my glasses on to shield my eyes. Grant was saying a final farewell to his girls, while the palm trees swayed and brushed against each other around him, like a tropical meditation soundtrack that calmed my nerves. I looked around at the powerlines, buildings, cars, and civilisation. All the things we would not see again until we made it to the other side. It was time for no regrets; it was time to launch.

We climbed aboard on February 9th at 11.30 a.m., and Grant started pedalling us into the channel. We quickly sped up to 4 knots, with the tide and wind helping to cast us out. The Sarasin bridge passed overhead again, and before we knew it, we had entered open water, with Phuket slowly fading behind us. Making the most of the phone reception, I sent Elise photos and messages, and Grant spoke to Stephanie. Inevitably our phones fell silent and were replaced by the whirring of the gears as Grant pedalled. We had agreed to two hour shifts, and as the sun set that evening and Phuket disappeared below the horizon, Grant called out from the deck, 'Two minutes mate.' It was my turn on shift; our new reality had set in.

Grants journal: I'm nervous about the stability of the boat at sea and how the gearbox will hold out, but also optimistic. Life now becomes simpler after a crazy six months of moving house and country, merging businesses, planning, and preparing for the expedition; life becomes simple, and it's time to adapt to life at sea. The cabin heat is bearable with the new 12 volt fan.

Losing sight of land, and having our entire world shrink to the size of a tiny boat, can be an exposing and vulnerable moment at the start of a trip. In everyday life, we are accustomed to roaming free, where if we forget something when we leave the house, we can easily buy it at the shop on the way to our destination. This trip was vastly different; we had everything we needed to survive on board and, hopefully, the skills to get us through. In my experience, the feeling of exposure and vulnerability transforms into competence and confidence after a few days. We learn that the true sense of security comes from within ourselves, not from the environment.

Our first 24 hours at sea passed as expected, completing two hour pedalling shifts with micro naps, and eating spliced in between. Grant succumbed to a 90 minute deep sleep in between one shift, and I managed two smaller blocks. On my Atlantic row, I adapted to three 90 minute periods of sleep and a power nap per day. This was enough to get me through a 55 day crossing, albeit while also losing 15 kilograms in weight.

We had covered 95 kilometres on day one, but then the wind blew in from the north during the night, and the current started pushing us north, both combined to slow our progress substantially. I devoured granola with powdered milk for breakfast, happy with our food selection to start each day, and then proceeded to make a hot brew for each of us. The ignition switch on the cooker failed to work, and after digging around for a lighter, I scorched the hair on my hand while lighting the gas. The heat generated by the small stove in the cabin created a sauna effect, and I was pouring sweat by the time our coffee was ready. The whole process was counterproductive; it was the last time we used the cooker for the entire trip.

Like our lap around Phuket, the afternoon shifts were the toughest due to the heat, and even with the bigger 12 volt fan, the cabin was scorching. Although hard on the legs, this made being out on the deck in the fresh air much better than being inside. The sun set on a sweaty day two, and we settled into our night shifts. So far, we had both avoided sea sickness, and our bodies seemed to adapt quickly to the constant rocking. I was violently seasick on my Atlantic crossing for three days but felt nothing on the Tasman crossing with Grant. I was grateful to avoid it this time as well; combined with the brutal temperatures, constant vomiting could have destroyed morale.

The distance between Phuket and Sri Lanka is roughly 1900 kilometres, as the crow flies, but it wasn't open water the entire way. Five hundred kilometres off Thailand's west coast and across the Andaman Sea, lay the Andaman and Nicobar Islands; a union territory of India consisting of 572 islands, of which only 37 were inhabited. We needed to navigate through or around these obstacles before making it into the Bay of Bengal. Some islands are a tourist's paradise with white sandy beaches and untouched natural rainforests. While many were off limits due to their strategic locations, and others were guarded due to tribes inhabiting them who were still untouched by the modern world.

North Sentinel Island, a tiny landmass seven kilometres wide and eight kilometres long, is the most famous of these forbidden islands. It is home to the Sentinelese tribe, an indigenous people in voluntary isolation who have often defended their way of life by force. Since 1996 the Indian government has made it illegal for fishermen, tourists, researchers, or other civilians to land on the island. The military maintains this administrative barrier with Navy patrols. Yet, in 2006 two fishermen made an emergency landing on the island and were killed by the Sentinelese, their bodies buried in the sand. Any attempt to retrieve the remains was met with a volley of arrows.

The most recent headline was in 2018 when a 26 year old missionary, John Allen Chau, from the United States paid a local fisherman to take him to the island and anchor offshore. He made two attempts in a kayak to preach to the locals who met him on the beach before he retreated, fearing for his life both times. Referring to them in his recovered journals, he wrote, 'Is this Satan's last stronghold,' he asked God, 'where none have heard or even had a chance to hear your name?' His third attempt was his last, and he was never seen again.

Before we reached these island obstacles, we were battling other forces of nature. In our naïve planning, we had predicted a pleasant crossing of the Andaman Sea, with following southeast winds helping us along. In reality, the benign surface of the water only concealed the volatile currents beneath that were wreaking havoc on our progress. At 9 p.m., the current was too strong to pedal against and even though we were aiming west, we were pushed southeast.

The following day the situation hadn't improved, and we started encountering strange phenomena that we nicknamed current bombs. We could see them coming on the horizon, wide bands of turbulent sea and chopped up white water that seemed to be moving fast towards us. When we converged, The Little Donkey was forced backwards at 2 to 3 knots and tossed in all directions. All we could do was hang on and try to keep pedalling forward. The current bombs were separate from the leading ocean currents, and would last fifteen minutes before releasing us back into the smooth water and westerly flow. On a two hour shift, we were being hit by three or more current bombs that drastically reduced our progress.

Sleep deprivation took its toll throughout my third night at sea, and I constantly fell asleep at the pedals. I would wake after a micro nap to find us facing the wrong way and going backwards. I'd slap my face and pull my chest hairs to wake up, only to fall asleep again minutes later. I couldn't wait to get inside the cabin to sleep, but when we finally changed shifts and I crawled inside, the heat kept me awake and sweating. It wasn't until after midnight that the temperature dropped enough to pass out for an hour of much needed sleep.

Following our fast start leaving Phuket's shores, our speed had slowed significantly, and we covered only 54 kilometres in 24 hours. Moving at such a meagre speed, we both started thinking about our food rations. We needed to maintain a 70 kilometre daily average if we were going to complete the crossing in 30 days or less and avoid rationing food. If we didn't pick up the pace, there would be some tough decisions to make.

Grants journal: We are both starting to suffer through the heat of the day, and we can't wait for the evening when the heat disappears. The night sky was beautiful though, very clear, and the stars were out in force. When not looking at the G.P.S. screen, I would tilt my head and look at the stars. Around 2300 hours I had an amazing gift of seeing a meteorite come whizzing through the sky above my head and burning up in a bright flash. Incredible to see.

From the natural phenomena above to the destructive human behaviour below, we started to see more and more rubbish in the water the further out into the sea we pedalled. Bottles, thongs, nets, ropes, bags, and plastic in thousands of colours and variations littered the water. In some sections, the surface currents had forced the rubbish together into veins that snaked their way across the sea and off into the distance. The propellor was constantly fouled on plastic bags and debris, requiring us to reach down through the moon pool and cut them away. What humans have done to our planet and continue to do is tragic. The tipping point, for better or worse, will undoubtedly occur in my lifetime.

We battled the current bombs and opposing winds for two more days until we had no option but to divert from our desired path and go where nature wanted us to, and where we could at least make some forward progress. This decision sent us on a southwest trajectory towards Sumatra; it was not ideal, but it felt great to be moving forward. By our fifth day at sea and 250 kilometres from Phuket, the heat was so intense that we both opted to be naked in the cabin between shifts. At first, having Grant's naked form lying a foot away from me felt weird, but after a few shifts, it became routine.

To make our situation even more miserable, we had both broken out in severe prickly heat rash from the constant sweating inside the tropical cabin, and our choice of dehydrated meals turned out to be inedible. Whoever approved this brand of meals to be sold for human consumption deserves a grim death; they were shocking. I can eat almost anything, especially in a survival situation, but after forcing down one of them, my stomach ballooned, which had undesirable aftereffects. We opted to feed them to the fish, and our food rationing had begun. On top of the constant itching, heat, sweat, and slow progress, our gearing system had persistent breakdowns.

To make any decent speed, we had to put some serious effort into the pedals, which transferred the force into the gears, and then into the prop shaft generating our thrust. The weak link was the gears. We frequently stopped to remove shattered bearings from the gear shafts when a metal on metal grinding sound alerted us to their fracture. The entire assembly needed constant lubrication if we were to lengthen its lifespan. We also had to change out the critical clutch bearing twice and only had two more in reserve. The clutch bearing allowed us to stop pedalling at any time and freewheel. Like on a bicycle when going downhill. Without a clutch bearing, when you stop pedalling, the pedals would keep going and injure you in the process.

We had a long way to go, and at the rate we replaced parts, we would run out before halfway; something had to change. This adventure quickly evolved into a battle for the ages. I hadn't suffered this much on an expedition before; the heat was all consuming, sleep was non-existent, and the slow progress eroded our confidence. Each consecutive current bomb drove us backwards, and no matter how hard we pedalled, we struggled to make any heading west.

Grants journal: The seeds of self-doubt started to seep into my mind. With the current like this, it is proving much tougher than I anticipated. What a failure this will feel like if this trip does not work out and ends in the first week. Luke suggests calling into an island to rest and reevaluate the project. There is no island close to us though, and at this pace, we are 7 - 10 days from reaching any land. Our progress slows until by mid-afternoon when not peddling, we are being blown back to shore at 1.5 knots, which is opposite to where we want to be going. I turn south and to my surprise, find we can make progress around 1.8 knots at 180 - 220 degrees heading. It's not the direction we want to go, but at least it's better than going backwards. And maybe if we drop further south, we can find better current to head west. Immediately the mood on the boat picks up, we have gone from losing hope to having hope again - from a simple change in heading. It has made me aware of the necessity to keep ourselves positive, focused, and not let the seeds of self-doubt manifest.

The sun's soft presence grew slowly on the horizon on the morning of day six. I had an hour remaining on my last night shift, and my mind and body wanted one thing, to rest. As I pedalled, a purple butterfly landed on my knee, and I wondered if I was micro napping again. Hundreds of kilometres from land, here was a fragile butterfly, a fellow explorer, and so out of place in the foreign environment; I felt an instant friendship. He hung out for 15 minutes going through the rotations of the pedals and enjoying a rest before he departed just as abruptly as he arrived. I watched him fly away, checked the time, and then announced to Grant, 'Two minutes mate.' It was his turn to suffer.

The midday heat was stifling, and I couldn't remain in the cabin for long in-between shifts. I stood for respite and noticed a fishing vessel approaching from behind us. It was a colourful wooden banana boat typical to this area, and onboard I counted a dozen men all watching us. My military mind immediately went into 'Actions On,' and I brainstormed quick plans with Grant in case they were hostile. They pulled alongside, their derelict and barely seaworthy craft cutting through the swell. They were trawling lines and had nets stowed on board, and looking at the crew's condition, it must be a rough life.

I waved hello, and they waved back, breaking the tension. They then started a game of charades and mimicked the action of drinking and smoking. 'Are they asking us if we need water?' I asked Grant.

'Doubtful mate, they want alcohol and smokes I'd say. They probably come from one of the Islamic areas of Sumatra where it's all illegal.'

With nothing to offer them, we pedalled on waving goodbye, and they continued their hunt for fish. Their job was getting increasingly more challenging from what I could see in the state of the water. We had been silently pedalling across the Andaman Sea for six days and were yet to encounter anything larger than a bait fish, it seemed to be void of marine life.

The beam on swell was tough on our bodies, but it didn't slow our progress now that we had found a friendly current. We covered 91 kilometres for the day and formulated a plan to navigate the Nicobar Islands ahead on our path. Professor Federico in Singapore and Elise in Bali sent us daily weather updates and predicted currents. As we all know, weather forecasts are rarely 100 per cent accurate, but we could come reasonably close between the two.

The most accurate data surprised us with a storm system due to thunder from the east in 24 hours; at about the same time we would need to pass between the islands. Not an ideal situation, but I was looking forward to the extra shove. Our weather guides advised us to turn west and aim for the southern tip of Great Nicobar Island. Once we cleared the land mass, the currents on the other side looked like they were all heading due west with nothing to hold them back. That's where we wanted to be. We changed heading and settled in for night shifts, with a tinder of hope we would clear the islands soon and the week of punishment and brutal currents would be behind us.

Fatigue was taking a toll on my mind, and hallucinations began like daydreams. At one point I thought we were going under a bridge; I caught myself, laughed at the impossibility, pulled on some chest hairs, and returned to work. This momentary lapse evolved into entire shifts where I believed, without a doubt, that someone was sitting next to me on the deck. It was a comforting feeling, a friend to share the pain with. When I snapped out of these moments, I felt slightly abandoned and then worried I was losing my mind entirely. I tried to sleep but found myself subconsciously talking to the other person sleeping beside me in a mirror image of the cabin. Mid-conversation with these fellow travellers, I would be brought back to reality by Grant, 'Two minutes mate.'

He was in a similar state, with the fatigue and lack of sleep chipping away at our veneer of sanity, yet throughout it all, we maintained the pace and got the job done.

Grants journal: I started having the first hallucinations, and Luke sounds drunk when I wake him up for his shift in the middle of the night. Slurring his words, wobbly and uncoordinated as we change shifts. He had some massive hallucinations during the night and chatted away to imaginary friends on deck. We are getting on really well though in tough conditions. We don't talk much, but when we do, we laugh and joke, and the mood is high. It would be terrible doing this with someone you didn't like.

Our hope in rounding the southern tip was dampened by a metal on metal grinding noise on the morning of day seven. The sprag clutch had blown again, and we needed to strip down the gearbox and replace it. Forty five minutes of grease and effort before we were back underway. The drive system was in peaceful harmony again, yet the sea state around us had grown angry. The predicted winds had arrived and, throughout the day, kept intensifying, developing into a big swell barrelling in from the east. Luckily, it was a following swell and not likely to capsize the donkey. However, we needed to enter professional mode and prepare for the worst case scenario.

Although dangerous, I loved moments where every sense was heightened and tweaked for optimal performance. With the following sea, we needed to be ninjas on the steering and maintain a straight line down the swell as we were picked up. This allowed us to surf down the face of the wave and gain adrenalin pumping speeds. If we were too slow, the bow could turn as we were lifted and capsize us, creating the scenario we wanted to avoid at all costs. We cleared the deck of superfluous items, donned lifejackets and safety lines, and settled in for a big night.

Grants journal: We pedalled our gut's out all night, being thrown around on the back deck in the rough water as we struggled to point the boat southwest to clear the island. My knees are in agony, and Luke damages his shoulder from hanging on to the side of the boat as he pedals in rough conditions. Just after midnight, we agree to drop to 90 minute shifts as two hours is too tiring when we are pedalling this hard. It's impossible to sleep inside the cabin when the boat is being thrown around like this. We are both now completely exhausted and running purely on adrenalin.

We tried holding a west heading towards the southern tip of the island, but as the evening wore on it became much harder to do, and we slowly lost speed. The wind and waves were heading west, and according to our basic understanding of weather patterns, we should have been going west as well, but underneath us, a much stronger current was heading north. We could make a very slow west heading by changing to 90 minute shifts to keep up the intensity. However, our bodies could not hold the tempo, and by midnight we had to admit defeat and turn north with the current. It was a big blow to morale after a massive effort to sneak around the southern tip.

The adrenalin wore off as the sea state calmed down slightly, and we succumbed to continuing north on the morning of day eight. The lack of sleep, food, and water had taken its toll, but we were not out of the woods by a long shot. We were heading north with the barren coastline of Great Nicobar Island close to our west and being pounded by the swell. Getting pushed onto the coast was a serious concern, and our new plan was to utilise the northern current and try to slip through a channel separating the Great and Little Nicobar Islands. This meant doubling down our effort on the pedals throughout the day and relying on luck that the current around the top of the island would pull us through.

Late that afternoon, I lay in the cabin desperate for sleep, yet pouring sweat and unable to fight the rising anxiety. The feeling grew into panic, and in my sleep deprived state, one thought took hold, I must get off the boat; I can't do this. I was accustomed to rising negative emotions, but this one swept me up like a tsunami, and I failed to fight its intensity. I stood up, cooled down, and lay down again. I tried to eat and sleep, but as the minutes ticked by, the depressed vortex tore me down. My mental strength wavered then shattered, and I crawled onto my knees and said to Grant.

'Mate, I'm really struggling, I think I'm done. I can't do this; I need to get off the boat.'

No thoughts of letting people down, of failing, or of regret held any sway over me, nothing broke through the fog, and all I had as an answer to my miserable condition was to get off the boat.

Now one would think the suddenness of my announcement would have unsettled Grant, but as a testament to his emotional intelligence and resilience, he calmly started to talk to me. He felt for me, and we slowly and methodically spoke about the options. If I was desperate to leave, I only had two choices. Head towards the immediate coast where there was a possible harbour and be dropped off. The risk of us being washed ashore was great, and the conditions were terrible. This option would also leave me on a remote island, deep in the jungle. Or, try and make it through the next few days and call for a ship to come and pick me up.

The logic and calmness of the conversation seemed to penetrate my echo chamber, and I knew immediately I would not put anyone at risk because I wanted out. The thought of placing Grant or rescue crews in danger sliced through the panic and desire for escape.

'I feel for you bro; what would you like to do.' Grant asked.

'Let's keep going, no one gets put at risk because of me. It's my turn on shift.'

I took over, and Grant went to sleep. As soon as I put my feet on the pedals and started to turn them, I burst into tears. Uncontrolled blubbering and a fountain of misery poured from me. Deep emotion that was buried and had tormented me for days spewed out, and I cried for an hour. At shift change, I crawled into the cabin and passed out. I slept for two hours, and when I woke up, I no longer wanted to quit. I was unfettered from my emotions, and all that remained was embarrassment that I had let myself break.

Grant made the ultimate gesture of mateship and teamwork by telling me to return to sleep for another hour while he kept pedalling. He knew I was over the hump, but also knew the added sleep would make me even stronger. An extra hour does not sound like much, but while suffering, like we were, and while weak and desperate for sleep himself, it was a huge sacrifice. He kept pushing and let me sleep. This type of action is what makes a great expedition partner and ultimately an unbeatable team. I would return his kindness in the weeks to come.

This was the first time I had ever been mentally broken. Nothing ever pushed me that far throughout my military career, mountaineering, ocean rows, B.A.S.E Jumping, desert crossings, or the ups and downs of life. This expedition had done it in eight days. Writing these words, a month post expedition, I have had time to reflect on this moment. The biggest lesson from it was that I could completely shatter and mentally break, and then with sleep and some food, be able to carry on and complete the mission. I was fortunate to learn this lesson in an environment where I couldn't physically quit because if I had, I would have regretted it for the rest of my life. I had become unbreakable by reaching my breaking point and overcoming it during this intense experience.

I was over my mental battle, but the battle of the islands was beginning. The north current pulled us closer and closer to the shore, and on sundown we were sucked into a narrow channel between the islands. We were in unknown shallow waters, in a boat that couldn't manoeuvre, and at the whim of strong wind and currents. Grant put in a sterling performance guiding us through the shallows, and we were finally heading west along the northern tip of Great Nicobar.

With an overwhelming uncertainty, we could not let our guard down, and at any moment we were expecting a current, or a wave, to destroy our plans and send us onto the rocks.

Grants journal: I am in a state of exhausted depression. The first 600 kilometres has nearly killed us. We have almost used all our spare parts. How on earth can we hold this together to make it over 1600 kilometres more? At 3 am in the morning, as we change shifts, we both decide we definitely cannot keep going like this, and we need to take a good long break for both of us to recover. We agree that once we reach better conditions with currents, we will take that break. (We never ended up taking any break, but psychologically it made us feel a little better just thinking about it.)

We finally relaxed when dawn arrived and were greeted with an open ocean, as far as the eyes could see to the west. We were released into the Bay of Bengal on the morning of day nine, and I allowed a seed of hope to plant itself in my mind. If we could survive what we had just endured, we could surely survive whatever came next.

◆◆◆

The following week brought emotional ups and downs and physical torture with the heat, but a consistency in the currents heading west. This allowed us to dial in our pedalling shifts and clock up the kilometres. 80 kilometre days grew to 90, then to over 100 kilometres in 24 hours. Slowly but surely, we were inching our way towards the coast of Sri Lanka, and safety. We needed to be gentle with the gearbox because our sprag clutch blew out again, and we were down to our last one. If we broke one more, we would be at the ocean's mercy and calling in a rescue.

The uncertainty of knowing the gearbox could blow at any time kept us both hypervigilant. We greased and lubricated the gears twice daily without fail. Then pulled out the clutch, cleaned it, and reassembled it every third day. We also backed off the power we forced into the pedals. Softly was the new approach, ticking off the hours and kilometres towards our goal. The adventure evolved into one continuous groundhog day of two hours on, two hours off pedalling shifts, and every spare moment between spent eating, sleeping, doing maintenance on the boat, and trying not to predict the future.

In the background, we were trying to organise spare parts to be dropped off to us. First, we thought we could find a local yachty that was sailing through from Thailand to drop them. Or a container ships captain sympathetic to our cause could be willing, but locating the parts we needed in Southeast Asia turned out quite challenging, and then even harder to get them to us in the ocean. Grant's wife, Stephanie, was working on the problem.

At least marine life was abundant in the Bay of Bengal. We were visited by Dolphins some evenings, a giant Manta Ray stopped by for breakfast once, and on some days we would pedal through enormous schools of mullet and flying fish. It was great to finally see some life where we initially thought it was barren. However, an eyesore of rubbish still coated the surface of the bay, and often whole trees were floating past in gyres of plastic with a collection of fish underneath calling it home.

Thunderstorms and rain squalls became frequent in the late afternoons and evenings, and it felt amazing to have freshwater soak into our skin and start to remedy the prickly heat rashes that coated our bodies. The friction rash under my arms and across my back was grim and kept me awake on nights when the boat was rocking from side to side. It was ghastly to look at, and Grant's skin was in a similar condition.

The night shifts became our only respite from the heat and discomfort, and we both started to navigate without the G.P.S. and the screen's intrusive glow. This allowed a universe of stars to shine in all their glory with zero light to counter them. We would pick one bright star on our heading and use it to guide the way, just like the early explorers and Polynesians would have done a thousand years before us.

We crossed the 1000 kilometre halfway point on day 14, and with our consistency at the pedals and the friendly westerly current, we counted down the distance to land in the west. Eight hundred kilometres to go, 620 kilometres, 500 kilometres, each morning we ticked off a distance earned with sweat, and it was a little victory in a much larger battle.

Due to having no spare parts and the fragility of the drive system, we couldn't risk manoeuvring ourselves into the southern shipping lanes to conduct water samples. The main traffic routes were 150 kilometres further south from where we currently drifted, and we feared the effort to get there would be too much for the gearbox. We were unwilling to risk a breakdown inside the shipping lanes, and after sending our concerns to Professor Federico, he agreed with us. Instead, on day 19 after covering 114 kilometres in 24 hours and 1620 kilometres since leaving Phuket, we took one water sample to prove the concept of science conducted at sea in a small craft.

With the final few hundred kilometres in our sights and some luck, we would be pedalling our way into the picturesque harbour of Galle on the south coast of Sri Lanka in under a week. Then it happened.

Grants journal: The gearbox blew up again, and we knew immediately what the problem was - the sprag clutch. With no more options, we fit back one of the broken sprag clutches. Now we are in a real pickle and have no idea if the broken one would even work well enough to pedal. We pedalled slowly, and it seemed to hold, but we knew we needed to be very gentle.

During my afternoon shift, we break the oars out to try rowing. I have rowed the boat using the emergency oars on a flat river, and it was ok. However, on the ocean, bumping around with waves and swell, it is hopeless. It confirms to us that rowing is not going to be the option to get us to Sri Lanka. It is pedal power or nothing.

The hits kept coming during the night when the pedalling seat snapped clean off its mounts after a week of beam on swell and constant rocking. Pedalling became a nightmare until we could configure a system of ropes and bungee cords to hold it in the boat's centre again. Sri Lanka's coast couldn't come quickly enough, and as the distance decreased by the day, our weather guides informed us there were some powerful southwest currents along the Sri Lankan coastline. It wasn't going to be as easy as we had hoped to make landfall.

We were not the first to attempt this crossing to Sri Lanka. A fellow ocean rower and explorer, Karlis Bardelis crossed from Malaysia to Sri Lanka in 2022 as part of his global circumnavigation under human power. Grant had spoken to him about the conditions, and he had told us the currents sweeping around the southern tip of the country were a huge obstacle. He experienced no wind and calm sea conditions, yet the currents were so strong that he had to row non-stop for over 48 hours to make it in and not be pushed back out to sea. We were now facing a similar battle to finish our mission.

Day 23 dawned, and we were 40 kilometres off the east coast; we could taste victory but couldn't yet see land. A thick fog obscured the horizon as we pedalled and fought to keep a westerly heading against the ever increasing strength of the southwest currents. Around midday, we entered the section Karlis had warned us about, and we immediately started losing ground south towards the open ocean. Holding a heading due west became impossible, and we were drifting at 2 knots south along the coast.

Elise, Stephanie, and Grant's daughters had arrived in Sri Lanka two days before and were trying to facilitate our arrival there. They had also managed to track down spare parts and were enquiring into having a local fishing vessel come out and drop them off to us. Although we were only 30 kilometres off the coast, we were still two days away from our chosen landing harbour in Galle, situated along the southern coast.

With spare parts on board, we could theoretically increase the pressure on the pedals and fight the currents. We had enquired about costs for delivery and the possible eventuation of rescue if we did break down, and the numbers were astronomical. 10k USD, up to 15k USD to come out and get us if we got into trouble. It seemed commercial profiteering at the expense of travellers was alive and well in the country. It was to be expected, considering Sri Lanka was in the grips of massive inflation, fuel shortages, corruption, and widespread unemployment. We decided to forget the resupply, continue as best we could towards the coast, and hope the gears held out.

Grants journal: As the afternoon wears on, we cannot get any closer than 22 kilometres to the coast. We realise we are in that southwest current which is now pushing us parallel to the coast. We pedal as hard as we dare, taking the broken sprag clutch into consideration, and even though we point the boat directly towards the coast we are being blown sideways through the water by a combination of a 2.5 knot current and 17 knots of northeast winds. By mid-afternoon, the situation becomes very clear. It does not look like we will get any closer than 22 kilometres to Sri Lanka. Having travelled over 2150 kilometres in 23 days, this looks to be the end of our human powered journey.

We received an update from Stephanie and Elise telling us they had been able to organise the Navy from the port of Hambantota to come out and drop us some parts for the gearbox. The best part was that they had agreed to do it for free. We agreed immediately, and they would be out to us in a couple of hours; their Navy destroyer would make light work of the distance when travelling at 40 knots. We were initially optimistic that we could finish the pedal to Galle, but while waiting for the parts, we checked our position, the weather forecast, and our drift.

We were still 22 kilometres from the closest coastline and had made zero progress over the previous few hours, yet we had lost a lot of distance south. The forecast was for increasing northerly winds, which would worsen our situation. We only had 40 more kilometres of coastline until we missed the southern tip of Sri Lanka. Our situation was bleak on paper, and even though our egos wanted to continue and try our luck, we had to take the emotion out of it, analyse the data, and make the right decision. The Navy was coming out to us as a favour, and we didn't want to be the guys who accepted their generosity and then asked for rescue 24 to 36 hours after they had been with us. Ultimately, it wasn't a tough decision, the data was clear, and once we talked it all through, we decided it was time to call it a day.

Grants journal: Around 6 pm in the evening, just before dark, we received a call on channel 16 on the V.H.F. radio from the Sri Lankan Naval vessel. We relayed our coordinates, and 10 minutes later, they were at our position when we released a flare, and they found us without issue. We had prepared the boat for towing, and we requested from them that instead of a parts drop off that they tow us into the safety of Hambantota port which they kindly agreed. With the wind picking up, the sea state was getting bumpy, but in the darkness, we soon had the boat tied on, and we transferred to the larger naval vessel as the tow-in commenced.

One minute we were standing in the Little Donkey holding a flare to the sky, watching the enormous Navy boat come steaming towards us. The next, we were on board the rolling deck with a crew of smiling faces offering us handshakes. The captain pushed the throttle down, and we turned towards the coast and our waiting family. We were invited below deck into the air-conditioned kitchen, and I was having sensory overload. The crew all wanted photos with us, and the cooks brought over two steaming plates of spicy food and hot coffee. Grant and I were blown away by their generosity.

In a few short days, we would forget the pain, the heat, the uncertainty, and the effort of covering 2150 kilometres in 23 days under human pedal power. Good sleep, food, and hot showers cleanse the memory of these details. But as we lifted spoonfuls of hot Sri Lankan food to our mouths in those first few minutes on board, starting to replenish the seven kilograms of weight I had lost, the experience was still vivid in our minds. It had been an expedition like no other and easily the most brutal trip I had ever done. I turned to Grant and said,

'Hey bro, thanks again for inviting me on this epic adventure, but I think you need to lose my number for at least a year yeah.'

He smiled and kept eating. A few seconds later, he looked up at me and said,

'Two minutes mate.'

CONCLUSION

Our glasses touched, and the fragile sound that often accompanied celebration echoed off the wooden walls of our home. Elise and I were back at Basecamp Tasmania, and it was time to recover from our recent expeditions, while also conducting sea trials on a craft we had built for the next adventure. The whisky warmed my throat and tasted sweet with a hint of spice. We have added a few more photos and memories to our living room wall since I wrote the introduction to this book; and the year ahead looks just as intense. I eased back into the couch, allowing the tension in my back to dissipate and leave goosebumps in its wake.

'The outriggers worked perfectly today.'

'They sure did. It's like a different boat,' Elise replied.

'It was unstable on the first trial and would have been a nightmare, this new setup will be perfect.'

During our cycle trip across Australia, when my parents joined us in their caravan, Dad and I had gotten to talking about river exploration. We discussed remote locations we would love to explore and the perfect design for a long distance self-sustaining vessel. That night I sketched out a concept, and over the next six months it came to life and eventually sat ready in our front yard.

We took an old, donated surf boat from a surf club in North Queensland, built for a five person rowing crew, and rebuilt her into a two person rowboat. With waterproof storage compartments, a reinforced hull, and outriggers for stability, she is a thing of beauty. Due to my reluctance to suffer as much as I had on the Bay of Bengal, we have also fitted her with an electric outboard, batteries, and solar panels to harness free energy from Mother Nature. Our rough plan is to row for a few hours each morning and afternoon, then utilise the outboard through the hottest part of each day.

I was initially sceptical about how much power an electric outboard could generate. However, after the sea trials I have total confidence in the technology. We can steam along at almost 3 knots when the sun is above us and lose next to no stored power from the batteries. It has a cruising speed 1 knot per hour faster than the best day pedalling The Little Donkey to Sri Lanka. Elise and I debated our route for weeks, and eventually, we settled for exploring one of the world's natural wonders, The Great Barrier Reef. We plan to tow the boat to Townsville in North Queensland, launch her, and travel all the way around Cape York following the coast. To finish in the Gulf of Carpentaria at the mining town of Weipa. It will be a two month journey through some of the most beautiful and wild country Australia has to offer, and my parents will follow along the coast for as long as they can.

'I'm worried about the Crocodiles up there,' Elise said as she sat beside me.

'Yeah, it's a risk all right; there have been two attacks in the last month. They are growing to over five metres long and 1000 kilograms in weight, we will have to keep a sharp eye out.'

'It is going to be amazing though; I can't wait.'

'What time is the ferry leaving Monday?' I asked.

'Evening departure from Devonport to Geelong, 6.30 p.m.'

'Ok cool, plenty of time for packing her up. Hey, did you hear about Simon from the market, heart attack and died. He was only 53.'

'I know, and then Maggie from down the road, stroke at 60. We really don't know how much time we have left.'

'Yep, they were going about life, planning their futures, and the next thing it's all over.'

I extracted myself from the couch, walked to the kitchen and returned with the bottle. I refilled our glasses and stood staring at our photos, a shrine to the adventure life.

'Well, we won't be wasting any time; we have some big trips coming up.' I said, restarting the conversation.

'Cheers to you old man,' Elise raised her glass.

We chinked our drinks again, harder than the first, as if to reinforce the point of not slowing down anytime soon.

'Cheers to you babe, and to five more years of living.'

Other Writing

The short story below burst forth from me one day in an hour of frantic writing. I couldn't tell you what the catalyst for it was, maybe it was simply time to let it out. A therapeutic release that needed a solid foundation perhaps before the tap could be opened. It reads like an unhinged fire hose, a testament to its rapid entry onto the page, and it is a brief history of my mental health journey since leaving the military many years ago. It is a story few people know in its entirety, and its insertion into this book was not guaranteed until the very last minute. I wasn't sure if I was ready to share it. However, as the title of my book makes clear, we don't know when our time will come, and if I only had five years to live, I want the story to be told.

A Soldier's Journey

I opened my eyes, bright sunlight piercing my coma, sweat beading down my face. My lips were parched, stuck together with cotton, the result of a long, dehydrated night. I remembered the beginning, a rubber arm grabbing the first offered beer after a fortnight of sobriety. I remembered the first bar, then club, then nothing. Darkness. Memories lost to a chamber in my mind filled with secrets, shame, and regret.

    I sat up, knocking a half-eaten pizza from my chest, ants scattered from their prize. The gutter made an ideal resting place for the man I was becoming, a vagrant, a drunk, a soldier falling through space and time. Lost was the teenager who joined the Army four years prior. He was a child, free of the horrors, the trauma, the drink, and the drugs. He was an idealist, he read too many books, tried too hard to be the champion, and hoped too much. I stood, stumbled, and fell. My knuckles were already skinned and bleeding, fighting again. My head ached from the booze and whatever else I put up my nose. The top of my skull was covered in lumps. Fists or kicks? It hardly seemed to matter now. Memory gone. I sat on the curb watching the world come slowly into focus. It wasn't a real world; it was a fake one, full of people who didn't know what I knew, people with hopes and dreams, stuck in a cycle society had built for them. A safe place where they would never see the horrors.

I shook my head; tears falling to the pavement. I had been here too many times lately, and I was spiralling. I wouldn't be at first parade again, and I knew what that would mean when I turned up at the barracks. My heart pounded with the thought.

'You are a fucken idiot,' I said aloud to the drunk. This wasn't me; I was better than this. I was 17 when I enlisted, a patriot, off to serve my country with honour. Who was I now, how did I get here, and how the hell was I going to get out?

◆◆◆

I had been out of the Army for 12 months as I walked a few paces behind my friends, we were ejected from the pub for fighting. I was the one fighting, my friends were pulling me away. The London streets were busy, I was still getting acclimated to the cold, it was a big change from North Queensland's humid climate. My hands were still shaking. I was drunk, but I hadn't disappeared into the black hole yet, that would come later. As the adrenalin wore off the sadness built up, tears fell from my eyes, and my friends turned their heads, embarrassed for me, not sure how to handle this 6 foot 100 kilogram veteran crying after a little tussle in a bar. I didn't know how to handle him either. I swallowed, wiped the evidence from my face and buried it deep, way down where I hoped it would stay, hidden amongst the violence, the dead body in the jungle, and the shame.

Six months after the bar room brawl, I lay on the bathroom floor; I had been awake for three days and didn't know if it was day or night. I welcomed Ibiza with open arms, the Spanish party island, it was to be a celebration of a good mate's birthday, yet once again it turned into drug fuelled self-destruction. My drug use was getting out of hand, I knew it, yet was powerless to stop. I wanted to tear my memories apart, shred them like confetti and watch them float away on the breeze. They always returned. The floor was cold, my body hot. I shivered. I was broken and due to fly back to London in a few hours. I couldn't fathom looking another human in the eye. The line between dream and reality was blurred, I slipped in and out through a revolving door. I felt the floor fall away and the heat burn my skin. I descended into the earth, down where I belonged, fires raging, deep in the pits of hell. I felt the flames scorch my skin and I smelled the char. I burst awake and screamed. Heart pounding. I looked around, was I in a dream now and being in hell was the reality? These days, I didn't know the difference.

◆◆◆

Two years after discharge from the military, my awareness returned when a burst of scorching water hit me squarely in the face. But there was no shower. Water didn't fall on me, it was blasted at me. I was naked, covered in my own filth. My body shook, and I groaned. A noise more animal than human. The police officers laughed. Finally, I lifted my head to see them. Three men, one with a hose washing me down. I was in lockup again. I had blacked out three days before and was on the junkie's autopilot, searching for chemicals to keep the train on the tracks. But I had well and truly derailed this time. I was hosed down and thrown a set of white overalls to wear, the same ones a painter might use. My clothes were discarded, taking their stories to the landfill. I was placed in the drunk tank and told to sleep it off. Sleep, I remember what that was like. Sixteen years old, playing football, fishing, and sleeping through the night. Those days seemed like someone else's life. I shivered. Nightmares tore at my mind like lions at a carcass. Bit by bit removing the foundation, bit by bit losing the parts that made me who I was, the guy I remembered, the one raised with love in the Outback, the young man who had a perfect start to life. I wanted that guy back.

Something cracked inside. More like an opening than a crack, a realisation. I knew if I stayed this course, I would be dead or calling prison home permanently. This wasn't who I wanted to be. I wanted to change.

The next morning, I was released. As I stumbled away, I knew what I had to do. I needed to ask for help, to call someone. My phone was back at the apartment, I had to get there to turn it all around. But first, I needed to get high.

Two days later with shaking hands, I made the phone call, and he picked up on the third ring. Liam was home in Sydney, woken by a desperate man on a long distance call. We served on operations together in the jungle, and he gave me an order which I followed like the disciplined soldier I once was. 'Get out of there, fly to Phuket, train at Tiger Muay Thai and turn your life around.' He was a mixed martial artist sending me to his happy place. I didn't know what the hell I was doing. My bag was packed in minutes, and flights were booked. I cowered in the back of an iconic black taxi on the way to Heathrow Airport and dabbed a wet finger at my remaining white powder, finishing it off, not quite ready to let go of one branch of life, before grabbing a new one. Greasy sweat oozed from my pores as I slid through customs and immigration. My paranoia was in overdrive, hoping I had thrown out all remnants of the drugs.

The plane lifted off, and panic erupted. Heading up, while inside I was coming down. I hoped the handful of painkillers would kick in soon. My anxious legs vibrated, and I noticed the passenger next to me looking at them. I held them still as best I could. My eyes grew heavy, I eased back in my chair, the tension dripping off my shoulders. The last week had been a rollercoaster. This was it, the turning point, the cliché rock bottom moment before the Incy Wincy spider story would become my reality. I was climbing the spout again, life was waiting, adventures, love, marriage, and a life of happiness. My last thought before passing out was, 'I have to survive the flight.'

❖❖❖

My story is not unique. The transition for any soldier back to civilian life can be a struggle. For combat veterans even more so. I waited a long time before asking for help, and even then, my path to recovery was very different. I had spent two months inside a Thai training camp getting the darkness beaten out of me. I couldn't fight, but every drop of sweat that hit the canvas was cleansing me of the drink, the drugs, and the shame. Dreams and aspirations that lay dormant for years started to emerge. A desire for adventure was reborn from my youth, and I grabbed hold of this desire with both hands. Hitching my recovery wagon to the pursuit of adventure. With new clarity, but still on rocky ground, I threw myself into work, saving money for what would be my first in a long list of expeditions. After years adrift, I found a safe harbour in high risk, physically gruelling expeditions. Climbing, mountaineering, ocean rowing, B.A.S.E Jumping, kayaking, long distance cycling, you name it. I did it all. I felt calmest in environments that made most people shake with fear. When Mother Nature tried her hardest to pluck me from the land of the living, that's when I was at peace. The military gave me a unique set of skills and moulded an extreme character that has found a resting place in the outdoors, where my demons remained silent.

They returned sometimes during periods in-between expeditions, in busy places full of people, in restaurants, and inside busy shopping centres. I once climbed a concrete wall to break out of a Westfield car park; the looks from people were like the ones I received as an addict. When sitting idle, I gathered a good team around me, composed of veterans on a similar journey, a psychiatrist, and some incredible people who volunteered their time to help lost sheep like me. I have found balance, mixed with highs and lows of a different nature. The journey has only just begun. Mental health, the black dog, the smiling sadness, whatever the title, it takes time, patience, knowledge, and vulnerability. I haven't felt the fires of hell in years, and I hope they never return.

❖❖❖

My heart was pounding, I couldn't breathe. I opened my crusty eyes and noticed the light. Was that a torch or the sun? My body ached from the punishment I had given it over the previous few days, I hadn't slept or eaten. I sipped from my water bottle and checked my watch, it was 1 a.m., it must have been a torch. I looked over at my beautiful wife lying beside me in the tent. We were 6100 metres in altitude, perched on a ledge at camp two on Ama Dablam, an infamous mountain in Nepal. My headache thumped as I pulled on my jacket, and poked my head outside the tent. The wind was howling, bitterly cold, I noticed other climbers preparing their gear for what would be a big summit day. The cold caused me to shiver, I slipped inside and back into my sleeping bag. I thought back over the last 15 years, from the jungles of Timor, to the cocaine fuelled streets of London, to the cold mountain nest I now found myself in. I was grateful. It would be an 18 hour summit day unlike anything I had experienced, brutal, and beautiful in the same breath. I smiled with excitement.

I have adopted a motto since getting clean all those years ago: One Life, One Chance. It's what I live by, and its finite nature keeps me focused and on track. The adventure list gets bigger every year, and I will not be slowing down anytime soon. I'm often asked why I do these adventures, and in the past I have replied with stoic answers and media clickbait. The truth is I do it for my own survival. It's where I find peace, where the demons are caged and don't try to pull me back into their world. Adventure has saved my life.

I pulled on my boots, clipped on my crampons, and looked towards the top; an icy wind whipped my face. The demons rattled their cage deep in my soul, and a whisper of doubt entered my mind. I took a step forward and heard the ice crunch under my boot, I thought to myself, 'I'll shut you bastards up,' and started to climb.

Life is the greatest gift.
It is yours alone, not something borrowed,
or on trial, and there is no secret.
Love and fear are the constant levellers,
and endurance perhaps the key.
Fate and destiny are our two wild cards; to find
them you must take a chance and gamble.
Time is the great unknown.
May it smile upon you and be your friend.

Clive Richmond

ACKNOWLEDGEMENTS

First and foremost, I want to thank my wife, Elise. Without you by my side on expeditions, and in life, I wouldn't be where I am today. This book is for you, my love. No expedition is a solo affair, and neither is producing a book. In no specific order I want to thank my expedition teammates from the last few years: Elise Richmond, Mingma Chirri, Yok Chaiwat, Lakpa Nuru, Kami Chirri, Pasang Geljin, Ang Pruba, Kim-Arild Karlsen, Vidar Hyrve, Kelly Hughes, Harriet Roberts, Stéphane Clark, Dylan James, Brett Fernon, Craig Edmunds, Al Kidner, and the mighty Grant Rawlinson. You are all amazing humans, and your characters give this book its unique flavour and edge, thank you for loving adventure as much as I do.

I want to thank my first draft editor Eamonn Halloway, and my forensic line editor Ernest Hocking for your diligent work. One day I will write in the correct tense. Thank you to my designer Nada Backovic, your artistic flare, and seamless layout allows my words to find their mark with ease. I want to thank my gypsy parents Clive and Mandy Richmond; their constant support, and unwavering love is a foundation I have built my life on. The seed of adventure was planted in me by watching you both live life on your own terms, and now we get to take on adventures together. Bring on the next ten years of craziness.

Thank you to my main sponsors, Stowe Australia, and Stamford Capital, for always backing my outlandish ideas, and then sharing in the hard earned lessons.

Lastly but certainly not least I want to thank you, the reader. You are the reason I put these words to paper year after year, and your emails and messages of support are cherished. I hope these stories continue to inspire your own epic adventures, and always remember; we only have One Life and One Chance, so get out there and make the most of it.

To purchase Lukes first book
ONE LIFE ONE CHANCE
visit his website www.olocadventures.com

To purchase Lukes second book
VODKA & SANDSTORMS
visit his website www.olocadventures.com

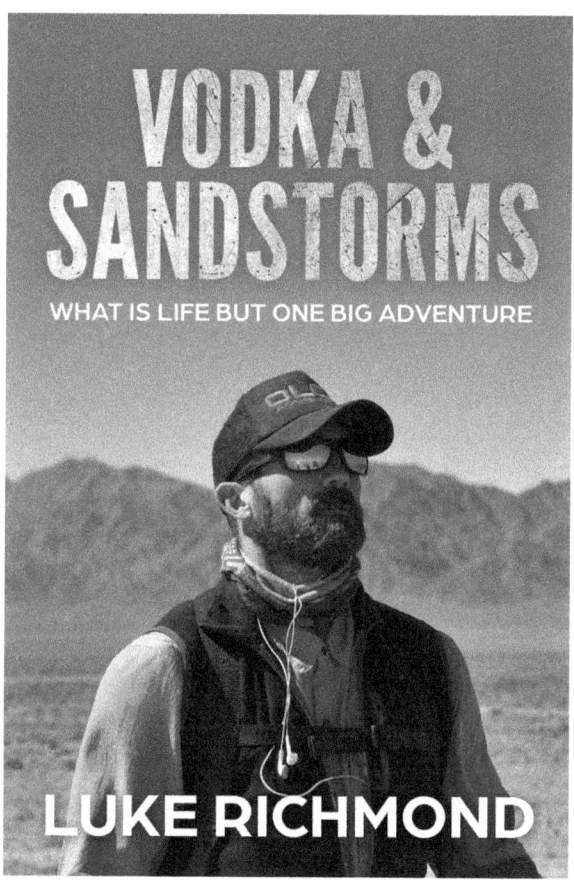

*Stay up to date with Luke's adventures
or get in touch with him at:*

EMAIL - Luke@olocadventures.com
WEBSITE - www.olocadventures.com
INSTAGRAM - Luke_olocadventures
FACEBOOK - Luke Richmond - Adventurer

Stowe Australia is a leading electrical and communications installation and service contractor with a pre-eminent industry reputation for performance, quality and reliability.

Your Certainty in Commercial Property Capital
With unrivalled market knowledge and capital partnerships from private investors to ASX-listed companies. Stamford Capital provides developers and investors with access to a broad range of financing options, and advice to ensure their transaction is successful.

www.ingramcontent.com/pod-product-compliance
Lightning Source LLC
LaVergne TN
LVHW041247080426
835510LV00009B/626